SONGS THE DEAD MEN SING

SONGS THE DEAD MEN SING

by

GEORGE R. R. MARTIN

LONDON
VICTOR GOLLANCZ LTD
1985

First published in the USA 1983
by Dark Harvest, Niles, Illinois

This edition first published
in Great Britain 1985 by Victor Gollancz Ltd,
14 Henrietta Street, London WC2E 8QJ

to Lisa Tuttle,
my favorite collaborator.
It's all your fault!

British Library Cataloguing in Publication Data
Martin, George R. R.
  Songs the dead men sing.
  I. Title
  813′.54[F]   PS3563.A7239
  ISBN 0-575-03566-8

Printed in Great Britain by
St Edmundsbury Press, Bury St Edmunds, Suffolk

CONTENTS

ACKNOWLEDGMENTS

The Monkey Treatment

Kenny Dorchester was a fat man.

He had not always been a fat man, of course. He had come into the world a perfectly normal infant of modest weight, but the normalcy was short-lived in Kenny's case, and before very long he had become a chubby-cheeked toddler well-swaddled in baby fat. From then on it was all downhill and upscale so far as Kenny was concerned. He became a pudgy child, a corpulent adolescent, and a positively porcine college student, all in good turn, and by adulthood he had left all those intermediate steps behind and graduated into full obesity.

People become obese for a variety of complex reasons, some of them physiological and some psychological. Kenny's reason was relatively simple: food. Kenny Dorchester loved to eat. Often he would paraphrase Will Rogers, winking broadly, and tell his friends that he had never met a food he didn't like. This was not precisely true, since Kenny loathed both liver and prune juice. Perhaps, if his mother had served them more often during his childhood, he would never have attained the girth and gravity that so haunted him at maturity. Unfortunately, Gina Dorchester was more inclined to lasagna and roast turkey with stuffing and sweet potatoes and chocolate pudding and veal cordon bleu and buttered corn-on the cob and stacks of blueberry pancakes (although not all in one meal) than she was to liver and prune juice, and once Kenny had expressed his preference in the matter by retching his liver back onto his plate, she obligingly never served liver and prune juice again. Thus, all unknowing, she set her son on the soft, suety road to the monkey treatment. But that was long ago and the poor woman really cannot be blamed, since it was Kenny himself who ate his way there.

Kenny loved pepperoni pizza, or plain pizza, or garbage pizza with everything on it including anchovies. Kenny could eat an entire slab of barbequed ribs, either beef or pork, and the spicier the sauce was the more he approved. He was fond of rare prime rib and roast chicken and Rock Cornish game hens stuffed with rice, and he was hardly the sort to object to a nice sirloin or a platter of fried shrimp or a hunk of kielbasa. He liked his burgers with everything on them, and fries and onion rings on the side, please. There was nothing you could do to his friend the potato that would turn him against it, but he was also partial to pasta and rice, to yams candied and un-, and even to mashed rutabagas. "Desserts are my downfall," he would sometimes say, for he liked sweets of all varieties, especially devil's food cake and cannoli and hot apple pie with cheese (Cheddar, please) or maybe cold strawberry pie with whipped cream. "Bread is my downfall," he would say at other times, when it seemed likely that no dessert was forthcoming, and so saying he would rip off another chunk of sourdough or butter up another crescent roll or reach for another slice of garlic bread, which was a particular vice. Kenny had a lot of particular vices. He thought himself an authority on both fine restaurants and fast-food franchises, and could discourse endlessly and knowledgably about either. He relished Greek food and Chinese food and Japanese food and Korean food and German food and Italian food and French food and Indian food, and was always on the look-out for new ethnic groups so he might "expand my cultural horizons." When Saigon fell, Kenny speculated about how many of the Vietnamese refugees would be likely to open restaurants. When Kenny traveled, he always made it a point to gorge himself on the area's specialty, and he could tell you the best places to eat in any of twenty-four major American cities, while reminiscing fondly about the meals he had enjoyed in each of them. His favorite writers were James Beard and Calvin Trillin.

"I live a tasty life!" Kenny Dorchester would proclaim, beaming. And so he did. But Kenny also had a secret. He did not often think of it and never spoke it, but it was there nonetheless, down at the heart of him beneath all those great rolls of flesh, and not all his sauces could drown it, nor could his trusty fork keep it at bay.

Kenny Dorchester did not *like* being fat.

Kenny was like a man torn between two lovers, for while he loved his food with an abiding passion, he also dreamed of other loves, of women, and he knew that in order to secure the one he would have to give up the other, and that knowledge was his secret pain. Often he wrestled with the dilemmas posed by his situation. It seemed to Kenny that while it might be preferable to be slender and have a woman than to be fat and have only a crawfish bisque, nonetheless the latter was not entirely to be spurned. Both were sources of happiness after all, and the real misery fell to those who gave up the one and failed to obtain the other. Nothing depressed or saddened Kenny so much as the sight of a fat person eating cottage cheese. Such pathetic human beings never seemed to get appreciably skinnier, Kenny thought, and were doomed to go through life bereft of both women and crawfish, a fate too grim to contemplate.

Yet despite all his misgivings, at times the secret pain inside Kenny Dorchester would flare up mightily, and fill him with a sense of resolve that made him feel as if anything might be possible. The sight of a particularly beautiful woman or the word of some new, painless, and wonderfully effective diet were particularly prone to trigger what Kenny thought of as his "aberrations." When such moods came, Kenny would be driven to diet.

Over the years he tried every diet there was, briefly and secretly. He tried Dr. Atkins' diet and Dr. Stillman's diet, the grapefruit diet and the brown rice diet. He tried the liquid protein diet, which was truly disgusting. He lived for a week on nothing but Slender and Sego, until he had run through all of the flavors and gotten bored. He joined a Pounds-Off club and attended a few meetings, until he discovered that the company of fellow dieters did him no good whatsoever, since all they talked about was food. He went on a hunger strike that lasted until he got hungry. He tried the fruit juice diet, and the drinking man's diet (even though he was not a drinking man), and the martinis-and-whipped-cream diet (he omitted the martinis). A hypnotist told him that his favorite foods tasted bad and he wasn't hungry anyway, but it was a damned lie, and that was that for hypnosis. He had his behavior modified so he put down his fork between bites, used small plates that looked full even with tiny portions, and wrote down every thing he ate in a notebook. That left his with stacks of notebooks, a great many small dishes to wash, and unusual manual dexterity in putting down and picking up his fork. His favorite diet was the one that said you could eat all you wanted of your favorite food, so long as you ate nothing *but* that. The only problem was that Kenny couldn't decide what was really his one true favorite, so he wound up eating ribs for a week, and pizza for a week, and Peking duck for a week (that was an expensive week), and losing no weight whatsoever, although he did have a great time.

Most of Kenny Dorchester's aberrations lasted for a week or two. Then, like a man coming out of a fog, he would look around and realized that he was absolutely miserable, losing relatively little weight, and in imminent danger of turning into one of those cottage-cheese fatties he so pitied. At that point he would chuck the diet, go out for a good meal, and be restored to his normal self for another six months, until his secret pain surfaced again.

Then, one Friday night, he spied Henry Moroney at the Slab.

The Slab was Kenny's favorite barbeque joint. It specialized in ribs, charred and meaty and served dripping with a sauce that Kenny approved of mightily. And on Fridays the Slab offered all the ribs you could eat for only $15.00, which was prohibitively high for most people but a bargain for Kenny, who could eat a great many ribs. On that particular Friday, Kenny had just finished his first slab and was waiting for the second, sipping beer and eating bread, when he chanced to look up and realized, with a start, that the slim haggard fellow in the next booth was, in fact, Henry Moroney.

Kenny Dorchester was nonplussed. The last time he had seen Henry Moroney they had both been unhappy Pounds-Off members, and Moroney had been the only one in the club who weighed more than Kenny did. A great fat whale of a man, Moroney had carried about the cruel nickname of "Boney," as he confessed to his fellow members. Only now the nickname seemed to fit. Not only was Moroney skinny enough to hint at a ribcage under his skin, but the table in front of him was absolutely littered with bones. That was the detail that intrigued Kenny Dorchester. All those bones. He began to count, and he lost track before very long, because all the bones were disordered, strewn about on empty plates in little puddles of drying sauce. But from the sheer mass of them it was clear that Moroney had put away at least four slabs of ribs, maybe five.

It seemed to Kenny Dorchester that Henry "Boney" Moroney knew the secret. If there was a way to lose hundreds of pounds and still be able to consume five slabs of ribs at a sitting, that was something Kenny desperately needed to know. So he rose and walked over to Moroney's booth and squeezed in opposite him. "It *is* you," he said.

Moroney looked up as if he hadn't noticed Kenny until that very second. "Oh," he said in a thin, tried voice. "You." He seemed very weary, but Kenny thought that was probably natural for someone who had lost so much weight. Moroney's eyes were sunk in deep gray hollows, his flesh sagged in pale empty folds, and he was slouching forward with his elbows on the table as if he were too exhausted to sit up straight. He looked terrible, but he had lost so much *weight* . . .

"You look wonderful!" Kenny blurted. "How did you do it? How? You must tell me, Henry, really you must."

"No," Moroney whispered. "No, Kenny. Go away."

Kenny was taken aback. "Really!" he declared. "That's not very friendly. I'm not leaving until I know your secret, Henry. You owe it to me. Think of all the times we've broken bread together."

"Oh, Kenny," Moroney said, in his faint and terrible voice. "Go, please, go, you don't want to know, it's too . . . too . . ." He stopped in mid-sentence, and a spasm passed across his face. He moaned. His head twisted wildly to the side, as if he were having some kind of a fit, and his hands beat on the table. "Oooooo," he said.

"Henry, what's wrong?" Kenny said, alarmed. He was certain now that Boney Moroney had overdone his diet.

"Ohhhh," Moroney sighed in sudden relief. "Nothing, nothing, I'm fine." His voice had none of the enthusiasm of his words. "I'm wonderful, in fact. Wonderful, Kenny. I haven't been so slim since . . . since . . . why, never. It's a miracle." He smiled faintly. "I'll be at my goal soon, and then it will be over. I think. Think I'll be at my goal. Don't know my weight, really." He put a hand to his brow. "I am slender, though, truly I am. Don't you think I look good?"

"Yes, yes," Kenny agreed impatiently. "But how? You must tell me. Surely not those Pounds-Off phonies . . ."

"No," said Moroney weakly. "No, it was the monkey treatment. Here, I'll write it down for you." He took out a pencil and scrawled an address on a napkin.

Kenny stuffed the napkin into a pocket. "The monkey treatment? I've never heard of that. What is it?"

Henry Moroney licked his lips. "They . . . " he started, and then another fit hit him, and his head twitched around grotesquely. "Go," he said to Kenny, "just go. It works, Kenny, yes, oh. The monkey treatment, yes. I can't say more. You have the address. Excuse me." He placed his hands flat on the table and pushed himself to his feet, then walked over to the cashier, shuffling like a man twice his age. Kenny Dorchester watched him go, and decided that Moroney had *definitely* overdone this monkey treatment, whatever it was. He had never had tics or spasms before, or whatever that had been.

"You have to have a sense of proportion about these things," Kenny said stoutly to himself. He patted his pocket to make sure the napkin was still there, resolved that he would handle things more sensibly than Boney Moroney, and returned to his own booth and his second slab of ribs. He ate four that night, figuring that if he was going to start a diet tomorrow he had better get in some eating while the eating was good.

The next day being Saturday, Kenny was free to pursue the monkey treatment and the dream of a new, slender him. He rose early, and immediately rushed to the bathroom to weigh himself on his digital scale, which he loved dearly because you didn't have to squint down at the numbers, since they lit up nice and bright and precise in red. This morning they lit up as 367. He had gained a few pounds, but he hardly minded. The monkey treatment would strip them off again soon enough.

Kenny tried to phone ahead, to make sure this place was open on Saturday, but that proved to be impossible. Moroney had written nothing but an address, and there was no diet center at that listing in the yellow pages, nor a health club, nor a doctor. Kenny looked in the white pages under "Monkey" but that yielded nothing. So there was nothing to do but go down there in person.

Even that was troublesome. The address was way down by the docks in a singularly unsavory neighborhood, and Kenny had a hard time getting the cab to take him there. He finally got his way by threatening to report the cabbie to the commissioner. Kenny Dorchester knew his rights.

Before long, though, he began to have his doubts. The narrow little streets they wound through were filthy and decaying, altogether unappetizing and it occured to Kenny that any diet center located down here might offer only dangerous quackery. The block in question was an old commercial strip gone to seed, and it put his hackles up even more. Half the stores were boarded closed, and the rest lurked behind filthy dark windows and iron gates. The cab pulled up in front of an absolutely miserable old brick storefront, flanked by two vacant lots full of rubble, its plate glass windows grimed over impenetrably. A faded Coca-Cola sign swung back and forth, groaning, above the door. But the number was the number that Boney Moroney had written down.

"Here you are," the cabbie said impatiently, as Kenny peered out the taxi window, aghast.

"This does not look correct," Kenny said. "I will investigate. Kindly wait here until I am certain this is the place."

The cabbie nodded, and Kenny slid over and levered himself out of the taxi. He had taken two steps when he heard the cab shift gears and pull away from the curb, screeching. He turned and watched in astonishment. "Here, you can't . . ." he began. But it did. He would most definitely report that man to the commissioner, he decided.

But meanwhile he was stranded down here, and it seemed foolish not to proceed when he had come this far. Whether he took the monkey treatment or not, no doubt they would let him use a phone to summon another cab. Kenny screwed up his resolution, and went on in the grimy, unmarked storefront. A bell tinkled as he opened the door.

It was dark inside. The dust and dirt on the windows kept out nearly all the sunlight, and it took a moment for Kenny's eyes to adjust. When they did, he saw to his horror that he had walked into someone's living room. One of those gypsy families that moved into abandoned stores, he thought. He was standing on a threadbare carpet, and around and about him was a scatter of old furniture, no doubt the best the Salvation Army had to offer. An ancient black-and-white TV set crouched in one corner, staring at him blindly. The room stank of urine. "Sorry," Kenny muttered feebly, terrified that some dark gypsy youth would come out of the shadows to knife him. "Sorry." He had stepped backwards, groping behind him for the doorknob, when the man came out of the back room.

"Ah!" the man said, spying Kenny at once from tiny bright eyes. "Ah, the monkey treatment!" He rubbed his hands together and grinned. Kenny was terrified. The man was the fattest, grossest human being that Kenny had ever laid eyes on. He had squeezed through the door sideways. He was fatter than Kenny, fatter than Boney Moroney. He literally dripped with fat. And he was repulsive in other ways as well. He had the complexion of a mushroom, and miniscule little eyes almost invisible amid rolls of pale flesh. His corpulence seemed to have overwhelmed even his hair, of which he had very little. Barechested, he displayed vast areas of folded, bulging skin, and his huge breasts flopped as he came forward quickly and seized Kenny by the arm. "The monkey treatment!" he repeated eagerly, pulling Kenny forward. Kenny looked at him, in shock, and was struck dumb by his grin. When the man grinned, his mouth seemed to become half his face, a grotesque semicircle full of shining white teeth.

"No," Kenny said at last, "no, I have changed my mind." Boney Moroney or no, he didn't think he cared to try this monkey treatment if it was administered by such as this. In the first place, it clearly could not be very effective, or else the man would not be so monsterously obese. Besides, it was probably dangerous, some quack potion of monkey hormones or something like that. *"NO!"* Kenny repeated more forcefully, trying to wrest his arm free from the grasp of the grotesquerie who held it.

But it was useless. The man was distinctly larger and infinitely stronger than Kenny, and he propelled him across the room with ease, oblivious to Kenny's protests, grinning like a maniac all the while.

"Fat man," he burbled, and as if to prove his point he reached out and seized one of Kenny's bulges and twisted it painfully. "Fat, fat, fat, no good. Monkey treatment make you thin."

"Yes, but . . ."

"Monkey treatment," the man repeated, and somehow he had gotten behind Kenny. He put his weight against Kenny's back and pushed, and Kenny staggered through a curtained doorway into the back room. The smell of urine was much stronger in there, strong enough to make him want to retch. It was pitch black, and from all sides Kenny heard rustlings and scurryings in the darkness. *Rats,* he thought wildly. Kenny was deathly afraid of rats. He fumbled about and propelled himself toward the square of dim light that marked the curtain he had come through.

Before he was quite there, a high-pitched chittering sounded suddenly from behind him, sharp and rapid as fire from a machine gun. Then another voice took it up, then a third, and suddenly the dark was alive with the terrible hammering noise. Kenny put his hands over his ears and staggered through the curtain, but just as he emerged he felt something brush the back of his neck, something warm and hairy. "Aieeee!" he screamed, dancing out into the front room where the tremendous bare-chested madman was waiting patiently. Kenny hopped from one foot to the other, screeching, "Aieeee, a rat, a rat on my back. Get it off, get it *off!*" He was trying to grab for it with both hand, but the thing was very quick, and shifted around so cleverly so that he couldn't get ahold of it. But he felt it there, alive, moving. "Help me, help me!" he called out. "A rat!"

The proprietor grinned at him and shook his head, so all his many chins went bobbing merrily. "No, no," he said. "No rat, fat man. Monkey. You get the monkey treatment." Then he stepped forward and seized Kenny by the elbow again, and drew him over to a full-length mirror mounted on the wall. It was so dim in the room that Kenny could scarcely make out anything in the mirror, except that it wasn't wide enough and chopped off both his arms. The man stepped back and yanked a pull-cord dangling from the ceiling, and a single bare lightbulb clicked on overhead. The bulb swung back and forth, back and forth, so the light shifted crazily. Kenny Dorchester trembled and stared at the mirror.

"Oh!" he said.

There was a monkey on his back.

Actually it was on his shoulders, its legs wrapped around his thick neck and twined together beneath his triple chin. He could feel its monkey hair scratching the back of his neck, could feel its warm little monkey paws lightly grasping his ears. It was a very tiny monkey. As Kenny looked into the mirror, he saw it peek out from behind his head, grinning hugely. It had quick darting eyes, coarse brown hair, and altogether too many shiny white teeth for Kenny's liking. Its long prehensile tail swayed about restlessly, like some hairy snake that had grown out of the back of Kenny's skull.

Kenny's heart was pounding away like some great air-hammer lodged in his chest and he was altogether distressed by this place, this man, and this monkey, but he gathered all his reserves and forced himself to be calm. It wasn't a rat, after all. The little monkey couldn't harm him. It had to be a trained monkey, the way it had perched on his shoulders. Its owner must let it ride around like this, and when Kenny had come unwillingly through the curtain, it had probably mistook him. All fat men look alike in the dark. Kenny grabbed behind him and tried to pull the monkey loose, but somehow he couldn't seem to get a grip on it. The mirror, reversing everything, just made it worse. He jumped up and down ponderously, shaking the entire room and making the furniture leap around every time he landed, but the monkey held on tight to his ears and could not be dislodged.

Finally, with what Kenny thought was incredible aplomb under the circumstances, he turned to the gross proprietor and said, "Your monkey, sir. Kindly help me remove it."

"No, no," the man said. "Make you skinny. Monkey treatment. You no want to be skinny?"

"Of course I do," Kenny said unhappily, "but this is absurd." He was confused. This monkey on his back seemed to be part of the monkey treatment, but that certainly didn't make very much sense.

"Go," the man said. He reached up and snapped off the light with a sharp tug that sent the bulb careening wildly again. Then he started toward Kenny, who backpedaled nervously. "Go," the man repeated, as he grabbed Kenny's arm again. "Out, out. You get monkey treatment, you go now."

"See here!" Kenny said furiously. "Let go of me! Get this monkey off me, do your hear? I don't want your monkey! Do you hear me? Quit pushing, sir! I tell you, I have friends with the police department, you aren't going to get away with this. Here now . . ."

But all his protestations were useless. The man was a veritable tidal wave of sweating, smelling pale flesh, and he put his weight against Kenny and propelled him helplessly towards the door. The bell rang again as he pulled it open and shoved Kenny out into the garish bright sunlight.

"I'm not going to pay for this!" Kenny said stoutly, staggering. "Not a cent, do you hear!"

"No charge for monkey treatment," the man said, grinning.

"At least let me call a cab," Kenny began, but it was too late, the man had closed the door. Kenny stepped forward angrily and tried to yank it back open, but it did not budge. Locked. "Open up in there!" Kenny demanded at the top of his lungs. There was no reply. He shouted again, and grew suddenly and uncomfortably aware that he was being stared at. Kenny turned around. Across the street three old winos were sitting on the stoop of a boarded-up store, passing a bottle in a brown paper bag and regarding him through wary eyes.

That was when Kenny Dorchester recalled that he was standing there in the street in broad daylight with a monkey on his back.

A flush crept up his neck and spread across his cheeks. He felt very silly. "A pet!" he shouted to the winos, forcing a smile. "Just my little pet!" They went staring on. Kenny gave a last angry look at the locked door, and set off down the street, his legs pumping furiously. He had to get to someplace private.

Rounding the corner, he came upon a dark, narrow alley behind two grey old tenement buildings, and ducked inside, wheezing for breath. He sat down heavily on a trash can, pulled out his handkerchief, and mopped his brow. The monkey shifted just a bit, and Kenny felt it move. "Off me!" he shouted, reaching up and back again to try to wrench it off by the scruff of its neck, only to have it elude him once more. He tucked away his handkerchief and groped behind his head with both hands, but he just couldn't get ahold of it. Finally, exhausted, he stopped, and tried to think.

The legs! he thought. The legs under his chins! That's the ticket! Very calmly and deliberately he reached up, and felt for the monkey's legs, and wrapped one big fleshy hand around each of them. He took a deep breath and then savagely tried to yank them apart, as if they were two ends of a giant wishbone.

The monkey attacked him.

One hand twisted his right ear painfully, until it felt like it was being pulled clean off his head. The other started hammering against his temple, beating a furious tattoo. Kenny Dorchester yelped in distress and let go of the monkey's legs -- which he hadn't budged for all his efforts. The monkey quit beating on him and released his ear. Kenny sobbed, half with relief and half with frustration. He felt wretched.

He sat there in that filthy alley for ages, defeated in his efforts to remove the monkey and afraid to go back to the street where people would point at him and laugh, or make rude insulting comments under their breath. It was difficult enough going through life as a fat man, Kenny thought. How much worse, then, to face the cruel world as a fat man with a monkey on his back. Kenny did not want to know. He resolved to sit there on that trash can in the dark alley until he died or the monkey died, rather than face shame and ridicule on the streets.

His resolve endured about an hour. Then Kenny Dorchester began to get hungry. Maybe people would laugh at him, but they had always laughed at him, so what did it matter? Kenny rose and dusted himself off, while the monkey settled itself more comfortably on his neck. He ignored it, and decided to go in search of a pepperoni pizza.

He did not find one easily. The absymal slum in which he had been stranded had a surfeit of winos, dangerous-looking teenagers, and burned-out or boarded-up buildings, but it had precious few pizza parlors. Nor did it have any taxis. Kenny walked down the main thoroughfare with brisk dignity, looking neither left nor right, heading for safer neighborhoods as fast as his plump little legs could carry him. Twice he came upon phone booths, and eagerly fetched out a coin to summon transportation, but both time the phones proved to be out of order. Vandals, thought Kenny Dorchester, were as bad as rats.

Finally, after what seemed like hours of walking, he stumbled upon a sleazy cafe. The lettering on the window said JOHN'S GRILL, and there was a neon sign above the door that said, simply, EAT. Kenny was very familiar with those three lovely letters, and he recognized the sign two blocks off. It called to him like a beacon. Even before he entered, he knew it was rather unlikely that such a place would include pepperoni pizza on its menu, but by that time Kenny had ceased to care.

As he pushed the door aside, Kenny experienced a brief moment of apprehension, partially because he felt very out of placed in the cafe, where the rest of the diners all appeared to be muggers, and partially because he was afraid they would refuse to serve his because of the monkey on his back. Acutely uncomfortable in the doorway, he moved quickly to a small table in an obscure corner, where he hoped to escape the curious stares. A gaunt grey-haired waitress in a faded pink uniform moved purposefully toward him, and Kenny sat with his eyes downcast, playing nervously with the salt, pepper, and ketchup, dreading the moment when she arrived and said, "Hey, you can't bring that thing in here!"

But when the waitress reached his table, she simply pulled a pad out of her apron's pocket and stood poised, pencil in hand. "Well?" she demanded. "What'll it be?"

Kenny stared up in shock, and smiled. He stammered a bit, then recovered himself and ordered a cheese omelet with a double side of bacon, coffee and a large glass of milk, and cinnamon toast. "Do hash browns come with?" he asked hopefully, but the waitress shook her head and departed.

What a marvelous kind woman, Kenny thought as he waited for his meal and shredded a paper napkin thoughtfully. What a wonderful place! Why, they hadn't even mentioned his monkey! How very polite of them.

The food arrived shortly. "Ahhhh," Kenny said as the waitress laid it out in front of him on the formica table top. He was ravenous. He selected a slice of cinnamon toast, and brought it to his mouth.

And a little monkey hand darted out from behind his head and snatched it clean away.

Kenny Dorchester sat in numb surprise for an instant, his suddenly empty hand poised before his mouth. He heard the monkey eating his toast, chomping noisily. Then, before Kenny had quite comprehended what was happening, the monkey's great long tail snaked in under his armpit, curled around his glass of milk, and spirited it up and away in the blink of an eye. *"Hey!"* Kenny said, but he was much too slow. Behind his back he heard slurping, sucking sounds, and all of a sudden the glass came vaulting over his left shoulder. He caught it before it fell and smashed, and set it down unsteadily. The monkey's tail came stealthily around and headed for his bacon. Kenny grabbed up a fork and stabbed at it, but the monkey was faster than he was. The bacon vanished, and the tines of the fork bent against the hard formica uselessly. By then Kenny knew he was in a race. Dropping the bent fork, he used his spoon to cut off a chunk of the omelet, dripping cheese, and he bent forward as he lifted it, quick as he could. The monkey was quicker. A little hand flashed in from somewhere, and the spoon had only a tantalizing gob of half-melted cheese remaining on it when it reached Kenny's mouth. He lunged back towards his plate, and loaded up again, but it didn't matter how fast he tried to be. The monkey had two paws and a tail, and once it even used a little monkey foot to snatch something away from him. In hardly any time at all, Kenny Dorchester's meal was gone. He sat there staring down at the empty, greasy plate, and he felt tears gathering in his eyes.

The waitress reappeared without Kenny noticing. "My, you sure are a hungry one," she said to him, ripping off his check from her pad and putting it in front of him. "Polished that off quicker than anyone I every saw."

Kenny looked up at her. "But I *didn't*," he protested. "The monkey ate it all!"

The waitress looked at him very oddly. "The monkey?" she said, uncertainly.

"The monkey," Kenny said. He did not care for the way she was staring at him, like he was crazy or something.

"What monkey?" she asked. "You didn't sneak no animals in here, did you? The Board of Health don't allow no animals in here, Mister."

"What do you mean, *sneak?*" Kenny said in annoyance. "Why, the monkey is right on my . . ." He never got a chance to finish. Just then the monkey hit him, a tremendous hard blow on the left side of his face. The force of it twisted his head half-around, and Kenny yelped in pain and shock.

The waitress seemed concerned. "You OK, Mister?" she asked. "You ain't gonna have a fit, are you, twitching like that?"

"I didn't twitch!" Kenny all but shouted. "The goddamned monkey hit

me! Can't you see?"

"Oh," said the waitress, taking a step backwards. "Oh, of course. Your monkey hit you. Pesky little things, ain't they?"

Kenny pounded his fists on the table in frustration. "Never mind," he said, "just never mind." He snatched up the check -- the monkey did not take that away from him, he noted -- and rose. "Here," he said, pulling out his wallet. "And you have a phone in this place, don't you? Call me a cab, all right? You can do that, can't you?"

"Sure," the waitress said, moving to the register to ring up his meal. Everyone in the cafe was staring at him. "Sure, Mister," he muttered. "A cab. We'll get you a cab right away."

Kenny waited, fuming. The cab driver made no comment on his monkey. Instead of going home, he took the cab to his favorite pizza place, three blocks from his apartment. Then he stormed right in and ordered a large pepperoni. The monkey ate it all, even when Kenny tried to confuse it by picking up one slice in each hand and moving them simultaneously toward his mouth. Unfortunately, the monkey had two hands as well, both of them faster than Kenny's. When the pizza was completely gone, Kenny thought for a moment, summoned over the waitress, and ordered a second. This time he got a large anchovy. He thought that was very clever. Kenny Dorchester had never met anyone else beside himself who liked anchovy pizza. Those little salty fishes would be his salvation, he thought. To increase the odds, when the pizza arrived Kenny picked up the hot pepper shaker and covered it with enough hot pepppers to ignite a major conflagration. Then, feeling confident, he tried to eat a slice.

The monkey liked anchovy pizza with lots of hot peppers. Kenny Dorchester almost wept.

He went from the pizza place to the Slab, from the Slab to a fine Greek restaurant, from the Greek restaurant to a local McDonald's, from McDonald's to a bakery that made the most marvelous chocolate eclairs. Sooner or later, Kenny Dorchester thought, the monkey would be full. It was only a very little monkey, after all. How much food could it eat? He would just keep on ordering food, he resolved, and the monkey would either reach its limit or rupture and die.

That day Kenny spent more than two hundred dollars on meals.

He got absolutely nothing to eat.

The monkey seemed to be a bottomless pit. If it had a capacity, that capacity was surely greater than the capacity of Kenny's wallet. Finally he was forced to admit defeat. The monkey could not be stuffed into submission.

Kenny cast about for another tactic, and finally hit on it. Monkeys were stupid, after all, even invisible monkeys with prodigious appetites. Smiling slyly, Kenny went to a neighborhood supermarket, and picked up a box of banana pudding (it seemed appropriate) and a box of rat poison. Humming a spry little tune, he walked on home, and set to work making the pudding, stirring in liberal amounts of the rat poison as it cooked. The poison was nicely odorless. The pudding smelled wonderful. Kenny poured it into some dessert cups to cool, and watched television for a hour or so. Finally he rose nonchalantly, went to the refrigerator, and got out a pudding and a nice big spoon. He sat back down in front of the set, spooned up a generous glob of pudding, and brought it to his open mouth. Where he paused. And paused. And waited.

The monkey did nothing.

Maybe it was full at last, Kenny thought. He put aside the poisoned pudding and rushed back to his kitchen, where he found a box of vanilla wafers hiding on a shelf, and a few forlorn fig newtons as well.

The monkey ate all of them.

A tear trickled down Kenny's cheek. The monkey would let him have all the poisoned pudding he wanted, it seemed, but nothing else. He reached back half-heartedly and tried to grab the monkey once again, thinking maybe all that eating would have slowed it down some, but it was a vain hope. The monkey evaded him, and when Kenny persisted the monkey bit his finger. Kenny yowled and snatched his hand back. His finger was bleeding. He sucked on it. That much, at least, the monkey permitted him.

When he had washed his finger and wrapped a band-aid around it, Kenny returned to his living room and seated himself heavily, weary and defeated, in front of his television set. An old rerun of *The Galloping Gourmet* was coming on. He couldn't stand it. He jabbed at his remoted control to change the channel, and watched blindly for hours, sunk in despair, weeping at the Betty Crocker commercials. Finally, during the late late show, he stirred a little at one of the frequent public service announcements. That was it, he thought; he had to enlist others, he had to get help.

He picked up his phone and punched out the Crisis Line number.

The woman who answered sounded kind and sympathetic and very beautiful, and Kenny began to pour out his heart to her, all about the monkey that wouldn't let him eat, about how nobody else seemed to notice the monkey, about... but he had barely gotten his heart-pouring going good when the monkey smashed him across the side of the head. Kenny moaned. "What's wrong?" the woman asked. The monkey yanked his ear. Kenny tried to ignore the pain and keep on talking, but the monkey kept hurting him until finally he shuddered and sobbed and hung up the phone.

This is a nightmare, Kenny thought, a terrible nightmare. And so thinking, he pushed himself to his feet and staggered off to bed, hoping that everything would be normal in the morning, that the monkey would have been nothing but part of some wretched dream, no doubt brought on by indigestion.

The merciless little monkey would not even allow him to sleep properly, Kenny discovered. He was accustomed to sleeping on his back, with his hands folded very primly on his stomach. But when he undressed and tried to assume that position, the monkey fists came raining down on his poor head like some furious hairy hail. The monkey was not about to be squashed between Kenny's bulk and the pillows, it seemed. Kenny squealed with pain and rolled over on his stomach. He was very uncomfortable this way and had difficulty falling asleep, but it was the only way the monkey would leave him alone.

The next morning Kenny Dorchester drifted slowly into wakefulness, his cheek mashed against the pillows and his right arm still asleep. He was afraid to move. It was all a dream, he told himself, there is no monkey, what a silly thing that would be, monkey indeed!, it was only that Boney Moroney had told him about this "monkey treatment" and he had slept on it and had a nightmare. He couldn't feel anything on his back, not a thing. This was just like any other morning. He opened one bleary eye. His bedroom looked perfectly normal. Still he was afraid to move. It was very peaceful lying here like this, monkeyless, and he wanted to savor the feeling. So Kenny lay very still for the longest time, watching the numbers on his digital clock change slowly.

Then his stomach growled at him. "There is no monkey!" he proclaimed loudly, and he sat up in bed.

He felt the monkey shift.

Kenny trembled and almost started to weep again, but he controlled himself with an effort. No monkey was going to get the best of Kenny Dorchester, he told himself. Grimacing, he donned his slippers and plodded into the bathroom.

The monkey peered out cautiously from behind his head while Kenny was shaving. He glared at it in the bathroom mirror. It seemed to have grown a bit, but was hardly surprising, considering how much it had eaten yesterday. Kenny toyed with the idea of trying to cut the monkey's throat, but decided that his Norelco electric shaver was not terribly well suited to that end. And even if he used a knife, trying to stab behind his own back while looking in the mirror was a dangerously uncertain proposition.

Before leaving the bathroom, Kenny was struck by a whim. He stepped on his scale.

The numbers lit up at once. 367. The same as yesterday, he thought. The monkey weighed nothing. He frowned. No, that had to be wrong. No doubt the little monkey weighed a pound or two, but its weight was offset by whatever poundage Kenny had lost. He had to have lost *some* weight, he reasoned, since he hadn't been allowed to eat anything for ever so long. He stepped off the scale, then got back on quickly, just to doublecheck. It still read 367. Kenny was certain that he had lost weight. Perhaps some good would come of his travails after all. The thought made him feel oddly cheerful.

Kenny grew even more cheerful at breakfast. For the first time since he had gotten his monkey, he managed to get some food in his mouth.

When he arrived at the kitchen, he debated between French toast and bacon and eggs, but only briefly. Then he decided that he would never get to taste either. Instead, with a somber fatalism, Kenny fetched down a bowl and filled it with corn flakes and milk. The monkey would probably steal it all anyway, he thought, so there was no sense going to any trouble.

Quick as he could he hurried the spoon to his mouth. The monkey grabbed it away. Kenny had expected it, had known it would happen, but when the monkey hand wrenched the spoon away he nonetheless felt a sudden and terrible grief. "No," he said useless. "No, no, no." He could hear the corn flakes crunching in that filthy monkey mouth, and he felt milk dripping down the back of his neck. Tears gathered in his eyes as he stared down at the bowl of corn flakes, so near and yet so far.

Then he had an idea.

Kenny Dorchester lunged forward and stuck his face right down in the bowl.

The monkey twisted his ear and shrieked and pounded on his temple, but Kenny didn't care. He was sucking in milk gleefully and gobbling up as many corn flakes as his mouth could hold. By the time the monkey's tail lashed around angrily and sent the bowl sailing from the table to shatter on the floor, Kenny had a huge wet mouthful. His cheeks bulged and milk dribbled down his chin, and somehow he'd gotten a corn flake up his right nostril, but Kenny was in heaven. He chewed and swallowed as fast as he could, almost choking on the food.

When it was all gone he licked his lips and rose triumphantly. "Ha, ha," he said. "Ha, ha, ha." He walked back to his bedroom with great dignity and dressed, sneering at the monkey in the full-length bedroom mirror. He had beaten it.

In the days and weeks that followed, Kenny Dorchester settled into a new sort of daily routine and an useasy accommodation with his monkey.

It proved easier than Kenny might have imagined, except at mealtimes. When he was not attempting to get food into his mouth, it was almost possible to forget about the monkey entirely. At work it sat peacefully on his back while Kenny shuffled his papers and made his phone calls. His co-workers either failed to notice the monkey or were sufficiently polite so as not to comment on it. The only difficulty came one day at coffee break, when Kenny foolheartedly approached the coffee vendor in an effort to secure a cheese danish. The monkey ate nine of them before Kenny could stagger away, and the man insisted that Kenny had done it when his back was turned.

Simply by avoiding mirrors, a habit that Kenny Dorchester now began to cultivate as assiduously as any vampire, he was able to keep his mind off the monkey for most of the day. He had only one difficulty, though it occured thrice daily; breakfast, lunch, and dinner. At those times the monkey asserted itself forcefully, and Kenny was forced to deal with it. As the weeks passed, he gradually fell into the habit of ordering food that could be served in bowls, so that he might practice what he termed his "Kellogg manuever." By this strategem, Kenny usually managed to get at least a few mouthfuls to eat each and every day.

To be sure, there *were* problems. People would stare at him rather strangely when he used the Kellogg manuever in public, and sometimes make rude comments on his table manners. At a chili emporium Kenny liked to frequent, the proprietor assumed he had suffered a heart attack when he dove towards his chili, and was very angry with him afterwards. On another occasion a bowl of soup left him with facial burns that made it look as though he was constantly blushing. And the last straw came when he was thrown bodily out of his favorite seafood restaurant in the world, simply because he plunged his face into a bowl of crawfish bisque and began sucking it up noisily. Kenny stood in the street and berated them loudly and forcefully, reminding them how much money he had spent there over the years. Thereafter he ate only at home.

Despite the limited success of his Kellogg maneuver, Kenny Dorchester still lost nine-tenths of every meal and ten-tenths of some to the voracious monkey on his back. At first he was constantly hungry, frequently depressed, and full of schemes for ridding himself of his monkey. The only problem with these schemes was that none of them seemed to work. One Saturday Kenny went to the monkey house at the zoo, hoping that his monkey might hop off to play with others of its kind, or perhaps go in pursuit of some attractive monkey of the opposite sex. Instead, no sooner had he entered the monkey house than all the monkeys imprisoned therein ran to the bars of their cages and began to chitter and scream and spit and leap up and down madly. His own monkey answered in kind, and when some of the caged monkeys began to throw peanut husks and other bits of garbage Kenny clapped his hands over his ears and fled. On another occasion he allowed himself to visit a local saloon, and order a number of boilermakers, a drink he understood to be particularly devastating. His intent was to get his monkey so blind drunk that it might be easily removed. This experiment too had rather unfortunate consequences. The monkey drank the boilermakers as fast as Kenny could order them, but after the third one it began to keep time to the disco music from the juke box by beating on the top of Kenny's head. The next morning it was Kenny who woke with the pounding headache; the monkey seemed fine.

After a time, Kenny finally put all his scheming aside. Failure had discouraged him, and moreover the matter seemed somehow less urgent that it had originally. He was seldom hungry after the first week, in fact. Instead he went through a brief period of weakness, marked by frequent dizzy spells, and then a kind of euphoria settled over him. He felt just wonderful, and even better, he was losing weight!

To be sure, it did not show on his scale. Every morning he climbed up on it, and every morning it lit up as 367. But that was only because it was weighing the monkey as well as himself. Kenny knew he was losing; he could almost feel the pounds and inches just melting away, and some of his co-workers in the office remarked on it as well. Kenny owned up to it, beaming. When they asked him how he was doing it, he winked and replied, "The monkey treatment! The mysterious monkey treatment!" He said no more than that. The one time he tried to explain, the monkey fetched him such a wallop it almost took his head off, and his friends began to mutter about his strange spasms.

Finally the day came when Kenny had to tell his cleaner to take in all his pants a few inches. That was one of the most delightful tasks of his life, he thought.

All the pleasure went right out of the moment when he exited the store, however, and chanced to glance briefly to his side and see his reflection in the window. At home Kenny had long since removed all his mirrors, so he was shocked at the sight of his monkey. It had grown. It was a little thing no longer. Now it hunched on his back like some evil deformed chimpanzee, and its grinning face loomed above his head instead of peering out behind it. The monkey was grossly fat beneath its sparse brown hair, almost as wide as it was tall, and its great long tail drooped all the way to the ground. Kenny stared at it with horror, and it grinned back at him. No wonder he had been having backaches recently, he thought.

He walked home slowly, all the jauntiness gone out of his step, trying to think. A few neighborhood dogs followed him up the street, barking at his monkey. Kenny ignored them. He had long since learned that dogs could see his monkey, just like the monkeys at the zoo. He suspected that drunks could see it as well. One man had stared at him for a very long time that night he had visited the saloon. Of course, the fellow might just have been staring at those vanishing boilermakers.

Back in his apartment Kenny Dorchester stretched out on his couch on his stomach, stuck a pillow underneath his chin, and turned on his television set. He paid no attention to the screen, however. He was trying to figure things out.

Even the Pizza Hut commercials were insufficiently distracting, although Kenny did absently mutter "Ah-h-h-h" like you were supposed to when the slice of pizza, dripping long strands of cheese, was first lifted from the pan.

When the show ended, Kenny got up and turned off the set and sat himself down at his dining room table. He found a piece of paper and a stubby little pencil. Very carefully, he block-printed a formula across the paper, and stared at it.

ME + MONKEY = 367 POUNDS

There were certain disturbing implications in that formula, Kenny thought. The more he considered them, the less he like them. He was definitely losing weight, to be sure, and that was not to be sneered at -- nonetheless, the grim inflexibility of the formula hinted that most of the gains traditionally attributed to weight loss would never be his to enjoy. No matter how much fat he shed, he would continue to carry around 367 pounds, and the strain on his body would be the same. As for becoming svelte and dashing and attractive to women, how could he even consider it so long as he had his monkey? Kenny thought of how a dinner date might go for him, and shuddered. "Where will it all end?" he said aloud.

The monkey shifted, and snickered a vile little snicker.

Kenny pursed his lips in firm disapproval. This could not go on, he resolved. He decided to go straight to the source on the morrow, and with that idea planted firmly in his mind, he took himself to bed.

The next day, after work, Kenny Dorchester returned by cab to the seedy neighborhood where he'd been subjected to the monkey treatment.

The storefront was gone.

Kenny sat in the back seat of the taxi (this time he had the good sense not to get out, and moreover had tipped the driver handsomely in advance) and blinked in confusion. A tiny wet blubbery moan escaped his lips. The address was right, he knew it, he still had the slip of paper that had brought him there in the first place. But where he had found a grimy brick storefront adorned by a faded Coca-Cola sign and flanked by two vacant lots, now there was only one large vacant lot, choked with weeds and rubbish and broken bricks. "Oh, no," Kenny said. "Oh, no."

"You OK?" asked the lady driving the cab.

"Yes," Kenny muttered. "Just . . . just wait, please. I have to think." He held his head in his hands. He feared he was going to develop a splitting headache. Suddenly he felt weak and dizzy. And very hungry. The meter ticked. The cabbie whistled. Kenny thought. The street looked just as he remembered it, except for the missing storefront. It was just as dirty, the old winos were still on their stoop, the . . .

Kenny rolled down the window. "You, sir!" he called out to one of the winos. The man stared at him. "Come here, sir!" Kenny yelled.

Warily the old man shuffled across the street.

Kenny fetched out a dollar bill from his wallet and pressed it into the man's hand. "Here, friend," he said, "Go and buy yourself some vintage Thunderbird, if you will."

"Why you givin' me this?" the wino said suspiciously.

"I wish you to answer me a question. What has become of the building that was standing there" -- Kenny pointed -- "a few weeks ago."

The man stuffed the dollar into his pocket quickly. "Ain't been no buildin' there fo' years," he said.

"I was afraid of that," Kenny said. "Are you certain? I was here in the not-so-distant past and I *distinctly* recall . . ."

"No buildin'," the wino said firmly. He turned and walked away, but after a few steps he paused and glanced back. "You're one of them fat guys," he said accusingly.

"What do you know about . . . ahem . . . overweight men?"

"See 'em wanderin' over there, all the time. Crazy, too. Yellin' at thin air, playin with some kind of animals. Yeah. I 'member you. You're one of them fat guys all right." He scowled at Kenny, confused. "Looks like you lost some of that blubber, though. Real good. Thanks for the dollar."

Kenny Dorchester watched him return to his stoop and begin conversing animatedly with his colleagues. With a tremulous sigh, Kenny rolled up the window, glanced at the empty lot again, and bid his driver take him home. Him and his monkey, that is.

Weeks went dripping by and Kenny Dorchester lived as if in a trance. He went to work, shuffled his papers, mumbled pleasantries to his coworkers, struggled and schemed for his meagre mouthfuls of food, avoided mirrors. The scale read 367. His flesh melted away from his at a precipitous rate. He developed slack droopy jowls, and his skin sagged all about his middle, looking as flacid and pitiful as a used condom. He began to have fainting spells, brought on by hunger. At times he staggered and lurched about the street, his thinning and weakened legs unable to support the weight of his growing monkey. His vision go blurry. Once he even thought that his hair had started to fall out, but that at least was a false alarm; it was the monkey who was losing hair, thank goodness. It shed all over the place, ruining his furniture, and even daily vacuuming didn't seem to help much. Soon Kenny stopped trying to clean up. He lacked energy. He lacked the energy for just about everything, in fact. Rising from a chair was a major undertaking. Cooking dinner was impossible torment -- but he did *that* anyway, since the monkey beat him severely when it was not fed. Nothing seemed to matter very much to Kenny Dorchester. Nothing but the terrible tale of his scale each morning, and the formula that he had scotch-taped to his bathroom wall.

ME + MONKEY = 367 POUNDS

He wondered how much was ME anymore, and how much was MONKEY, but he did not really want to find out. One day, following the dictates of a kind of feeble whim, Kenny made a sudden grab for the monkey's legs under his chin, hoping against hope that it had gotten slow and obese and that he would be able to yank it from his back. His hands closed on nothing. On his own pale flesh. The monkey's legs did not seem to be there, though Kenny could still feel its awful crushing weight. He patted his neck and breast in dim confusion, staring down at himself, and noting absently that he could see his feet. He wondered how long that had been true. They seemed to be perfectly nice feet, Kenny Dorchester thought, although the legs to which they were attached were alarmingly gaunt.

Slowly his mind wandered back to the quandry at hand -- what had become of the monkey's legs? Kenny frowned and puzzled and tried to work it all out in his head, but nothing occured to him. Finally he slid his newly-rediscovered feet into a pair of bed slippers and shuffled to the closet where he had stored all of his mirrors. Closing his eyes, he reached in, fumbled about, and found the full-length mirror that had once hung on his bedroom wall. It was a large, wide mirror. Working entirely by touch, Kenny fetched it out, carried it a few feet, and painstakingly propped it up against a wall. Then he held his breath and opened his eyes.

There in the mirror stood a gaunt, gray, skeletal looking fellow, hunched over and sickly. On his back, grinning, was a thing the size of a gorilla. A very obese gorilla. It had a long pale snakelike tail, and great long arms, and it was as white as a maggot and entirely hairless. It had not legs. It was . . . *attached* to him now, growing right out of his back. Its grin was terrible, and filled up half of its face. It looked very like the gross proprietor of the monkey treatment emporium, in fact. Why had he never noticed that before? Of course, of course.

Kenny Dorchester turned from the mirror, and cooked the monkey a big rich dinner before going to bed.

That night he dreamed of how it had all started, back in the Slab when he had met Boney Moroney. In his nightmare a great evil white thing rode atop Moroney's shoulders, eating slab after slab of ribs, but Kenny politely pretended not to notice while he and Boney made bright, spritely conversation. Then the thing ran out of ribs, so it reached down and lifted one of Boney's arms and began to eat his hand. The bones crunched nicely, and Moroney kept right on talking. The creature had eaten its way up to the elbow when Kenny woke screaming, covered with a cold sweat. He had wet his bed too.

Agonizingly he pushed himself up and staggered to the toilet, where he dry-heaved for ten minutes. The monkey, angry at being wakened, gave him a desultory slap from time to time.

And then a furtive light came into Kenny Dorchester's eyes. "Boney," he whispered. Hurriedly he scrambled back to his bedroom on hands and knees, rose, and threw on some clothes. It was three in the morning, but Kenny knew there was no time to waste. He looked up an address in his phone book, and called a cab.

Boney Moroney lived in a tall modern highrise by the river, with moonlight shining brightly off its silver-mirrored flanks. When Kenny staggered in, he found the night doorman asleep at his station, which was just as well. Kenny tiptoed past him to the elevators and rode up to the eighth floor. The monkey on his back had begun stirring now, and seemed uneasy and ill-tempered.

Kenny's finger trembled as he pushed the round black button set in the door to Moroney's apartment, just beneath the eyehole. Musical chimes sounded loudly within, startling in the morning stillness. Kenny leaned on the button. The music played on and on. Finally he heard footsteps, heavy and threatening. The peephole opened and closed again. Then the door swung open.

The apartment was black, though the far wall was made entirely of glass, so the moonlight illuminated the darkness softly. Outlined against the stars and the light of the city stood the man who had opened the door. He was hugely, obscenely fat, and his skin was a pasty fungoid white, and he had little dark eyes set deep into crinkles in his broad suety face. He wore nothing but a vast pair of striped shorts. His breasts flopped about against his chest when he shifted his weight. And when he smiled, his teeth filled up half his face. A great crescent moon of teeth. He smiled when he saw Kenny, and Kenny's monkey. Kenny felt sick. The thing in the door weighed twice as much as the one on his back. Kenny trembled. "Where is he?" he whispered softly. "Where is Boney? What have you done to him?"

The creature laughed, and its pendulous breasts flounced about wildly as it shook with mirth. The monkey on Kenny's back began to laugh too, a higher thinner laughter as sharp as the edge of knife. It reached down and twisted Kenny's ear cruelly. Suddenly a vast fear and a vast anger filled Kenny Dorchester. He summoned all the strength left in his wasted body and pushed forward, and somehow, somehow, he barged past the obese colossus who barred his way and staggered into the interior of the apartment. "Boney," he called, "where are you, Boney? It's me, Kenny."

There was no answer. Kenny went from room to room. The apartment was filthy, a shambles. There was no sign of Boney Moroney anywhere. When Kenny came panting back to the living room, the monkey shifted abruptly, and threw him off balance. He stumbled and fell hard. Pain went shooting up through his knees, and he cut open one outstretched hand on the edge of the chrome-and-glass coffee table. Kenny began to weep.

He heard the door close, and the thing that lived here moved slowly toward him. Kenny blinked back tears and stared at the approach of those two mammoth legs, pale in the moonlight, sagging all around with fat. He looked up and it was like gazing up the side of a mountain. Far, far above him grinned those terrible mocking teeth. *"Where is he?"* Kenny Dorchester whispered. "What have you done with poor Boney?"

The grin did not change. The thing reached down a meaty hand, fingers as thick as a length of kielbasa, and snagged the waistband of the baggy striped shorts. It pulled them down clumsily, and they settled to the ground like a parachute, bunching around its feet.

"Oh, no," said Kenny Dorchester.

The thing had no genitals. Hanging down between its legs, almost touching the carpet now that it had been freed from the confines of the soiled shorts, was a wrinkled droopy bag of skin, long and gaunt, growing from the creature's crotch. But as Kenny stared at it in horror, it thrashed feebly, and stirred, and the loose folds of flesh separated briefly into tiny arms and legs.

Then it opened its eyes.

Kenny Dorchester screamed and suddenly he was back on his feet, lurching away from the grinning obscenity in the center of the room. Between its legs, the thing that had been Boney Moroney raised its pitiful stick-thin arms in supplication. "Oh, nooooo," Kenny moaned, blubbering, and he danced about wildly, the vast weight of his monkey heavy of his back. Round and round he danced in the dimness, in the moonlight, searching for an escape from this madness.

Beyond the plate glass wall the lights of the city beckoned.

Kenny paused and panted and stared at them. Somehow the monkey must have known what he was thinking, for suddenly it began to beat on him wildly, to twist at his ears, to rain savage blows all around his head. But Kenny Dorchester paid no mind. With a smile that was almost beatific, he gathered the last of his strength and rushed pell-mell toward the moonlight.

The glass shattered into a million glittering shards, and Kenny smiled all the way down.

It was the smell that told him he was still alive, the smell of disinfectant, and the feel of starched sheets beneath him. A hospital, he thought amidst a haze of pain. He was in a hospital. Kenny wanted to cry. Why hadn't he died? Oh, why, oh, why? He opened his eyes and tried to say something.

Suddenly a nurse was there, standing over him, feeling his brow and looking down with concern. Kenny wanted to beg her to kill him, but the words would not come. She went away and when she came back she had others with her.

A chubby young man said, "You'll be all right, Mr. Dorchester, but you have a long way to go. You're in a hospital. You're a very lucky man. You fell eight stories. You ought to be dead."

I want to be dead, Kenny thought, and he shaped the words very very carefully with his mouth, but no one seemed to hear them. Maybe the monkey has taken over, he thought. Maybe I can't even talk any more.

"He wants to say something," the nurse said.

"I can see that," said the chubby young doctor. "Mr. Dorchester, please don't strain yourself. Really. If you are trying to ask about your friend, I'm afraid he wasn't as lucky as you. He was killed by the fall. You would have died as well, but fortunately you landed on top of him."

Kenny's fear and confusion must have been obvious, for the nurse put a gentle hand on his arm. "The other man," she said patiently. "The fat one. You can thank God he was so fat, too. He broke your fall like a giant pillow."

And finally Kenny Dorchester understood what they were saying, and began to weep, but now he was weeping for joy, and trembling.

Three days later, he managed his first word. "Pizza," he said, and it came weak and hoarse from between his lips, and then louder still, and before long he was pushing the nurse's call button and shouting and pushing and shouting. "Pizza, pizza, pizza, pizza," he chanted, and he would not be calm until they ordered one for him. Nothing had ever tasted so good.

...for a single yesterday

Keith was our culture, what little we had left. He was our poet and our troubadour, and his voice and his guitar were our bridges to the past. He was a time-tripper too, but no one minded that much until Winters came along.

Keith was our memory. But he was also my friend.

He played for us every evening after supper. Just beyond sight of the common house, there was a small clearing and a rock he liked to sit on. He'd wander there at dusk, with his guitar, and sit down facing west. Always west; the cities had been east of us. Far east, true, but Keith didn't like to look that way. Neither did the rest of us, to tell the truth.

Not everybody came to the evening concerts, but there was always a good crowd, say three-fourths of the people in the commune. We'd gather around in a rough circle, sitting on the ground or lying in the grass by ones and twos. And Keith, our living hi-fi in denim and leather, would stroke his beard in vague amusement and begin to play.

He was good, too. Back in the old days, before the Blast, he'd been well on his way to making a name for himself. He'd come to the commune four years ago for a rest, to check up on old friends and get away from the musical rat race for a summer. But he'd figured on returning.

Then came the Blast. And Keith had stayed. There was nothing left to go back to. His cities were graveyards full of dead and dying, their towers melted tombstones that glowed at night. And the rats—human and animal—were everywhere else.

In Keith, those cities still lived. His songs were all of the old days, bittersweet things full of lost dreams and loneliness. And he sang them with love and longing. Keith would play requests, but mostly he stuck to his kind of music. A lot of folk, a lot of folk-rock, and a few straight rock things and show tunes. Lightfoot and Kristofferson and Woody Guthrie were particular favorites. And once in a while he'd play his own compositions, written in the days before the Blast. But not often.

Two songs, though, he played every night. He always started with "They Call the Wind Maria" and ended with "Me and Bobby McGee." A few of us got tired of the ritual, but no one ever objected. Keith seemed to think the songs fit us, somehow, and nobody wanted to argue with him.

Until Winters came along, that is. Which was in a late-fall evening in the fourth year after the Blast.

His first name was Robert, but no one ever used it, although the rest of us were all on a first name basis. He'd introduced himself as Lieutenant Robert Winters the evening he arrived, driving up in a jeep with two other men. But his Army didn't exist anymore, and he was looking for refuge and help.

That first meeting was tense. I remember feeling very scared when I heard the jeep coming, and wiping my palms on my jeans as I waited. We'd had visitors before. None of them very nice.

I waited for them alone. I was as much a leader as we had in those days. And that wasn't much. We voted on everything important, and nobody gave orders. So I wasn't really a boss, but I was a greeting committee. The rest scattered, which was good sense. Our last visitors had gone in big for slugging people and raping the girls. They'd worn black-and-gold uniforms and called themselves the Sons of the Blast. A fancy name for a rat pack. We called them SOB's too, but for other reasons.

Winters was different, though. His uniform was the good ol' U.S. of A. Which didn't prove a thing, since some Army detachments are as bad as the rat packs. It was our own friendly Army that went through the area in the first year after the Blast, scorching the towns and killing everyone they could lay their hands on.

I don't think Winters was part of that, although I never had the courage to flat-out ask him. He was too decent. He was big and blond and straight, and about the same age as the rest of us. And his two "men" were scared kids, younger than most of us in the commune. They'd been through a lot, and they wanted to join us. Winters kept saying that he wanted to help us rebuild.

We voted them in, of course. We haven't turned anyone away yet, except for a few rats. In the first year, we even took in a half-dozen citymen and nursed them while they died of radiation burns.

Winters changed us, though, in ways we never anticipated. Maybe for the better. Who knows? He brought books and supplies. And guns, too, and two men who knew how to use them. A lot of the guys on the commune had come there to get away from guns and uniforms, in the days before the Blast. So Pete and Crazy Harry took over the hunting, and defended us against the rats that drifted by from time to time. They became our police force and our army.

And Winters became our leader.

I'm still not sure how that happened. But it did. He started out making suggestions, moved on to leading discussions, and wound up giving orders. Nobody objected much. We'd been drifting ever since the Blast, and Winters gave us a direction. He had big ideas, too. When I was spokesman, all I worried about was getting us through until tomorrow. But Winters wanted to rebuild. He wanted to build a generator, and hunt for more survivors, and gather them together into a sort of village. Planning was his bag. He had big dreams for the day after tomorrow, and his hope was catching.

I shouldn't give the wrong impression, though. He wasn't any sort of a tin tyrant. He led us, yeah, but he was one of us, too. He was a little different from us, but not *that* different, and he became a friend in time. And he did his part to fit in. He even let his hair get long and grew a beard.

Only Keith never liked him much.

Winters didn't come out to concert rock until he'd been with us over a week. And when he did come, he stood outside the circle at first, his hands shoved into his pockets. The rest of us were lying around as usual, some singing, some just listening. It was a bit chilly that night, and we had a small fire going.

Winters stood in the shadows for about three songs. Then, during a pause, he walked closer to the fire. "Do you take requests?" he asked, smiling uncertainly.

I didn't know Winters very well back then. But I knew Keith. And I tensed a little as I waited for his answer.

But he just strummed the guitar idly and stared at Winters' uniform and his short hair. "That depends," he said at last. "I'm not going to play 'Ballad of the Green Berets,' if that's what you want."

An unreadable expression flickered over Winters' face. "I've killed people, yes," he said. "But that doesn't mean I'm proud of it. I wasn't going to ask for that."

Keith considered that, and looked down at his guitar. Then, seemingly satisfied, he nodded and raised his head and smiled. "Okay," he said. "What do you want to hear?"

"You know 'Leavin' on a Jet Plane?" Winters asked.

The smile grew. "Yeah. John Denver. I'll play it for you. Sad song, though. There aren't any jet planes anymore, Lieutenant. Know that? 'S true. You should stop and think why."

He smiled again, and began to play. Keith always had the last word when he wanted it. Nobody could argue with his guitar.

A little over a mile from the common house, beyond the fields to the west, a little creek ran through the hills and the trees. It was usually dry in the summer and the fall, but it was still a nice spot. Dark and quiet at night, away from the noise and the people. When the weather was right, Keith would drag his sleeping bag out there and bunk down under a tree. Alone.

That's also where he did his timetripping.

I found him there that night, after the singing was over and everyone else had gone to bed. He was leaning against his favorite tree, swatting mosquitoes and studying the creekbed.

I sat down next to him. "Hi, Gary," he said, without looking at me.

"Bad times, Keith?" I asked.

"Bad times, Gary," he said, staring at the ground and idly twirling a fallen leaf. I watched his face. His mouth was taut and expressionless, his eyes hooded.

I'd known Keith for a long time. I knew enough not to say anything. I just sat next to him in silence, making myself comfortable in a pile of fresh-fallen leaves. And after a while he began to talk, as he always did.

"There ought to be water," he said suddenly, nodding at the creek. "When I was a kid, I lived by a river. Right across the street. Oh, it was a dirty little river in a dirty little town, and the water was as polluted as all hell. But it was still water. Sometimes, at night, I'd go over to the park across the street, and sit on a bench, and watch it. For hours, sometimes. My mother used to get mad at me."

He laughed softly. "It was pretty, you know. Even the oil slicks were pretty. And it helped me think. I miss that, you know. The water. I always think better when I'm watching water. Strange, right?"

"Not so strange," I said.

He still hadn't looked at me. He was still staring at the dry creek, where only darkness flowed now. And his hands were tearing the leaf into pieces. Slow and methodical, they were.

"Gone now," he said after a silence. "The place was too close to New York. The water probably glows now, if there is any water. Prettier than ever, but I can't go back. So much is like that. Every time I remember something, I have to remember that it's gone now. And I can't go back, ever. To anything. Except . . . except with that . . . ." He nodded toward the ground between us. Then he finished with the leaf, and started another.

I reached down by his leg. The cigar box was where I expected it. I held it in both hands, and flipped the lid with my thumbs. Inside, there was the needle, and maybe a dozen small bags of powder. The powder looked white in the starlight. But seen by day, it was pale, sparkling blue.

I looked at it and sighed. "Not much left," I said.

Keith nodded, never looking. "I'll be out in a month, I figure." His voice sounded very tired. "Then I'll just have my songs, and my memories."

"That's all you've got now," I said. I closed the box with a snap and handed it to him. "Chronine isn't a time machine, Keith. Just a hallucinogen that happens to work on memory."

He laughed. "They used to debate that, way back when. The experts all said chronine was a memory drug. But they never *took* chronine. Neither have you, Gary. But I know. I've timetripped. It's not memory. It's more. You go back, Gary, you really do. You live it again, whatever it was. You can't change anything, but you know it's real, all the same."

He threw away what was left of his leaf, and gathered his knees together with his arms. Then he put his head atop them and looked at me. "You ought to timetrip someday, Gary. You really ought to. Get the dosage right, and you can pick your yesterday. It's not a bad deal at all."

I shook my head. "If I wanted to timetrip, would you let me?"

"No," he said, smiling but not moving his head. "I found the chronine. It's mine. And there's too little left to share. Sorry, Gary. Nothing personal, though. You know how it is."

"Yeah," I said. "I know how it is. I didn't want it anyway."

"I knew that," he said.

Ten minutes of thick silence. I broke it with a question. "Winters bother you?"

"Not really," he said. "He seems okay. It was just the uniforms, Gary. If it wasn't for those damn bastards in uniforms and what they did, I *could* go back. To my river, and my singing."

"And Sandi," I said.

His mouth twisted into a reluctant smile. "And Sandi," he admitted. "And I wouldn't even need chronine to keep my dates."

I didn't know what to say to that. So I didn't say anything. Finally, wearying, Keith slid forward a little, and lay back under the tree. It was a clear night. You could see the stars through the branches.

"Sometimes, out here at night, I forget," he said softly, more to himself than to me. "The sky still looks the same as it did before the Blast. And the stars don't know the difference. If I don't look east, I can almost pretend it never happened."

I shook my head. "Keith, that's a game. It *did* happen. You can't forget that. You know you can't. And you can't go back. You know that, too."

"You don't listen, do you, Gary? I *do* go back. I really do."

"You go back to a dream world, Keith. And it's dead, that world. You can't keep it up. Sooner or later you're going to have to start living in reality."

Keith was still looking up at the sky, but he smiled gently as I argued. "No, Gary. You don't see. The past is as real as the present, you know. And when the present is bleak and empty, and the future more so, then the only sanity is living in the past."

I started to say something, but he pretended not to hear. "Back in the city, when I was a kid, I never saw this many stars," he said, his voice distant. "The first time I got into the country, I remember how shocked I was at all the extra stars they'd gone and stuck in my sky." He laughed softly. "Know when that was? Six years ago, when I was just out of school. Also last night. Take your pick. Sandi was with me, both times."

He fell silent. I watched him for a few moments, then stood up and brushed myself off. It was never any use. I couldn't convince him. And the saddest part of it was, I couldn't even convince myself. Maybe he was right. Maybe, for him, that was the answer.

"You ever been in the mountains?" he asked suddenly. He looked up at me quickly, but didn't wait for an answer. "There was this night, Gary—in Pennsylvania, in the mountains. I had this old beat-up camper, and we were driving through, bumming it around the country.

"Then, all of a sudden, this fog hit us. Thick stuff, gray and rolling, all kind of mysterious and spooky. Sandi loved stuff like that, and I did too, kind of. But it was hell to drive through. So I pulled off the road, and we took out a couple of blankets and went off a few feet.

"It was still early, though. So we just lay on the blankets together, and held each other, and talked. About us, and my songs, and that great fog, and our trip, and her acting, and all sorts of things. We kept laughing and kissing, too, although I don't remember what we said that was so funny. Finally, after an hour or so, we undressed each other and made love on the blankets, slow and easy, in the middle of that dumb fog."

Keith propped himself up on an elbow and looked at me. His voice was bruised, lost, hurt, eager. And lonely. "She was beautiful, Gary. She really was. She never liked me to say that, though. I don't think she believed it. She liked me to tell her she was pretty. But she was more than pretty. She *was* beautiful. All warm and soft and golden, with red-blond hair and these dumb green eyes that were either green or gray, depending on her mood. That night they were gray, I think. To match the fog." He smiled, and sank back, and looked up at the stars again.

"The funniest thing was the fog," he said. Very slowly. "When we'd finished making love, and we lay back together, the fog was gone. And the stars were out, as bright as tonight. The stars came out for us. The silly goddamn voyeuristic stars came out to watch us make it. And I told her that, and we laughed, and I held her warm against me. And she went to sleep in my arms, while I lay there and looked at the stars and tried to write a song for her."

"Keith . . ." I started.

"Gary," he said. "I'm going back there tonight. To the fog and the stars and my Sandi."

"Damnit, Keith," I said. "Stop it. You're getting yourself hooked."

Keith sat up again and began unbuttoning his sleeve. "Did you ever think," he said, "that maybe it's not the drug that I'm addicted to?"

And he smiled very broadly, like a cocky, eager kid.

Then he reached for his box, and his timetrip. "Leave me alone," he said.

That must have been a good trip. Keith was all smiles and affability the next day, and his glow infected the rest of us. The mood lasted all week. Work seemed to go faster and easier than usual, and the nightly song sessions were as boisterous as I can remember them. There was a lot of laughter, and maybe more honest hope than we'd had for quite a while.

I shouldn't give Keith all the credit, though. Winters was already well into his suggestion-making period, and things were happening around the commune. To begin with, he and Pete were already hard at work building another house—a cabin off to the side of the common house. Pete had hooked up with one of the girls, and I guess he wanted a little more privacy. But Winters saw it as the first step toward the village he envisioned.

That wasn't his only project, either. He had a whole sheaf of maps in his jeep, and every night he'd drag someone off to the side and pore over them by candlelight, asking all sorts of questions. He wanted to know which areas we'd searched for survivors, and which towns might be worth looting for supplies, and where the rat packs liked to run, and that sort of thing. Why? Well, he had some "search expeditions" in mind, he said.

There was a handful of kids on the commune, and Winters thought we ought to organize a school for them, to replace the informal tutoring they'd been getting. Then he thought we ought to build a generator and get the electricity going again. Our medical resources were limited to a good supply of drugs and medicines; Winters thought that one of us should quit the fields permanently and train himself as a village doctor. Yeah, Winters had a lot of ideas, all right. And a good portion of 'em were pretty good, although it was clear that the details were going to require some working out.

Meanwhile, Winters had also become a regular at the evening singing. With Keith in a good mood, that didn't pose any real problems. In fact, it livened things up a little.

The second night that Winters came, Keith looked at him very pointedly and swung into "Vietnam Rag," with the rest of us joining in. Then he followed it up with "Universal Soldier." In between lyrics, he kept flashing Winters this taunting grin.

Winters took it pretty well, however. He squirmed and looked uncomfortable at first, but finally entered into the spirit of the thing and began to smile. Then, when Keith finished, he stood up. "If you're so determined to cast me as the commune's very own friendly reactionary, well I guess I'll have to oblige," he said. He reached out a hand. "Give me that guitar."

Keith looked curious but willing. He obliged. Winters grabbed the instrument, strummed it a few times uncertainly, and launched into a robust version of "Okie from Muskogee." He played like his fingers were made of stone, and sang worse. But that wasn't the point.

Keith began laughing before Winters was three bars into the song. The rest of us followed suit. Winters, looking very grim and determined, plowed on through to the bitter end, even though he didn't know all the words and had to fake it in spots. Then he did the Marine hymn for an encore, ignoring all the hissing and moaning.

When he was finished, Pete clapped loudly. Winters bowed, smiled and handed the guitar back to Keith with an exaggerated flourish.

Keith, of course, was not one to be topped easily. He nodded at Winters, took the guitar, and promptly did "Eve of Destruction."

Winters retaliated with "Welfare Cadillac." Or tried to. Turned out he knew hardly any of the words, so he finally gave that up and settled for "Anchors Aweigh."

That sort of thing went on all night, as they jousted back and forth, and everybody else sat around laughing. Well, actually we did more than laugh. Generally we had to help Winters with his songs, since he didn't really know any of them all the way through. Keith held his own without us, of course.

It was one of the more memorable sessions. The only thing it really had in common with Keith's usual concerts was that it began with "They Call the Wind Maria," and ended with "Me and Bobby McGee."

But the next day, Keith was more subdued. Still some kidding around between him and Winters, but mostly the singing slipped back into the older pattern. And the day after, the songs were nearly all Keith's kind of stuff, except for a few requests from Winters, which Keith did weakly and halfheartedly.

I doubt that Winters realized what was happening. But I did, and so did most of the others. We'd seen it before. Keith was getting down again. The afterglow from his latest timetrip was fading. He was getting lonely and hungry and restless. He was itching, yet again, for his Sandi.

Sometimes, when he got that way, you could almost see the hurt. And if you couldn't see it, you could hear it when he sang. Loud and throbbing in every note.

Winters heard it too. He'd have had to be deaf to miss it. Only I don't think he understood what he heard, and I know he didn't understand Keith. All he knew was the anguish he heard. And it troubled him.

So, being Winters, he decided to do something about it. He came to Keith.

I was there at the time. It was midmorning, and Keith and I had come in from the field for a break. I was sitting on the well with a cup of water in my hand, and Keith was standing next to me talking. You could tell that he was getting ready to timetrip again, soon. He was very down, very distant, and I was having trouble reaching him.

In the middle of all this, Winters comes striding up, smiling, in his Army jacket. His house was rising quickly, and he was cheerful about it, and he and Crazy Harry had already mapped out the first of their "search expeditions."

"Hello, men," he said when he joined us at the well. He reached for the water, and I passed my cup.

He took a deep drink and passed it back. Then he looked at Keith. "I enjoy your singing," he said. "I think everybody else does, too. You're very good, really." He grinned. "Even if you are an anarchistic bastard."

Keith nodded. "Yeah, thanks," he said. He was in no mood for fooling around.

"One thing, though, has been bothering me," Winters said. "I figured maybe I could discuss it with you, maybe make a few suggestions. Okay?"

Keith stroked his beard and paid a little more attention. "Okay. Shoot, Colonel."

"It's your songs. I've noticed that most of them are pretty . . . down, let's say. Good songs, sure. But sort of depressing, if you know what I mean. Especially in view of the Blast. You sing too much about the old days, and things we've lost. I don't think that's good for morale. We've got to stop dwelling so much on the past if we're ever going to rebuild."

Keith stared at him, and slumped against the well. "You gotta be kidding," he said.

"No," said Winters. "No, I mean it. A few cheerful songs would do a lot for us. Life can still be good and worthwhile if we work at it. You should tell us that in your music. Concentrate on the things we still have. We need hope and courage. Give them to us."

But Keith wasn't buying it. He stroked his beard, and smiled, and finally shook his head. "No, Lieutenant, no way. It doesn't work like that. I don't sing propaganda, even if it's well-meant. I sing what I feel."

His voice was baffled. "Cheerful songs, well... no. I can't. They don't work, not for me. I'd like to believe it, but I can't, you see. And I can't make other people believe it. I don't. Life is pretty empty around here, the way I see it. And not too likely to improve. And... well, as long as I see it that way, I've got to sing it that way. You see?"

Winters frowned. "Things aren't *that* hopeless," he said. "And even if they were, we can't admit it, or we're finished."

Keith looked at Winters, at me, then down into the well. He shook his head again, and straightened. "No," he said simply, gently, sadly. And he left us at the well to stalk silently in the fields.

Winters watched him go, then turned to me. I offered him more water, but he shook his head. "What do you think, Gary?" he said. "Did I have a point? Or did I?"

I considered the question, and the asker. Winters sounded very troubled and very sincere. And the blond stubble on his chin made it clear that he was trying his best to fit in. I decided to trust him, a little.

"Yes," I said. "I know what you were driving at. But it's not that easy. Keith's songs aren't just songs. They mean things to him."

I hesitated, then continued. "Look, the Blast was hell for everybody, I don't have to tell you that. But most of us out here, we chose this kind of life, 'cause we wanted to get away from the cities and what they stood for. We miss the old days, sure. We've lost people, and things we valued, and a lot that made life joyful. And we don't much care for the constant struggle, or for having to live in fear of the rat packs. Still, a lot of what we valued is right here on the commune, and it hasn't changed that much. We've got the land, and the trees, and each other. And freedom of a sort. No pollution, no competition, no hatred. We like to remember the old days, and the *good* things in the cities—that's why we like Keith's singing—but now has its satisfactions too.

"Only, Keith is different. He didn't choose this way, he was only visiting. His dreams were all tied up with the cities, with poetry and music and people and noise. And he's lost his world; everything he did and wanted to do is gone. And... and well, there was this girl. Sandra, but he called her Sandi. She and Keith lived together for two years, traveled together, did everything together. They only split for a summer, so she could go back to college. Then they were going to join up again. You understand?"

Winters understood. "And then the Blast?"

"And then the Blast. Keith was here, in the middle of nowhere. Sandi was in New York City. So he lost her, too. I think sometimes that if Sandi had been with him, he'd have gotten over the rest. She was the most important part of the world he lost, the world they shared together. With her here, they could have shared a new world and found new beauties and new songs to sing. But she wasn't here, and . . . ."

I shrugged.

"Yeah," said Winters solemnly. "But it's been four years, Gary. I lost a lot too, including my wife. But I got over it. Sooner or later, mourning has to stop."

"Yes," I said. "For you, and for me. I haven't lost that much, and you . . . you think that things will be good again. Keith doesn't. Maybe things were *too* good for him in the old days. Or maybe he's just too romantic for his own good. Or maybe he loved harder than we did. All I know is that *his* dream tomorrow is like his yesterday, and mine isn't. I've never found anything I could be that happy with. Keith did, or thinks he did. Same difference. He wants it back."

I drank some more water, and rose. "I've got to get back to work," I said quickly, before Winters could continue the conversation. But I was thoughtful as I walked back to the fields.

There was, of course, one thing I hadn't told Winters, one important thing. The timetripping. Maybe if Keith was forced to settle for the life he had, he'd come out of it. Like the rest of us had done.

But Keith had an option; Keith could go back. Keith still had his Sandi, so he didn't *have* to start over again.

That, I thought, explained a lot. Maybe I should have mentioned it to Winters. Maybe.

Winters skipped the single that night. He and Crazy Harry were set to leave the next morning, to go searching to the west. They were off somewhere stocking their jeep and making plans.

Keith didn't miss them any. He sat on his rock, warmed by a pile of burning autumn leaves, and outsung the bitter wind that had started to blow. He played hard and loud, and sang sad. And after the fire went out, and the audience drifted off, he took his guitar and his cigar box and went off toward the creek.

I followed him. This time the night was black and cloudy, with the smell of rain in the air. And the wind was strong and cold. No, it didn't sound like people dying. But it moved through the trees and shook the branches and whipped away the leaves. And it sounded . . . restless.

When I reached the creek, Keith was already rolling up his sleeve.

I stopped him before he took his needle out. "Hey, Keith," I said, laying a hand on his arm. "Easy. Talk first, okay?"

He looked at my hand and his needle, and returned a reluctant nod. "Okay, Gary," he said. "But short. I'm in a rush. I haven't seen Sandi for a week."

I let go of his arm and sat down. "I know."

"I was trying to make it last, Gar. I only had a month's worth, but I figured I could make it last longer if I only timetripped once a week." He smiled. "But that's hard."

"I know," I repeated. "But it would be easier if you didn't think about her so much."

He nodded, put down the box, and pulled his denim jacket a little tighter to shut out the wind. "I think too much," he agreed. Then, smiling, he added, "such men are dangerous."

"Ummm, yeah. To themselves, mostly." I looked at him, cold and huddled in the darkness. "Keith, what will you do when you run out?"

"I wish I knew."

"I know," I said. "Then you'll forget. Your time machine will be broken, and you'll have to live today. Find somebody else and start again. Only it might be easier if you'd start now. Put away the chronine for a while. Fight it."

"Sing cheerful songs?" he asked sarcastically.

"Maybe not. I don't ask you to wipe out the past, or pretend it didn't happen. But try to find something in the present. You know it can't be as empty as you pretend. Things aren't black and white like that. Winters was part right, you know—there *are* still good things. You forget that."

"Do I? What do I forget?"

I hesitated. He was making it hard for me. "Well . . . you still enjoy your singing. You know that. And there could be other things. You used to enjoy writing your own stuff. Why don't you work on some new songs? You haven't written anything to speak of since the Blast."

Keith had picked up a handful of leaves and was offering them to the wind, one by one. "I've thought of that. You don't know how much I've thought of that, Gary. And I've *tried.* But nothing comes." His voice went soft right then. "In the old days, it was different. And you know why. Sandi would sit out in the audience every time I sang. And when I did something new, something of mine, I could see her brighten. If it was good, I'd know it, just from the way she smiled. She was proud of me, and my songs."

He shook his head. "Doesn't work now, Gary. I write a song now, and sing it, and . . . so what? Who cares? You? Yeah, maybe you and a few of the others come up after and say, 'Hey, Keith, I liked that.' But that's not the same. My songs were *important* to Sandi, the same way her acting was important to me. And now my songs aren't important to anyone. I tell myself that shouldn't matter. I should get my own satisfaction from composing, even if no one else does. I tell myself that a lot. But saying it doesn't make it so."

Sometimes I think, right then, I should have told Keith that his songs were the most important thing in the world to me. But hell, they weren't. And Keith was a friend, and I couldn't feed him lies, even if he needed them.

Besides, he wouldn't have believed me. Keith had a way of recognizing truth.

Instead, I floundered. "Keith, you could find someone like that again, if you tried. There are girls in the commune, girls as good as Sandi, if you'd open yourself up to them. You could find someone else."

Keith gave me a calm stare, more chilling than the wind. "I don't need someone else, Gary," he said. He picked up the cigar box, opened it, and showed me the needle. "I've got Sandi."

Twice more that week Keith timetripped. And both times he rushed off with a feverish urgency. Usually he'd wait an hour or so after the singing, and discreetly drift off to his creek. But now he brought the cigar box with him, and left even before the last notes of "Me and Bobby McGee" had faded from the air.

Nobody mentioned anything, of course. We all knew Keith was timetripping, and we all knew he was running out. So we forgave him, and understood. Everybody understood, that is, except Pete, Winters' former corporal. He, like Winters and Crazy Harry, hadn't been filled in yet. But one evening at the singing, I noticed him looking curiously at the cigar box that lay by Keith's feet. He said something to Jan, the girl he'd been sleeping with. And she said something back. So I figured he'd been briefed.

I was too right.

Winters and Crazy Harry returned a week, to the day, after their departure. They were not alone. They brought three young teen-agers, a guy and two girls, whom they'd found down west, in company with a group of rats. "In company," is a euphemism, of course. The kids had been slaves. Winters and Crazy had freed them.

I didn't ask what had happened to the rats. I could guess.

There was a lot of excitement that night and the night after. The kids were a little frightened of us, and it took a lot of attention to convince them that things would be different here. Winters decided that they should have their own place, and he and Pete began planning a second new cabin. The first one was nearing its crude completion.

As it turned out, Winters and Pete were talking about more than a cabin. I should have realized that, since I caught Winters looking at Keith very curiously and thoughtfully on at least two occasions.

But I didn't realize it. Like everyone else, I was busy getting to know the newcomers and trying to make them feel at ease. It wasn't simple, that.

So I didn't know what was going on until the fourth evening after Winters' return. I was outside, listening to Keith sing. He'd just barely finished "They Call the Wind Maria," and was about to swing into a second song, when a group of people suddenly walked into the circle. Winters led them, and Crazy Harry was just behind him with the three kids. And Pete was there, with his arm around Jan. Plus a few others who hadn't been at the concert when it started but had followed Winters from the common house.

Keith figured they wanted to listen, I guess. He began to play. But Winters stopped him.

"No, Keith," he said. "Not right now. We've got business to take care of now, while everybody's together. We're going to talk tonight."

Keith's fingers stopped, and the music faded. The only sounds were the wind and the crackle of the nearby burning leaves. Everyone was looking at Winters.

"I want to talk about timetripping," Winters said.

Keith put down his guitar and glanced at the cigar box at the base of concert rock. "Talk," he said.

Winters looked around the circle, studying the impassive faces, as if he was weighing them before speaking. I looked too.

"I've been told that the commune has a supply of chronine," Winters began. "And that you use it for timetripping. Is that true, Keith?"

Keith stroked his beard, as he did when he was nervous or thoughtful. "Yeah," he said.

"And that's the *only* use that's ever been made of this chronine?" Winters said. His supporters had gathered behind him in what seemed like a phalanx.

I stood up. I didn't feel comfortable arguing from the ground. "Keith was the first one to find the chronine," I said. "We were going through the town hospital after the Army had gotten through with it. A few drugs were all that were left. Most of them are in the commune stores, in case we need them. But Keith wanted the chronine. So we gave it to him, all of us. Nobody else cared much."

Winters nodded. "I understand that," he said very reasonably. "I'm not criticizing that decision. Perhaps you didn't realize, however, that there are other uses for chronine besides timetripping."

He paused. "Listen, and try to judge me fairly, that's all I ask," he said, looking at each of us in turn. "Chronine is a powerful drug; it's an important resource, and we need all our resources right now. And timetripping—anyone's timetripping— is an *abuse* of the drug. Not what it was intended for."

That was a mistake on Winters' part. Lectures on drug abuse weren't likely to go over big in the commune. I could feel the people around me getting uptight.

Rick, a tall, thin guy with a goatee who came to the concerts every night, took a poke at Winters from the ground. "Bullshit," he said. "Chronine's time travel, Colonel. Meant to be used for tripping."

"Right," someone else said. "And we gave it to Keith. I don't want to timetrip, but he does. So what's wrong with it?"

Winters defused the hostility quickly. "Nothing," he said. "*If* we had an unlimited supply of chronine. But we don't. Do we, Keith?"

"No," Keith said quietly. "Just a little left."

The fire was reflected in Winters' eyes when he looked at Keith. It made it difficult to read his expression. But his voice sounded heavy. "Keith, I know what those time trips mean to you. And I don't want to hurt you, really I don't. But we need that chronine, all of us."

"How?" That was me. I wanted Keith to give up chronine, but I'd be damned before I'd let it be taken from him. "How do we *need* the chronine?"

"Chronine is not a time machine," Winters said. "It is a memory drug. And there are things we *must* remember." He glanced around the circle. "Is there anyone here who ever worked in a hospital? An orderly? A candy-striper? Never mind. There might be, in a group this size. And they'd have seen things. Somewhere in the back of their skulls they'd *know* things we need to know. I'll bet some of you took shop in high school. I'll bet you learned all sort of useful things. But how much do you remember? With chronine, you could remember it all. We might have someone here who once learned to make arrows. We might have a tanner. We might have someone who knows how to build a generator. We might have a *doctor!"*

Winters paused and let that sink in. Around the circle, people shifted uneasily and began to mutter.

Finally Winters continued. "If we found a library, we wouldn't burn the books for heat, no matter how cold it got. But we're doing the same thing when we let Keith timetrip. *We're* a library—all of us here, we have books in our heads. And the only way to read those books is with chronine. We should use it to help us remember the things we must know. We should hoard it like a treasure, calculate every recall session carefully, and make sure—make *absolutely* sure—that we don't waste a grain of it."

Then he stopped. A long, long silence followed; for Keith, an endless one. Finally Rick spoke again. "I never thought of that," he said reluctantly. "Maybe you have something. My father was a doctor, if that means anything.'

Then another voice, and another; then a chorus of people speaking at once, throwing up half-remembered experiences that might be valuable, might be useful. Winters had struck paydirt.

He wasn't smiling, though. He was looking at me. I wouldn't meet his eyes. I couldn't. He had a point—an awful, awful point. But I couldn't admit that, I couldn't look at him and nod my surrender. Keith was my friend, and I had to stand by him.

And of all of us in the circle, I was the only one standing. But I couldn't think of anything to say.

Finally Winters' eyes moved. He looked at concert rock. Keith sat there, looking at the cigar box.

The hubbub went on for at least five minutes, but at last it died of its own weight. One by one the speakers glanced at Keith, and remembered, and dropped off into awkward silence. When the hush was complete, Keith rose and looked around, like a man coming out of a bad dream.

"No," he said. His voice was hurting and disbelieving; his eyes moved from person to person. "You can't. I don't . . . don't *waste* chronine. You know that, all of you. I visit Sandi, and that's not wasting. I need Sandi, and she's gone. I have to go back. It's my only way, my time machine." He shook his head.

My turn. "Yes," I said, as forcefully as I could manage. "Keith's right. Waste is a matter of definition. If you ask me, the biggest waste would be sending people back to sleep through college lectures a second time."

Laughter. Then other voices backed me. "I'm with Gary," somebody said. "Keith needs Sandi, and we need Keith. It's simple. I say he keeps the chronine."

"No way," someone else objected. "I'm as compassionate as anyone, but *hell*— how many of our people have died over the last few years' cause we've bungled it when they needed doctoring? You remember Doug, two years ago? You shouldn't need chronine for that. A bad appendix, and he dies. We butchered him when we tried to cut it out. If there's a chance to prevent that from happening again—even a long shot—I say we gotta take it."

"No guarantee it won't happen anyway," the earlier voice came back. "You have to hit the right memories to accomplish anything, and even *they* may not be as useful as you'd like."

"Shit. We have to *try* . . . ."

"I think we have an obligation to Keith . . . ."

"I think Keith's got an obligation to *us* . . . ."

And suddenly everybody was arguing again, hassling back and forth, while Winters and Keith and I stood and listened. It went on and on, back and forth over the same points. Until Pete spoke.

He stepped around Winters, holding Jan. "I've heard enough of this," he said. "I don't even think we got no argument. Jan here is gonna have my kid, she tells me. Well, damnit, I'm not going to take any chances on her or the kid dying. If there's a way we can learn something that'll make it safer, we take it. Especially I'm not gonna take no chances for a goddamn weakling who can't face up to life. Hell, Keithie here wasn't the only one hurt, so how does *he* rate? I lost a chick in the Blast too, but I'm not begging for chronine to dream her up again. I got a new chick instead. And that's what you better do, Keith."

Keith stood very still, but his fists were balled at his sides. "There are differences, Pete," he said slowly. "Big ones. My Sandi was no chick, for one thing. And I loved her, maybe more than you can ever understand. I know you don't understand pain, Pete. You've hardened yourself to it, like a lot of people, by pretending that it doesn't exist. So you convinced everybody you're a tough guy, a strong man, real independent. And you gave up some of your humanity, too." He smiled, very much in control of himself now, his voice sure and steady. "Well, I won't play that game. I'll cling to my humanity, and fight for it if I must. I loved once, really loved. And now I hurt. And I won't deny either of those things, or pretend that they mean any less to me than they do."

He looked to Winters. "Lieutenant, I want my Sandi, and I won't let you take her away from me. Let's have a vote."

Winters nodded.

It was close, very close. The margin was only three votes. Keith had a lot of friends.

But Winters won.

Keith took it calmly. He picked up the cigar box, walked over, and handed it to Winters. Pete was grinning happily, but Winters didn't even crack a smile.

"I'm sorry, Keith," he said.

"Yeah," said Keith. "So am I." There were tears on his face. Keith was never ashamed to cry.

There was no singing that night.

Winters didn't timetrip. He sent men on "search expeditions" into the past, all very carefully planned for minimum risk and maximum reward.

We didn't get any doctor out of it. Rick made three trips back without coming up with any useful memories. But one of the guys remembered some valuable stuff about medicinal herbs after a trip back to a bio lab, and another jaunt recalled some marginally good memories about electricity.

Winters was still optimistic, though. He'd turned to interviewing by then, to decide who should get to use the chronine next. He was very careful, very thorough, and he always asked the right questions. No one went back without his okay. Pending that approval, the chronine was stored in the new cabin, where Pete kept an eye on it.

And Keith? Keith sang. I was afraid, the night of the argument, that he might give up singing, but I was wrong. He couldn't give up song, any more than he could give up Sandi. He returned to concert rock the very next evening, and sang longer and harder than ever before. The night after that he was even better.

During the day, meanwhile, he went about his work with a strained cheerfulness. He smiled a lot, and talked a lot, but he never *said* anything much. And he never mentioned chronine, or timetripping, or the argument.

Or Sandi.

He still spent his nights out by the creek, though. The weather was getting progressively colder, but Keith didn't seem to mind. He just brought out a few blankets and his sleeping bag, and ignored the wind, and the chill, and the increasingly frequent rains.

I went out with him once or twice to sit and talk. Keith was cordial enough. But he never brought up the subjects that really mattered, and I couldn't bring myself to force the conversations to places he obviously didn't want to go. We wound up discussing the weather and like subjects.

These days, instead of his cigar box, Keith brought his guitar out to the creek. He never played it when I was there, but I heard him once or twice from a distance, when I was halfway back to the common house after one of our fruitless talks. No singing, just music. Two songs, over and over again. You know which two.

And after a while, just one. "Me and Bobby McGee." Night after night, alone and obsessed, Keith played that song, sitting by a dry creek in a barren forest. I'd always liked the song, but now I began to fear it, and a shiver would go through me whenever I heard those notes on the frosty autumn wind.

Finally, one night, I spoke to him about it. It was a short conversation, but I think it was the only time, after the argument, that Keith and I ever really reached each other.

I'd come with him to the creek, and wrapped myself in a heavy woolen blanket to ward off the cold, wet drizzle that was dripping from the skies. Keith lay against his tree, half into his sleeping bag, with his guitar on his lap. He didn't even bother to shield it against the damp, which bothered me.

We talked about nothing, until at last I mentioned his lonely creek concerts. He smiled. "You know why I play that song," he said.

"Yeah," I said. "But I wish you'd stop."

He looked away. "I will. After tonight. But tonight I play it, Gary. Don't argue, please. Just listen. The song is all I have left now, to help me think. And I've needed it, 'cause I been thinking a lot."

"I warned you about thinking," I said jokingly.

But he didn't laugh. "Yeah. You were right, too. Or I was, or Shakespeare . . . whoever you want to credit the warning to. Still, sometimes you can't help thinking. It's part of being human. Right?"

"I guess."

"I know. So I think with my music. No water left to think by, and the stars are all covered. And Sandi's gone. Really gone now. You know, Gary . . . if I kept on, day to day, and didn't think so much, I might forget her. I might even forget what she looked like. Do you think Pete remembers his chick?"

"Yes," I said. "And you'll remember Sandi. I'm sure of that. But maybe not quite so much . . . and maybe that's for the best. Sometimes it's good to forget."

Then he looked at me. Into my eyes. "But I don't *want* to forget, Gary. And I won't. I won't."

And then he began to play. The same song. Once. Twice. Three times. I tried to talk, but he wasn't listening. His fingers moved on, fiercely, relentlessly. And the music and the wind washed away my words.

Finally I gave up and left. It was a long walk back to the common house, and Keith's guitar stalked me through the drizzle.

Winters woke me in the common house, shaking me from my bunk to face a grim, gray dawn. His face was even grayer. He said nothing; he didn't want to wake the others, I guess. He just beckoned me outside.

I yawned and stretched and followed him. Just outside the door, Winters bent and handed me a broken guitar.

I looked at it blankly, then up at him. My face must have asked the question.

"He used it on Pete's head," Winters said. "And took the chronine. I think Pete has a mild concussion, but he'll probably be all right. Lucky. He could be dead, real easy."

I held the guitar in my hands. It was shattered, the wood cracked and splintered, several strings snapped. It must have been a hell of a blow. I couldn't believe it. "No," I said. "Keith . . . no, he couldn't . . ."

"It's his guitar," Winters pointed out. "And who else would take the chronine?" Then his face softened. "I'm sorry, Gary. I really am. I think I understand why he did it. Still I want him. Any idea where he could be?"

I knew, of course. But I was scared. "What . . . what will you do?"

"No punishment," he said. "Don't worry. I just want the chronine back. We'll be more careful next time."

I nodded. "Okay," I said. "But nothing happens to Keith. I'll fight you if you go back on your word, and the others will too."

He just looked at me, very sadly, like he was disappointed that I'd mistrust him. He didn't say a thing. We walked the mile to the creek in silence, me still holding the guitar.

Keith was there, of course. Wrapped in his sleeping bag, the cigar box next to him. There were a few bags left. He'd used only one.

I bent to wake him. But when I touched him and rolled him over, two things hit me. He'd shaved off his beard. And he was very, very cold.

Then I noticed the empty bottle.

We'd found other drugs with the chronine, way back when. They weren't even guarded. Keith had used sleeping pills.

I stood up, not saying a word. I didn't need to explain. Winters had taken it all in very quickly. He studied the body and shook his head.

"I wonder why he shaved?" he said finally.

"I know," I said. "He never wore a beard in the old days, when he was with Sandi."

"Yes," said Winters. "Well, it figures."

"What?"

"The suicide. He always seemed unstable."

"No, Lieutenant," I said. "You've got it all wrong. Keith didn't commit suicide."

Winters frowned. I smiled.

"Look," I said. "If you did it, it would be suicide. You think chronine is only a drug for dreaming. But Keith figured it for a time machine. He didn't kill himself. That wasn't his style. He just went back to his Sandi. And this time, he made sure he stayed there."

Winters looked back at the body. "Yes," he said. "Maybe so." He paused. "For his sake, I hope that he was right."

The years since then have been good ones, I guess. Winters is a better leader than I was. The timetrips never turned up any knowledge worth a damn, but the search expeditions proved fruitful. There are more than two hundred people in town now, most of them people that Winters brought in.

It's a real town, too. We have electricity and a library, and plenty of food. And a doctor—a real doctor that Winters found a hundred miles from here. We got so prosperous that the Sons of the Blast heard about us and came back for a little fun. Winters had his militia beat them off and hunt down the ones who tried to escape.

Nobody but the old commune people remember Keith. But we still have singing and music. Winters found a kid named Ronnie on one of his trips, and Ronnie has a guitar of his own. He's not in Keith's league, of course, but he tries hard, and everybody has fun. And he's taught some of the youngsters how to play.

Only thing is, Ronnie likes to write his own stuff, so we don't hear many of the old songs. Instead we get postwar music. The most popular tune, right now, is a long ballad about how our army wiped out the Sons of the Blast.

Winters says that's a healthy thing; he talks about new music for a new civilization. And maybe he has something. In time, I'm sure, there will be a new culture to replace the one that died. Ronnie, like Winters, is giving us tomorrow.

But there's a price.

The other night, when Ronnie sang, I asked him to do "Me and Bobby McGee." But nobody knew the words.

The Needle Men

Living in Uptown, Jerry had seen a lot of things never dreamt of in places like Forest Park and Wilmette. But he had learned to mind his own business as well, so it was no wonder that he hardly thought twice about the guy with the needle until he bumped into the cops on the steps of his building.

He hadn't really seen anything suspicious, after all. It was a Friday night when it happened, and Jerry had been down on Rush street, checking out the action at some singles bars, with a notable lack of success. He'd had a few Michelobs too many and was close to getting sloshed, so when the cute brunette he'd been talking to went off with someone else, he made up his mind to call it a night. He rode the el back to Argyle, staring pensively out at the weathered sooty brick and grey windows of the buildings near the tracks, blinking whenever blue-white sparks came crackling off the third rail to etch hard, intense shadows on the tenement walls.

From the Argyle el stop it was a short walk to the six-flat where Jerry shared an apartment with three roommates. Even at midnight, Argyle was lively; country music blasted out the open doors of redneck bars, dim female silhouettes writhed in the windows of the strip joints, the 24-hour coffee shops were open and crowded. Jerry had to step over one derelict, passed out in front of a grocery store. A second sidled up to him by the drugstore, mumbling something in a rasping boozy voice, but he shied off when Jerry threw him a look. It was that kind of neighborhood. "Yeasty," Jerry liked to call it; hillbillies and Hispanics and blacks and a lot of Orientals, pushed together cheek-to-jowl and hating every minute of it. On the other side of Sheridan, along Marine Drive, the high-rises stood, full of young marrieds and singles. Respectability was kind of nibbling at the edges of the area, chewing up the old overcrowded tenements and spitting out renovated condos, but Jerry figured the process of digestion would take a long long time.

In the meantime, rents were cheap, at least by Chicago standards. Jerry was a struggling free-lance journalist, so cheap mattered. Besides, he figured he needed to see the seemy side of life, seething and bubbling, and Uptown had plenty of that.

The shortest way from the el to his building cut through an alley just on the far side of Sheridan, and brought him up the back stairs. The alley was dark, but that had long since stopped bothering him; you only had to look at him to know Jerry wasn't worth mugging. So that Friday night he ducked into the alley, as he had a thousand times before, and that was where he saw the guy with the hypo.

There wasn't much to it. The guy was shutting the trunk of his car, a battered old black Javelin, just as Jerry came around the corner and started towards the rickety wooden staircase at the back of his six-flat. Jerry didn't see him very well, and didn't try. Just a white guy, youngish, with a little dark moustache, wearing one of those sports coats with leather patches at the elbows. He and Jerry traded a brief, wary glance, the way two strangers will when they meet in an alley in Uptown, and then the guy started around the car to the driver's side. As he did, he slid something into his jacket pocket, and Jerry glimpsed it briefly; a hypodermic needle. He thought nothing of it. The neighborhood was full of junkies.

As he climbed wearily up the stairs to the back door of his third floor apartment, he heard the car growl and turn over below him, and the headlights speared out and lit up the alley for a few moments. Jerry was pleased. He was just drunk enough so he was having difficulty getting his key into the lock, and the light helped. "A-*ha,*" he said, pushing it in and turning. By the time the door closed behind him, the Javelin was gone.

Jerry didn't give the incident another thought until the night the cops arrived.

It was near dusk. He'd eaten at a Siamese restaurant down south of Lawrence and was walking back, savoring the coolness of the evening. Coming up from the south like he was brought him to the front of his building, but long before he got there he saw there was commotion. A cop car was sitting right outside his door, a crowd had gathered around the steps, and two cops were trying to calm down some crazy lady. When he got closer, he saw that the crazy lady was Mrs. Monroe, the black woman who lived in 2-East with an army of kids.

Jerry pushed through the crowd and walked right up. Mrs. Monroe was crying, and trying to say something, but nothing sensible was coming out. One of the cops, a fat one with a red face, scowled at Jerry when he approached. *"Hey,"* he barked.

"I live here," Jerry said. "What's going on?"

"It's none of your concern," said the beer-bellied cop. "Her kid run off, is all. Now get on by if you're going in. We'll handle her."

Jerry shrugged, looked curiously at the sobbing Mrs. Monroe, and went on through the front door. Like all the other six-flats on the block, his had a tiled entry hall, mailboxes and doorbells on the walls, a second door barring the way to the stairs. You needed a key or a buzz from upstairs to get past that one. Between the two doors, watching the scene on the steps, were a couple of his neighbors. The Gumbo Granny was in her rocker. She and the old wicker chair with its faded flowered cushion came crawling out of 1-East every morning, and she sat there until dark, rocking and watching the street and rocking and smoking her pipe and rocking and holding incoherent conversations with whoever entered or left the building. Jerry nodded, but he knew better than to try to talk to her.

But the girl from 2-West was also standing there, and that was a different matter. She was a short, attractive blond, about 25 or so. She'd only moved in about a month ago, with a couple of female roommates. He had the vague impression they were grad students at Northwestern, or something like that. The rest of them were pretty plain, but the blond had a cute smile and a nice ass. She was standing casually by the door, wearing a white turtleneck sweater and a pair of tight jeans, listening to the argument outside. Jerry took out his key and hesitated. This seemed like a perfect opportunity to get to know her. "Do you know what happened?" he asked her, nodding towards Mrs. Monroe and the cops.

She turned and brushed a strand of hair from her eyes. Her hair was very long and very straight and very blond, just the way Jerry liked it. "One of her kids is missing," she said. "The oldest one, I think."

"Chollie," Jerry said. That was what everyone called him. He was a slight, well-mannered kid, always dribbling a basketball around the block, though Jerry had never seen him actually play the game. He was about sixteen, he thought; shy, maybe a little simple-minded. "Do they know what happened to him?"

"The police think it's just a runaway," she said. "That's what the fat one said, anyway. That was what set her off. They aren't very concerned.

He hasn't been gone very long, I guess."

"How long is that?"

"She said she sent him out around eleven last Friday, to get some milk. No one has seen him since."

"Tough," said Jerry, shaking his head. "Chollie didn't strike me like the sort to run away. He was always so quiet. I hope nothing happened to him."

"Well, the police told her that no bodies of that description have turned up, anyway."

"Thank God for that much," Jerry said.

"Dey ain't gone to be no body," said the Gumbo Granny, rocking back and forth and sucking on her pipe.

"Excuse me?" the blond said.

Jerry had to stifle a groan. It was always a mistake to speak to the Gumbo Granny. Once you acknowledged her, she got going, and once she got going she didn't stop. She was an old, *old* black women, a tiny little monkey of a woman with dry, wrinkled brown skin and pink palms. She was nearly bald, and she had a pink spot around her left eye, a patch of pinkness in the middle of that wizened old face. It made her look a little bit like a dog Jerry remembered from the *Our Gang* comedies he'd watched as a kid, only with the colors switched around. She was half-senile and didn't make sense most of the time, and even when she did you couldn't always understand her, since she talked funny. Evidently she'd come up from New Orleans at some point, though she'd lived in the building as long as anyone could remember. It was on account of New Orleans that the younger people in the building started calling her the Gumbo Granny. There was no name on her mailbox, but then she never got any mail.

When the blonde spoke to her, the Gumbo Granny took the pipe out of her mouth and rocked slowly back and forth, nodding to herself. "He's gone, lawdy, lawdy. He's gone. I tells 'em and I tells 'em, but dey don't lissen." She shook her small head, and rocked.

"Did you see something?" the blonde asked, frowning. "Do you know where the boy's gone?"

Jerry started to tell her not to pay attention to the old woman, that she was crazy as a loon, but before he could the Gumbo Granny was off again. "Yessum, I knows, I knows. I tells 'em, yessum. Won't get me out in dem streets at night, no, no, lawdy. Ain't findin' no body, no, no." She nodded to herself, her old tired eyes all wrinkled up and wise. "Dey got him, yessum, dey got ol' Chollie. I tells 'em, but dey don't lissen. Dey got him."

"Who?" said the blonde.

The Gumbo Granny peered around warily, as if to make sure there was no one lurking in the shadows beneath the stairs, and then she leaned forward in her rocker and whispered, "Dem needle mens got him." She nodded, satisfied, and settled back in her chair again, sucking on her pipe as she rocked and creaked, rocked and creaked. Outside the police had finally stopped the flow of Mrs. Monroe's tears, and they were talking quietly now. The crowd of spectators on the sidewalk had begun to drift away in search of other, livelier diversions. It was clear that not much was going to come of this one.

"The needle men," said Jerry, curious despite himself. He'd probably regret asking, he thought, but he heard himself say, "Who are the needle men?"

The Gumbo Granny smiled conspiratorially. "We had 'um down in New Orleans, yessuh, yessuh. Dey's tricky, dem needle mens, I knows all dey ways, you don't see me goin' out at night, nosuh, nosuh. Dey's hidin' out dere, awaitin', and dey got needles, dem big *looooong* kind long as you arm, and all sharp, with stuffs on 'em, yessuh, stuffs. Dey jump out at you, dey do, and poke you with dem needles, and you's done, lawdy, you's never seen again. Ain't findin' no body, not when dem needle mens gets you." She cackled.

The blond from 2-West smiled. "A morbid thought," she said drily.

"Needle men," said Jerry. "She's crazy." The Gumbo Granny rocked away as if she never heard him. He and the blonde traded sympathetic smiles, the kind that say let's-indulge-the-pitiful-old-thing. "Why would these needle men stab Mrs. Monroe's boy?" the blonde asked. "Are they ghosts?"

"Lawdy, no. No, no, no. Don't you know nothin'?" The old woman rocked and clucked. "You's so young, don't know nothin' though, nothin'. I tells 'em, but they don't lissen. Dem needle mens ain't no ha'nts. Dey's from Charity."

"Charity?"

"Hospital, yessum, yessum. Charity Hospital. It's bodies dey wants, bodies, fo' de students to cut up on, so dey creeps out with dem *looooong* needles with de stuffs on de end, and dey stabs the black folks and drags 'em back. Nobody misses no po' black folks, nosuh. I seen 'em hidin' in de bushes, hidin' in de alleys, dem needle mens with dem needles, but dey ain't a-gettin' me. My daddy learned me, yessuh, and I knows 'em, yes I do. Chollie wouldn't lissen, but I tells 'em, I knows. Knowed 'em down in New Orleans when I was just a littlest girl, knowed how to spy 'em then. Knows 'em up here too, yes I do. Ain't gone get ol' me with dem needles, drag me off fo' dem practice doctuhs to cut up on."

She rocked and smoked away. Outside the fat policeman was

questioning Mrs. Monroe and filling out a form.

"He'll come back, I bet," Jerry said, with a glance through the door. "Maybe there was fight or something, but Chollie was a good kid."

The blonde shrugged.

"My name is Jerry McCulloch, by the way," he said, smiling. "I'm a writer. Live in 3-West."

"Hi," she said, returning his smile. She was awfully pretty. He loved her hair. "I'm Kris. Kris Shelby."

"You're downstairs of us, right? With a couple of other girls?"

She nodded. "It's a long way from school, but the rent is low enough to make up for the el fares, and the apartment is bigger than anything we could have gotten near campus. Tuition is so high these days, you have to do all sorts of things to make ends meet." She wrinkled her nose. "Like living in this neighborhood, even."

Jerry nodded with sympathy.

"What do you write?" Kris asked. She had nice green eyes, he noticed. Very cool and alert.

"Anything they'll pay me for," he said with practiced modesty. "I sold a piece to the *Tribune* magazine once, on the abandoned coal tunnels beneath the Loop. There's a whole honeycomb of them, haven't been used for years. Maybe you read it?" Kris shook her head. "Well, it's not important. I do just odds and ends, really. Right now I'm working on a piece I'm hoping to sell to the *Reader*. Who knows?" He shrugged. "What about you?"

"What about me?" Kris said, lightly. She smiled.

Jerry stammered, and restrained an urge to ask about her hometown or her major. That was the kind of inane talk that always got him spurned down on Rush street. He decided not to come on too strong. He looked at his watch. "Hey, I got to go," he said. "Glad we met. Now if it gets too loud upstairs, you'll know who to bitch at."

She nodded. "See you around," she said, turning her attention back to the street.

Jerry started up the stairs. At the first landing, he turned back and called down to her, "Hey, Kris." When she looked up, he said, "Watch out for them needle men!" She smiled and nodded, and Jerry was feeling very good as he bounded up the stairs to the third floor. Harold and his latest true love were in the living room, listening to the stereo and making out on the couch. Alan was watching some old movie on the tube in his room. "How was that restaurant?" he called out when Jerry passed.

"Not bad." Jerry leaned through the open door. "I met that blonde from downstairs. Kris."

"Nice," said Alan.

"Yeah," Jerry said, grinning. He went back to the kitchen to get himself a beer. The light in the fridge was burned out, and he hadn't bothered flicking on the overhead, so he found himself fumbling around in back. Finally he found a Bud.

He yanked off the tab there in the darkened kitchen, and was just lifting the can to his lips when a car went past in the alley down below. All Jerry could see was the wash of its lights against the back of the buildings across the way, a dim, moving reflection.

That was when he finally remembered the guy with the needle.

He had a restless night. It was all so silly. The junkie in the leather-patched sports coat and the Gumbo Granny's needle men and Chollie Monroe had nothing to do with one another, that was obvious. Even so, it made Jerry feel strange. It *had* been Friday night, after all. He frowned and drank another Bud and went to bed.

He tossed and turned for more than an hour, his water bed sloshing softly underneath him every time he moved. Finally he drifted off to sleep. When he woke again, it was the middle of the night, and the apartment was dark and dead and quiet. A cool breeze was blowing in the open window, and the rippling curtains threw long shadows across his bed. Jerry stirred groggily and moved to shut the window a bit, and there he was, standing outside the window, a man in a sports coat with leather patches at the elbows. He had a dead white face, and he was smiling a terrible thin smile. As Jerry watched, his arm came through the open window. He was holding a long slender needle.

Jerry screamed, and wrenched away, and all of a sudden he was tangled in his sheets on the floor, and Harold was standing in the doorway in his jockey shorts, saying, "Hey, you okay?"

"He's coming in the window," Jerry said breathlessly, from the floor.

Harold glanced at the open window, where the curtains twisted lazily in the breeze. "You moron," he said. "We're on the third floor."

Everybody had a big laugh about Jerry's nightmare the next morning, when they were all bumping into one another trying to make breakfast. Everybody but Jerry, that is. He just scowled at them and drank his coffee, and then he went off to the Post Office to check his box. You had to have a Post Office box in this neighborhood, the way the mail was always getting ripped off.

He went down the front stairs, expecting that he'd have to listen to the Gumbo Granny spin more wild stories about deranged needle men. Fortunately she wasn't there; her rocker was in the entryway, but she wasn't in it. Jerry blessed his good fortune and went on by.

He was sitting in a booth at the coffee shop on Lawrence, sorting through his mail and waiting for a cheese omelette, when it suddenly hit him how odd that was. All the years he'd lived in that building he'd never seen the Gumbo Granny's rocker without the Gumbo Granny. In the morning she brought it out with her. In the evening she took it in with her. In between they were always there, rocking. Always.

A kind of shiver went through him. "No," he said aloud.

"What do mean *no?*" the waitress said. She was standing there with his cheese omelette in hand. "This is what you ordered, buster."

"Uh, yeah," said Jerry, abashed. "I didn't mean you."

The waitress looked at him strangely, set down his order, and walked off.

"No," Jerry repeated, picking up his fork.

But that evening, when he returned to the apartment, the rocker was still there. Empty. Jerry ignored it.

The next day he came and went by the back stairs. He tried not to think about the rocker, The Gumbo Granny, needle men, or anything like that. He was down in the Loop all day, and after dark he went drinking for a couple of hours, but it was no use. He couldn't even concentrate on the women around him. He kept staring into his beer and seeing that empty rocker.

When he came up the alley near to midnight, he saw something even more chilling. Parked in the shadows across from his building was an old, battered black Javelin. Half-drunk as he was, it startled him. He stopped in his tracks and stared at it. It was empty. Jerry looked around warily. Seeing no one, he approached the car. The trunk was locked.

He retreated upstairs, and went to bed. "No," he said loudly to himself, in the privacy of his bedroom. But before he went to sleep, he closed and locked his window.

The following morning he had to force himself to go out at all. He felt ridiculously nervous, with the rocker in front and the Javelin in back, but finally he laughed and said, "This is absurd," and went down the front way.

The Gumbo Granny's rocker was still in the entryway, still vacant. And now Jerry noticed something else as well. The old lady's pipe was lying on the tiles next to the rocker, in a smear of black ash.

He was standing there by the mailboxes, looking at it, when Kris came down. "Hi, Jerry," she said. "You're leaning against my mailbox."

He moved aside. "Uh," he said, as Kris got out her mail, "have you seen her lately? In the last couple days?"

"Who?" said Kris.

"Her. The old lady. The Gumbo Granny."

Kris looked at the rocker and wrinkled her nose. "No, I don't think so. Why?"

"She never leaves her rocker there like that. Never. She's always in it. But it's been there for three days now. I haven't seen her once in all that time."

Kris brushed back a fallen strand of hair, and smiled mischievously. "Maybe the needle men got her," she said. She opened the inner door and started back upstairs, but when Jerry did not move she looked back at him. "Jerry," she asked, "is anything wrong?"

"No," he said quickly. "No, nothing." If he told her half of the crazy stuff going through his head, he knew, he'd *never* get anywhere with her.

Kris shrugged and went upstairs.

The police made him hold for ten minutes and transferred him four times before he finally got connected with someone willing to talk to him. "I'm trying to get some information, officer," Jerry said. "I'm a reporter, and I need some figures on the number of disappearances from the Uptown area. Not killings, just cases where somebody vanished, with no body or anything, you understand?"

"What kind of time period you asking about? This week? This month? All year? You'll have to be more precise."

"Oh, hell, I don't know. This month, say. Can you get me the figures?"

"A lot of people vanish. Kids run off to New York or L.A. or God knows where, men skip out on alimony and child support, people duck collection agencies. We can't begin to keep track of 'em all, let alone find 'em. Not if they don't want to be found. What do you want this for, anyway?"

"It's a story I'm working on," Jerry said. "I'm a reporter."

"Yeah?" The voice sounded suspicious. "Who you with?"

"I'm kind of freelancing."

"I see," the policeman said. "Well, you better come downtown and talk to someone else. You got to be accredited, you know. We don't give out information to every joker who calls up and says he's from the press."

A kid vanished earlier this week. Charlie Monroe, Chollie they called him. Can you tell me if he's been found?"

"What business is it of yours? You family or something?"

Jerry didn't reply.

"Look, I can't help you. You better come downtown." Click.

Jerry hung up, frowning.

The rocker and pipe were gone the next morning, but somehow that failed to make Jerry feel any better. He knocked on the door of 1-East, a little warily, but still hoping that the Gumbo Granny herself would come scuffling to the door to tell him she'd been sick. He would have settled for a relative, telling him that she'd died. But there was no answer.

He spent the day at his typewriter, working on an assignment he'd pulled from the features editor of a neighborhood weekly, but he wasn't able to work up much enthusiasm about the gyros-pizza war for the stomachs of North Side singles. It was such a stupid story, anyway. Now if these damned needle men were only real, and he could prove it, expose them — *that* would be a story worth doing. Better even than his tunnels under the Loop. It could even get him a staff writer job someplace. At the very least it was a certain sale.

Jerry pushed his typewriter away from him and sat thinking. The typewriter was an electric. It kept humming, like it was impatient, rushing him. He turned it off.

Then he found his notebook and took the el up to Evanston, to check out the library at Northwestern.

That night Jerry returned in a fever. He'd filled twelve pages of his notebook in his close, careful script. He was so full with the story he felt he just *had* to talk to someone before he went nuts. But Alan was off somewhere, no telling when he'd be back, and Steve was still out of town. Harold was in his bedroom, but the door was closed, and when Jerry put his ear to it he heard thumping and low moans. Harold wouldn't like being interrupted. Besides, he was still giving Jerry a hard time over that nightmare. No sense giving him more ammunition.

"Damn," he said. He glanced at his notebook again. Then he said, "What the hell," and went down to the second floor.

One of the roommates answered the door, a heavy, bovine sort with mousy brown hair and bad acne. "Kris is studying for a big test," she told him. "She won't want to be disturbed." She sniffed. "Her class standing is low enough as is."

"Never mind that," Jerry said, "I have to talk to her." He insisted until he was let into the apartment. The other roommate was in a corner of the darkened living room, studying under a tensor lamp. She looked up at him vaguely from behind coke-bottle glasses while the pudgy one went to fetch Kris.

"Hi," Kris said. "What's the matter?"

"I want to tell you something," he said. "Come on, I'll buy you a drink."

Across Sheridan was a small bar patronized by the Marine Drive crowd, about the only place in the immediate vicinity where you could drink without listening to country music or worrying about knife fights. A bouncer kept out the derelicts, the rednecks, and other undesireables. He gave Jerry a long glance, but finally passed them when Kris smiled at him. Jerry led her to a small table by the window, ordered a pitcher of dark beer and a couple of shrimp cocktails, and opened his notebook.

"They were *real,*" he said in an excited whisper.

"Who?" Kris asked. "No, wait. I bet I know. The needle men."

Jerry nodded. "I was working all day, reading old books about life in New Orleans, folklore, looking over some newspaper microfilms. Nothing was ever proved about these needle men, but there were stories. For years and years, from the turn of the century or earlier well into the twenties. It was a black superstition, especially. If it was a superstition. They preyed on blacks, you see, because they were all so poor, and nobody much cared whether a few of them vanished or not. The police just laughed at the needle men stories, but the blacks passed the warnings along, word of mouth. It was just like the Gumbo Granny said. They were supposed to be medical students. They carried these long needles, tipped with poison or anaesthethic, something like that, and they skulked around in alleys and parks and such. Just a scratch from one of those needles was supposed to be enough. The victim would go under in seconds, and other needle men would come and cart him off to Charity Hospital or the medical schools, wherever cadavers were needed for demonstration and dissection. Later on, a lot of blacks wouldn't go to movies, because the needle men liked to operate inside of theaters. They'd come and sit behind you, you see, and push their needles through the back of your seat. A little prick in the small of the back, that's all it would take. Then they'd carry you out like you were drunk or sick, and you'd never be seen again. No bodies to be found, of course."

Kris speared a tiny shrimp with her toothpick, dipped it in cocktail sauce, and nibbled at it delicately, a pinky stuck out. Her hair fell around her shoulders in a gorgeous honey-colored cascade, lit by dim reflections from the lights above the bar. But her green eyes regarded him skeptically, and for a moment Jerry thought he'd blown it for good with his talk of the needle men. She was going to laugh, or shrug him off as a crackpot, or . . . he wasn't sure.

Instead she finished the shrimp, drank a bit of her beer, and said, "Well, it's an interesting story. Colorful. You can probably make an article out of it."

"Exactly what I'm going to do!" Jerry said.

"It'll have to be a kind of historical feature for some New Orleans magazine, though," she said. "You know, quaint old bogey men."

"No, no," Jerry said. "You don't understand. That's just the background. I'm going to bring all up to date, work in the modern stuff. Here and now. In Chicago."

Kris ate another shrimp and smiled. "That kind of story you might sell to the *Enquirer,* but nowhere else. Don't you think you're being silly?"

"No!" Jerry said stoutly.

"You really think these needle men exist? Not only in New Orleans around the turn of the century, but here and now, today, in Chicago? Is that what you think? And they carried off Chollie Monroe to provide some medical school with an experimental cadaver?" She shook her head, smiling. "You don't look like the sort of person to go off the deep end."

Jerry flushed. "It's not just Chollie," he insisted. "They got the Gumbo Granny, too. They had to. She knew all about them, you see. And there's more. Listen to me." He told her all about the guy with the hypodermic needle, and the black Javelin.

Kris listened to him politely enough, sipping her beer and nibbling on shrimp, but when he had finished she did not look convinced. "A sports coat with leather patches, you say? I think I've seen him in the alley too. I know I've seen the car. But that doesn't mean anything. He probably lives in one of the other buildings around here. What's so mysterious about that? There's a white Mustang back there a lot too. It belongs to my roommate." She wrinkled her nose. "The hypodermic — well, maybe he is a junkie. Or a doctor. I don't know. Either one is more likely than being a needle man, don't you think?"

"Even so," Jerry said, confused, "what about the Gumbo Granny?"

"Ah," said Kris, smiling, "that I happen to know about. I mentioned it to my roommate, Sheila, after I saw you by the mailboxes. The old lady had a stroke, Jerry. That's all. Just a stroke. The day after that fuss with the Monroe boy. She was out there in the morning, rocking, and she had her attack. Someone found her, called the hospital, the ambulance came and carted her away. Of course they wouldn't think to remove the rocker. So it stayed there, for days and days."

"It's gone now."

Kris smiled. "You know this neighborhood as well as I do. It finally got stolen, obviously. *You* put a perfectly good piece of furniture down there, and see how long it stays around."

Jerry sat back and shut his notebook. Suddenly he felt very confused. Kris was making a lot of sense, and his story was disintegrating around him. "What hospital is she in?" he asked.

"How should I know?" Kris said.

"Well," said Jerry. "Maybe you're right. I ought to check it out, though. This story could really make me." He brightened. "I know, I can call around to all the hospitals, until I find her."

"Asking for the Gumbo Granny?" Kris said. She smiled. "The staffs will love you. And won't you feel foolish when you find her?"

"Yes," Jerry admitted, ruefully. He tasted his beer. The head was gone, faded while they'd talked. "Still, it's worth doing. I mean, what if she *isn't* in a hospital? Then I'd be right, maybe." He scratched his head. "Your roommate saw an ambulance take the old lady away, right? They said she'd had a stoke?"

"Right."

"Well, what if one of these needle men came in, gave her an injection. She was too old to resist. She'd go under like *that.*" He snapped his fingers. "And then, what would be simpler than to pull right up with an ambulance, and carry out the old lady in broad daylight. She had no relatives, like poor Chollie. Who could object? If the needle men are med students, the ambulance drivers are probably in with them, right? Certainly they could get an ambulance easy enough."

Kris laughed and shook her head. "Oh, come on. Listen to yourself, Jerry. You're kind of cute, and I thought you were bright, but you're talking like a real paranoid. The Gumbo Granny had nothing on you!" She leaned across the table and took his hand. "Listen to me," she said, giving him a small, affectionate squeeze. "All this theorizing is bad enough, but your whole motive is crazy. Contraband corpses for medical schools? Body snatching? Come *on.* That stuff might have been great in the days of Burke and Hare, maybe even in 19th century New Orleans, but today? Are these needle men part of the faculties of the med schools, or do they just drive up, lift the bodies out of the trunks of their car, and dicker with the professors? I'm sure medical schools can get bodies in simpler ways, don't you think?"

Jerry grinned at her. "It so happens." he said, squeezing her hand back, and delighted by the warmth of it, "that I thought of that. It puzzled me for a bit too, but finally I figured it all out. It will be in my article."

"Yes?" Kris said, patiently.

"Transplants," Jerry said proudly.

She raised an eyebrow.

"No, really," he said. "Think about it. The old needle men, they just wanted bodies, like the old lady said. For the teaching hospitals and med schools. They needed 'em for dissection and weren't choosy about how they got them. Today, of course, that demand isn't there, and there are channels and procedures and such. But still, the needle men are out there. *Why,* I asked myself. Why, for transplants. Just watch late night TV sometime, you see all those public service spots, donate your kidneys here, leave your eyes there. You go to get a driver's license and they try to sign you up as an organ donor. Really, the demand is there. A lot of people need kidneys and livers and stuff, and there aren't enough to go around. You figure some rich people would be willing to pay almost anything to live, right? So there's got to be a black market in body parts, even if no one writes about it. The needle men. Only now they just put their victims to sleep instead of killing them, you see. The bodies get taken somewhere, still alive, and cut up for transplants. I bet there's money in it. A *lot* of money."

"And Uptown is full of these needle men?" Kris said.

"What better place? Today when I got off the el, a guy was lying passed out on the stairs. If some other guy had been helping him off, I never would have looked twice. We got so many runaways and such the police don't even count 'em. I know, I called them. There's gang wars, there's race trouble between the Orientals and the hillbillies and the blacks, there's fights in the bars most nights. Illegal aliens are working everywhere, nobody's got any records on them but their employers, and if one of them vanishes — well, he just got caught by immigration, or skipped town. Down in the all-black ghettoes, maybe a white needle man would stand out, like they used to in New Orleans. But Uptown is so damn mixed that nobody stands out. Think about it. This is prime territory."

Kris let go of his hand and poured them both more beer. "Drink up," she said, "I've got to get back and study. I can see there is no dissuading you from this. You've got every crazy detail worked out, don't you?"

"It's not crazy," Jerry said. "At least I don't think it is."

You can't prove a word of any of it, Jerry."

"Not now," Jerry said, "but I'll get proof, one way or the other.

This story will make a real name for me, I'm not about to let it slip through my fingers. The needle men don't know I'm on to them. I'm going to start checking up on runaways and disappearances, that kind of thing. And I'm going to watch that damn Javelin real carefully. From my back stairs, I can see the whole alley. I'll buy binoculars. And a gun. Yes. I'd better start carrying a gun."

"You start wandering the alley with binoculars and a gun and the police will be locking *you* up, not your needle men. Don't you think you're taking this folk tale a little too..." She stopped. "Oh my God," she said, looking out the window.

Jerry looked out too. Across the street was another tavern, a rough noisy place Jerry had never dared enter. Two men had just come out of it. A white man in a corduroy jacket with leather patches on the elbows was helping a black youth into a waiting car. The black seemed to be drunk or unconscious. The car, Jerry noted, was a black Javelin.

"Oh, it's just coincidence," Kris said, but her voice sounded as if even she no longer believed it. She licked her lips. "He's just drunk. There are a thousand explanations."

"We'd better get back," Jerry said. "The needle men are out tonight." He paid the bill and ushered Kris out of there. In the alley, every shadow seemed to hold a smiling shape with a long, long needle, but they hurried past and up the back stairs, and nothing leaped out at them. Both of them were breathing hard when they reached Kris' landing. From the stairs, Jerry tried to tell himself.

He put his arms around her and bent to kiss her, hoping she'd permit it. Her enthusiasm took him by surprise. When they finally broke apart, Kris was studying him from those wide, green eyes. "Oh, damn you," she said. "It's silly, but now you've got me seeing needle men everywhere." She wrinkled her nose. "I hate to admit it, but I'm frightened."

Jerry stood dumbfounded, not knowing what to say.

"I don't know how to ask this," Kris said. "Will you stay the night? With me? It'd make me sleep easier."

Jerry tried to keep from grinning. "Oh, sure," he said. "Me too."

"Thanks," Kris said. She turned and unlocked the door. Her apartment had the same layout as his own, but it was a lot neater. Better furnished, too. She and her roommates did a lot better than him. Kris didn't let him admire the decor, however. She led him straight to the bedroom, oddly enough the one right below his own.

Books were strewn all over the bed. She gathered them up and set them on a nightstand, then turned and touched the light switch. A dimmer. Illumination went down to a soft glow, and Kris turned to him with a smile. "Naked fear makes me horny," she said. "What are you waiting for?"

"Uh," said Jerry. He grinned. "Sure." Then it was a race to get undressed, and they tumbled into bed together laughing.

Afterwards, Jerry felt better than he had for years; a girl like Kris, a story like the needle men. Things were really coming together for him. He said as much to her, as she nestled up against him and he stroked her soft, fine hair.

"Ummmm," she said, raising her head. "The needle men. Did you have to mention them again? I'd managed to forget about them for a few moments." She laughed. "It all seems silly now. Are you really going through with it?"

"Of course," he said, wounded.

She sighed. "Good luck," she said. She kissed his chest lightly, and her hand started doing interesting things lower down. "Can you stay the whole night, or will your roommates call the police? Maybe you should go up and tell them where you are. We don't want them thinking you've been carried off by the needle men." She giggled.

"They don't know anything about the needle men," Jerry said, "and they don't care where I spend my nights. We're not that close. You know how it is sometimes." He smiled. "I'll stay. Hell, I'll move in if you want me."

I'll have to think about that one," Kris said. She sat up suddenly, and climbed out of bed. "Excuse," she said.

"Hey, where you going?" Jerry asked.

"The little girl's room," she said. "Don't worry. I'll be back." She padded to the door, nude. Even in the vague, dim light, she was lovely. Her long hair moved behind her as she walked.

She was gone a long time. Jerry got restless. For a moment, he even felt afraid. He thought he heard a door open and close somewhere, and he had a sudden vision of the needle man, creeping up the back stairs with his long, sharp needle in hand, jimmying the lock, stealing down the hall, slowly, quietly. He could be out there right now, white-faced, grinning, needle poised and ready for Kris to emerge from the bathroom. Or maybe he'd already gotten her, maybe she was lying at his feet even now, and he was about to open the door and come in for Jerry too.

"God," Jerry said. He was giving himself the shivers. He shifted in bed, saw Kris' books stacked up on the nightstand, picked up one on impulse. It was hard to read anything in the dim light, but if it would take his mind off the needle men it was worth the eyestrain.

He flipped through a few pages, frowned, flipped, stared. "Oh," he said, in a small whimper. "Oh, no. No."

That was when the door opened. They were standing there, all of them, Kris and her roommates, smiling. Kris had the needle. "You never asked me my major, Jerry," she said. "I'm in med school, second year. You'd be amazed at how expensive it is." She shrugged and came towards him.

Meathouse Man

(I)   In the Meathouse

They came straight from the ore-fields that first time, Trager with the others, the older boys, the almost-men who worked their corpses next to his. Cox was the oldest of the group, and he'd been around the most, and he said that Trager had to come even if he didn't want to. Then one of the others laughed and said that Trager wouldn't even know what to do, but Cox the kind-of leader shoved him until he was quiet. And when payday came, Trager trailed the rest to the meathouse, scared but somehow eager, and he paid his money to a man downstairs and got a room key.

He came into the dim room trembling, nervous. The others had gone to other rooms, had left him alone with her (no, *it*, not her but *it*, he reminded himself, and promptly forgot again). In a shabby gray cubicle with a single smoky light.

He stank of sweat and sulfur, like all who walked the streets of Skrakky, but there was no help for that. It would be better if he could bathe first, but the room did not have a bath. Just a sink, a double bed with sheets that looked dirty even in the dimness, a corpse.

She lay there naked, staring at nothing, breathing shallow breaths. Her legs were spread; ready. Was she always that way, Trager wondered, or had the man before him arranged her like that? He didn't know. He knew how to do it (he did, he *did*, he'd read the books Cox gave him, and there were films you could see, and all sorts of things), but he didn't know much of anything else. Except maybe how to handle corpses. That he was good at, the youngest handler on Skrakky, but he had to be. They had forced him into the handlers' school when his mother died, and they made him learn, so that was the thing he did. This, this he had never done (but he knew how, yes, yes, he *did*); it was his first time.

He came to the bed slowly and sat to a chorus of creaking springs. He touched her and the flesh was warm. Of course. She was not a corpse, no, really, no; the body was alive enough, a heart beat under the heavy white breasts, she breathed. Only the brain was gone, ripped from her, replaced with a deadman's synthabrain. She was meat now, an extra body for a corpse handler to control, just like the crew he worked each day under sulfur skies. She was not a woman. So it did not matter that Trager was just a boy, a jowly frog-faced boy who smelled of Skrakky. She (no, remember?) would not care, could not care.

Emboldened, aroused and hard, the boy stripped off his corpse handler's clothing and climbed in bed with the female meat. He was very excited; his hands shook as he stroked her, studied her. Her skin was very white, her hair dark and long, but even the boy could not call her pretty. Her face was too flat and wide, her mouth hung open, and her limbs were loose and sagging with fat.

On her huge breasts, all around the fat dark nipples, the last customer had left tooth-marks where he'd chewed her. Trager touched the marks tenatively, traced them with a finger. Then, sheepish about his hesitations, he grabbed one breast, squeezed it hard, pinched the nipple until he imagined a real girl would squeal with pain. The corpse did not move. Still squeezing, he rolled over on her and took the other breast into his mouth.

And the corpse responded.

She thrust up at him, hard, and meaty arms wrapped around his pimpled back to pull him to her. Trager groaned and reached down between her legs. She was hot, wet, excited. He trembled. How did they do that? Could she really get excited without a mind, or did they have lubricating tubes stuck into her, or what?

Then he stopped caring. He fumbled, found his penis, put it into her, thrust. The corpse hooked her legs around him and thrust back. It felt good, real good, better than anything he'd ever done to himself, and in some obscure way he felt proud that she was so wet and so excited.

It only took a few strokes; he was too new, too young, too eager to last long. A few strokes was all he needed—but it was all she needed too. They came together, a red flush washing over her skin as she arched against him and shook soundlessly.

Afterwards she lay again like a corpse.

Trager was drained and satisfied, but he had more time left, and he was determined to get his money's worth. He explored her thoroughly, sticking his fingers everywhere they would go, touching her everywhere, rolling it over, looking at everything. The corpse moved like dead meat.

He left her as he'd found her, lying face up on the bed with her legs apart. Meathouse courtesy.

The horizon was a wall of factories, all factories, vast belching factories that sent red shadows to flick against the sulfur-dark skies. The boy saw but hardly noticed. He was strapped in place high atop his automill, two stories up on a monster machine of corroding yellow-painted metal with savage teeth of diamond and duralloy, and his eyes were blurred with triple images. Clear and strong and hard he saw the control panel before him, the wheel, the fuel-feed, the bright handle of the ore-scoops, the banks of lights that would tell of trouble in the refinery under his feet, the brake and emergency brake. But that was not all he saw. Dimly, faintly, there were echoes; overlaid images of two other control cabs, almost identical to his, where corpse hands moved clumsily over the instruments.

Trager moved those hands, slow and careful, while another part of his mind held his own hands, his real hands, very still. The corpse controller hummed thinly on his belt.

On either side of him, the other two automills moved into flanking positions. The corpse hands squeezed the brakes; the machines rumbled to a halt. On the edge of the great sloping pit, they stood in a row, shabby pitted juggernauts ready to descend into the gloom. The pit was growing steadily larger; each day new layers of rock and ore were stripped away.

Once a mountain range had stood here, but Trager did not remember that.

The rest was easy. The automills were aligned now. To move the crew in unison was a cinch, any decent handler could do *that.* It was only when you had to keep several corpses busy at several different tasks that things got tricky. But a good corpsehandler could do that, too. Eight-crews were not unknown to veterans; eight bodies linked to a single corpse controller moved by a single mind and eight synthabrains. The deadmen were each tuned to one controller, and only one; the handler who wore that controller and thought corpse-thoughts in its proximity field could move those deadmen like secondary bodies. Or like his own body. If he was good enough.

Trager checked his filtermask and earplugs quickly, then touched the fuel-feed, engaged, flicked on the laser-knives and the drills. His corpses echoed his moves, and pulses of light spit through the twilight of Skrakky. Even through his plugs he could hear the awful whine as the ore-scoops revved up and lowered. The rock-eating maw of an automill was even wider than the machine was tall.

Rumbling and screeching, in perfect formation, Trager and his corpse crew descended into the pit. Before they reached the factories on the far side of the plain, tons of metal would have been torn from the earth, melted and refined and processed, while the worthless rock was reduced to powder and blown out into the already-unbreathable air. He would deliver finished steel at dusk, on the horizon.

He was a good handler, Trager thought as the automills started down. But the handler in the meathouse—now she must be an artist. He imagined her down in the cellar somewhere, watching each of her corpses through holos and psi circuits, humping them all to please her patrons. Was it just a fluke then, that his fuck had been so perfect? Or was she always that good? But how, *how,* to move a dozen corpses without even being near them, to have them doing different things, to keep them all excited, to match the needs and rhythm of each customer so exactly?

The air behind him was black and choked by rock-dust, his ears were full of screams, and the far horizon was a glowering red wall beneath which yellow ants crawled and ate rock. But Trager kept his hard-on all across the plain as the automill shook beneath him.

The corpses were company-owned; they stayed in the company deadman depot. But Trager had a room, a slice of the space that was his own in a steel-and-concrete warehouse with a thousand other slices. He only knew a handful of his neighbors, but he knew all of them too; they were corpse handlers. It was a world of silent shadowed corridors and endless closed doors. The lobby-lounge, all air and plastic, was a dusty deserted place where none of the tenants ever gathered.

The evenings were long there, the nights eternal. Trager had bought extra light-panels for his particular cube, and when all of them were on they burned so bright that his infrequent visitors blinked and complained about the glare. But always there came a time when he could read no more, and then he had to turn them out, and the darkness returned once more.

His father, long gone and barely remembered, had left a wealth of books and tapes, and Trager kept them still. The room was lined with them, and others stood in great piles against the foot of the bed and on either side of the bathroom door. Infrequently he went out with Cox and the others, to drink and joke and prowl for real women. He imitated them as best he could, but he always felt out of place. So most of his nights were spent at home, reading and listening to the music, remembering and thinking.

That week he thought long after he'd faded his light panels into black, and his thoughts were a frightened jumble. Payday was coming again, and Cox would be after him to return to the meathouse, and yes, yes, he wanted to. It had been good, exciting; for once he had felt confident and virile. But it was so easy, cheap, *dirty*. There had to be more, didn't there? Love, whatever that was? It had to be better with a real women, had to, and he wouldn't find one of those in a meathouse. He'd never found one outside, either, but then he'd never really had the courage to try. But he had to try, *had* to, or what sort of life would he ever have?

Beneath the covers he masturbated, hardly thinking of it, while he resolved not to return to the meathouse.

But a few days later, Cox laughed at him and he had to go along. Somehow he felt it would prove something.

A different room this time, a different corpse. Fat and black, with bright orange hair; less attractive than his first, if that was possible. But Trager came to her ready and eager, and this time he lasted longer. Again, the performance was superb. Her rhythm matched his stroke for stroke, she came with him, she seemed to know exactly what he wanted.

Other visits; two of them, four, six. He was a regular now at the meathouse, along with the others, and he had stopped worrying about it. Cox and the others accepted him in a strange half-hearted way, but his dislike of them had grown, if anything. He was better than they were, he thought. He could hold his own in a meathouse, he could run his corpses and his automills as good as any of them, and he still thought and dreamed. In time he'd leave them all behind, leave Skrakky, be something. They would be meathouse men as long as they would live, but Trager knew he could do better. He believed. He would find love.

He found none in the meathouse, but the sex got better and better, though it was perfect to begin with. In bed with the corpses, Trager was never dissatisfied: he did everything he'd ever read about, heard about, dreamt about. The corpses knew his needs before he did. When he needed it slow, they were slow. When he wanted to have it hard and quick and brutal, then they gave it to him that way, perfectly. He used every orifice they had; they always knew which one to present to him.

His admiration of the meathouse handler grew steadily for months, until it was almost worship. Perhaps somehow he could meet her, he thought at last. Still a boy, still hopelessly naive, he was sure he would love her. Then he would take her away from the meathouse to a clean corpseless world where they could be happy together.

One day, in a moment of weakness, he told Cox and the others. Cox looked at him, shook his head, grinned. Somebody else snickered. Then they all began to laugh. "What an *ass* you are, Trager," Cox said at last. "There is no fucking *handler!* Don't tell me you never heard of a feedback circuit?"

He explained it all, to laughter; explained how each corpse was tuned to a controller built into its bed, explained how each customer handled his own meat, explained why non-handlers found meathouse women dead and still. And the boy realized suddenly why the sex was always perfect. He was a better handler than even he had thought.

That night, alone in his room with all the lights burning white and hot, Trager faced himself. And turned away, sickened. He was good at his job, he was proud of that, but the rest . . .

It was the meathouse, he decided. There was a trap there in the meathouse, a trap that could ruin him, destroy life and dreams and hope. He would not go back; it was too easy. He would show Cox, show all of them. He could take the hard way, take the risks, feel the pain if he had to. And maybe the joy, maybe the love. He'd gone the other way too long.

Trager did not go back to the meathouse. Feeling strong and decisive and superior, he went back to his room. There, as years passed, he read and dreamed and waited for life to begin.

(1) When I Was One-and-Twenty

Josie was the first.

She was beautiful, had always been beautiful, knew she was beautiful; all that had shaped her, made her what she was. She was a free spirit. She was aggressive, confident, conquering. Like Trager, she was only twenty when they met, but she had lived more than he had, and she seemed to have the answers. He loved her from the first.

And Trager? Trager before Josie, but years beyond the meathouse? He was taller now, broad and heavy with both muscle and fat, often moody, silent and self-contained. He ran a full five-crew in the ore fields, more than Cox, more than any of them. At night, he read books; sometimes in his room, sometimes in the lobby. He had long since forgotten that he

went there to meet someone. Stable, solid, unemotional; that was Trager.
He touched no one, and no one touched him. Even the tortures had
stopped, though the scars remained *inside.* Trager hardly knew they were
there; he never looked at them.

He fit in well now. With his corpses.

Yet—not completely. Inside, the dream. Something believed, something hungered, something yearned. It was strong enough to keep him
away from the meathouse, from the vegetable life the others had all
chosen. And sometimes, on bleak lonely nights, it would grow stronger
still. Then Trager would rise from his empty bed, dress, and walk the
corridors for hours with his hands shoved deep into his pockets while
something twisted clawed and whimpered in his gut. Always, before his
walks were over, he would resolve to do something, to change his life
tomorrow.

But when tomorrow came, the silent gray corridors were half
forgotten, the demons had faded, and he had six roaring, shaking
automills to drive across the pit. He would lose himself in routine, and it
would be long months before the feelings came again.

Then Josie. They met like this:

It was a new field, rich and unmined, a vast expanse of broken rock and
rubble that filled the plain. Low hills a few weeks ago, but the company
skimmers had leveled the area with systematic nuclear blast mining, and
now the automills were moving in. Trager's five-crew had been one of the
first, and the change had been exilerating at first. The old pit had been just
about worked out; here there was a new terrain to contend with, boulders
and jagged rock fragments, baseball-sized fists of stone that came
shrieking at you on the dusty wind. It all seemed exciting, dangerous.
Trager, wearing a leather jacket and filtermask and goggles and earplugs,
drove his six machines and six bodies with a fierce pride, reducing
boulders to powder, clearing a path for the later machines, fighting his
way yard by yard to get whatever ore he could.

And one day, suddenly, one of the eye echoes suddenly caught his
attention. A light flashed red on a corpse-driven automill. Trager
reached, with his hands, with his mind, with five sets of corpse-hands. Six
machines stopped, but still another light went red. Then another, and
another. Then the whole board, all twelve. One of his automills was out.
Cursing, he looked across the rock field towards the machine in question,
used his corpse to give it a kick. The lights stayed red. He beamed out for
a tech.

By the time she got there—in a one-man skimmer that looked like a
tear drop of pitted black metal—Trager had unstrapped, climbed down
the metal rungs on the side of the automill, walked across the rocks to

where the dead machine stopped. He was just starting to climb up when Josie arrived; they met at the foot of the yellow-metal mountain, in the shadow of its treads.

She was field-wise, he knew at once. She wore a handler's coverall, earplugs, heavy goggles, and her face was smeared with grease to prevent dust abrasion. But still she was beautiful. Her hair was short, light brown, cut in a shag that was jumbled by the wind; her eyes, when she lifted the goggles, were bright green. She took charge immediately.

All business, she introduced herself, asked him a few questions, then opened a repair bay and crawled inside, into the guts of the drive and the ore-smelt and the refinery. It didn't take her long; ten minutes, maybe, and she was back outside.

"Don't go in there," she said, tossing her hair from out in front of her goggles with a flick of her head. "You've got a damper failure. The nukes are running away."

"Oh," said Trager. His mind was hardly on the automill, but he had to make an impression, made to say something intelligent. "Is it going to blow up?" he asked, and as soon as he said it he knew that *that* hadn't been intelligent at all. Of course it wasn't going to blow up; runaway nuclear reactors didn't work that way, he knew that.

But Josie seemed amused. She smiled—the first time he saw her distinctive flashing grin– and seem to see him, *him,* Trager, not just a corpsehandler. "No," she said. "It will just melt itself down. Won't even get hot out here, since you've got shields built into the walls. Just don't go in there."

"All right." Pause. What could he say now? "What do I do?"

"Work the rest of your crew, I guess. This machine'll have to be scrapped. It should have been overhauled a long time ago. From the looks of it, there's been a lot of patching done in the past. Stupid. It breaks down, it breaks down, it breaks down, and they keep sending it out. Should realize that something is wrong. After that many failures, it's sheer self-delusion to think the thing's going to work right next time out."

"I guess," Trager said. Josie smiled at him again, sealed up the panel, and started to turn.

"Wait," he said. It came out before he could stop it, almost in spite of him. Josie turned, cocked her head, looked at him questioningly. And Trager drew a sudden strength from the steel and the stone and the wind; under sulfur skies, his dreams seemed less impossible. Maybe, he thought. Maybe.

"Uh. I'm Greg Trager. Will I see you again?"

Josie grinned. "Sure. Come tonight." She gave him the address.

He climbed back into his automill after she had left, exulting in his six strong bodies, all fire and life, and he chewed up rock with something near to joy. The dark red glow in the distance looked almost like a sunrise.

When he got to Josie's, he found four other people there, friends of hers. It was a party of sorts. Josie threw a lot of parties and Trager—from that night on—went to all of them. Josie talked to him, laughed with him, *liked* him, and suddenly his life was no longer the same.

With Josie, he saw parts of Skrakky he had never seen before, did things he had never done:

: he stood with her in the crowds that gathered on the streets at night, stood in the dusty wind and sickly yellow light between the windowless concrete buildings, stood and bet and cheered himself hoarse while grease-stained mechs raced yellow rumbly tractor-trucks up and down and down and up.

: he walked with her through the strangely silent and white and clean underground Offices, and sealed air-conditioned corridors where off-worlders and paper-shufflers and company executives lived and worked.

: he prowled the rec-malls with her, those huge low buildings so like a warehouse from the outside, but full of colored lights and game rooms and cafeterias and tape shops and endless bars where handlers made their rounds.

: he went with her to dormitory gyms, where they watched handlers less skillful than himself send their corpses against each other with clumsy fists.

: he sat with her and her friends, and they woke dark quiet taverns with their talk and with their laughter, and once Trager saw someone looking much like Cox staring at him from across the room, and then he smiled and leaned a bit closer to Josie.

He hardly noticed the other people, the crowds that Josie surrounded herself with; when they went out on one of her wild jaunts, six of them or eight or ten, Trager would tell himself that he and Josie were going out, and that some others had come along with them.

Once in a great while, things would work out so they were alone together, at her place, or his. Then they would talk. Of distant worlds, of politics, of corpses and life on Skrakky, of the books they both consumed, of sports or games or friends they had in common. They shared a good deal. Trager talked a lot with Josie. And never said a word.

He loved her, of course. He suspected it the first month, and soon he was convinced of it. He loved her. This was the real thing, the thing he had been waiting for, and it had happened just as he knew it would.

But with his love: agony. He could not tell her. A dozen times he tried; the words would never come. What if she did not love him back?

His nights were still alone, in the small room with the white lights and the books and the pain. He was more alone than ever now; the peace of his routine, of his half-life with his corpses, was gone, stripped from him. By day he rode the great automills, moved his corpses, smashed rock and melted ore, and in his head rehearsed the words he'd say to Josie. And dreamed of those that she'd speak back. She was trapped too, he thought. She'd had men, of course, but she didn't love them, she loved him. But she couldn't tell him, any more than he could tell her. When he broke through, when he found the words and the courage, then everything would be all right. Each day he said that to himself, and dug swift and deep into the earth.

But back home, the sureness faded. Then, with awful despair, he knew that he was kidding himself. He was a friend to her, nothing more, never would be more. Why did he lie to himself? He'd had hints enough. They had never been lovers, never would be; on the few times he'd worked up the courage to touch her, she would smile, move away on some pretext, so he was never quite sure that he was being rejected. But he got the idea, and in the dark it tore at him. He walked the corridors weekly now, sullen, desperate, wanting to talk to someone without knowing how. And all the old scars woke up to bleed again.

Until the next day. When he would return to his machines, and believe again. He must believe in himself, he knew that, he shouted it out loud. He must stop feeling sorry for himself. He must do something. He must tell Josie. He would.

And she would love him, cried the day.

And she would laugh, the nights replied.

Trager chased her for a year, a year of pain and promise, the first year that he had ever *lived*. On that the night-fears and the day-voice agreed; he was alive now. He would never return to the emptiness of his time before Josie; he would never go back to the meathouse. That far, at least, he had come. He could change, and someday he would be strong enough to tell her.

Josie and two friends dropped by his room that night, but the friends had to leave early. For an hour or so they were alone, talking about nothing. Finally she had to go. Trager said he'd walk her home.

He kept his arm around her down the long corridors, and he watched her face, watched the play of light and shadow on her cheeks as they walked from light to darkness. "Josie," he started. He felt so fine, so good, so warm, and it came out. "I love you."

And she stopped, pulled away from him, stepped back. Her mouth opened, just a little, and something flickered in her eyes. "Oh, Greg," she said. Softly. Sadly. "No, Greg, no, don't, don't." And she shook her head.

Trembling slightly, mouthing silent words, Trager held out his hand. Josie did not take it. He touched her cheek, gently, and wordless she spun away from him.

Then, for the first time ever, Trager shook. And the tears came.

Josie took him to her room. There, sitting across from each other on the floor, never touching, they talked.

J: . . . *known it for a long time . . . tried to discourage you, Greg, but I didn't just want to come right out and . . . I never wanted to hurt you . . . a good person . . . don't worry . . .*

T: . . . *knew it all along . . . that it would never . . . lied to myself . . . wanted to believe, even if it wasn't true . . . I'm sorry, Josie, I'm sorry, i'm sorry, i'm—sorryimsorryimsorry . . .*

J: . . . *afraid you would go back to what you were . . . don't, Greg, promise me . . . can't give up . . . have to believe . . .*

T: *why? . . .*

J: . . . *stop believing, then you have nothing . . . dead . . . you can do better . . . a good handler . . . get off Skrakky, find something . . . no life here . . . someone . . . you will, you will, just believe, keep on believing . . .*

T: . . . *you . . . love you forever, Josie . . . forever . . . how can I find someone . . . never anyone like you, never . . . special . . .*

J: . . . *oh, Greg . . . lots of people . . . just look . . . open*

T: (laughter) . . . *open? . . . first time I ever talked to anyone . . .*

J: . . . *talk to me again, if you have to . . . I can talk to you . . . . had enough lovers, everyone wants to go to bed with me, better just to be friends . . .*

T: . . . *friends . . .* (laughter) . . . (tears) . . .

(II) Promises of Someday

The fire had burned out long ago, and Stevens and the forester had retired, but Trager and Donelly still sat around the ashes on the edge of the clear zone. They talked softly, so as not to wake the others, yet their words hung long in the restless night air. The uncut forest, standing dark behind them, was dead still; the wildlife of Vendalia had all fled the noise that the fleet of buzztrucks made during the day.

"... a full six-crew, running buzztrucks, I know enough to know that's not easy," Donelly was saying. He was a pale, timid youth, likeable but self-conscious about everything he did. Trager heard echoes of himself in Donelly's stiff words. "You'd do well in the arena."

Trager nodded, thoughtful, his eyes on the ashes as he moved them with a stick. "I came to Vendalia with that in mind. Went to the gladiatorials once, only once. That was enough to change my mind. I could take them, I guess, but the whole idea made me sick. Out here, well, the money doesn't even match what I was getting on Skrakky, but the work is, well, clean. You know?"

"Sort of," said Donelly. "Still, you know, it isn't like they were real people out there in the arena. Only meat. All you can do is make the bodies as dead as the minds. That's the logical way to look at it."

Trager chuckled. "You're too logical, Don. You ought to *feel* more. Listen, next time you're in Gidyon, go to the gladiatorials and take a look. It's ugly, *ugly*. Corpses stumbling around with axes and swords and morningstars, hacking and hewing at each other. Butchery, that's all it is. And the audience, the way they cheer at each blow. And *laugh*. They *laugh*, Don! No." He shook his head, sharply. "No."

Donelly never abandoned an argument. "But why not? I don't understand, Greg. You'd be good at it, the best. I've seen the way you work your crew."

Trager looked up, studied Donelly briefly while the youth sat quietly, waiting. Josie's word came back; open, be open. The old Trager, the Trager who lived friendless and alone and closed inside a Skrakky handlers' dorm, was gone. He had grown, changed.

"There was a girl," he said, slowly, with measured words. Opening. "Back on Skrakky, Don, there was a girl I loved. It, well, it didn't work out. That's why I'm here, I guess. I'm looking for someone else, for something better. That's all part of it, you see." He stopped, paused, tried to think his words out. "This girl, Josie, I wanted her to love me. You know." The words came hard. "Admire me, all that stuff. Now, yeah, sure, I could do good running corpses in the arena. But Josie could never love someone who had a job like *that*. She's gone now, of course, but still... the kind of person I'm looking for, I couldn't find them as an arena corpsemaster." He stood up, abruptly. "I don't know. That's what's important, though, to me. Josie, somebody like her, someday. Soon, I hope."

Donelly sat quiet in the moonlight, chewing his lip, not looking at

Trager, his logic suddenly useless. While Trager, his corridors long gone, walked off alone into the woods.

They had a tight-knit group; three handlers, a forester, thirteen corpses. Each day they drove the forest back, with Trager in the forefront. Against the Vendalian wilderness, against the blackbriars and the hard gray ironspike trees and the bulbous rubbery snaplimbs, against the tangled hostile forest, he would throw his six-crew and their buzztrucks. Smaller than the automills he'd run on Skrakky, fast and airborne, complex and demanding, those were buzztrucks. Trager ran six of them with corpse hands, a seventh with his own. Before his screaming blades and laser knives, the wall of wilderness fell each day. Donelly came behind him, pushing three of the mountain-sized rolling mills, to turn the fallen trees into lumber for Gidyon and other cities of Vendalia. Then Stevens, the third handler, with a flame-cannon to burn down stumps and melt rocks, and the soilpumps that would ready the fresh-clear land for farming. The forester was their foreman. The procedure was a science.

Clean, hard, demanding work; Trager thrived on it by day. He grew lean, almost athletic; the lines of his face tightened and tanned, he grew steadily browner under Vendalia's hot bright sun. His corpses were almost part of him, so easily did he move them, fly their buzztrucks. As an ordinary man might move a hand, a foot. Sometimes his control grew so firm the echoes so clear and strong, that Trager felt he was not a handler working a crew at all, but rather a man with seven bodies. Seven strong bodies that rode the sultry forest winds. He exulted in their sweat.

And the evenings, after work ceased, they were good too. Trager found a sort of peace there, a sense of belonging he had never known on Skrakky. The Vendalian foresters, rotated back and forth from Gidyon, were decent enough, and friendly. Stevens was a hearty slab of a man who seldom stopped joking long enough to talk about anything serious. Trager always found him amusing. And Donelly, the self-conscious youth, the quiet logical voice, he became a friend. He was a good listener, empathetic, compassionate, and the new open Trager was a good talker. Something close to envy shone in Donelly's eyes when Trager spoke of Josie and exorcised his soul. And Trager knew, or thought he knew, that Donelly was himself, the old Trager, the one before Josie who could not find the words.

In time, though, after days and weeks of talking, Donelly found his words. Then Trager listened, and shared another's pain. And he felt good about it. He was helping; he was lending strength; he was needed.

Each night around the ashes, the two men traded dreams. And wove a hopeful tapestry of promises and lies.

Yet still the nights would come.

Those were the worst times, as always; those were the hours of Trager's long lonely walks. If Josie had given Trager much, she had taken something too, she had taken the curious deadness he had once had, the trick of not-thinking, the pain-blotter of his mind. On Skrakky, he had walked the corridors infrequently; the forest knew him far more often.

After the talking all had stopped, after Donelly had gone to bed, that was when it would happen, when Josie would come to him in the loneliness of his tent. A thousand nights he lay there with his hands hooked behind his head, staring at the plastic tent film while he relived the night he'd told her. A thousand times he touched her cheek, and saw her spin away.

He would think of it, and fight it, and lose. Then, restless, he would rise and go outside. He would walk across the clear area, into the silent looming forest, brushing aside low branches and tripping on the underbrush; he would walk until he found water. Then he would sit down, by a scum-choked lake or a gurgling stream that ran swift and oily in the moonlight. He would fling rocks into the water, hurl them hard and flat into the night to hear them when they splashed.

He would sit for hours, throwing rocks and thinking, till finally he could convince himself the sun would rise.

Gidyon; the city; the heart of Vendalia, and through it of Slagg and Skrakky and New Pittsburg and all the other corpseworlds, the harsh ugly places where men would not work and corpses had to. Great towers of black and silver metal, floating aerial sculpture that flashed in the sunlight and shone softly at night, the vast bustling spaceport where freighters rose and fell on invisible firewands, malls where the pavement was polished, ironspike wood that gleamed a gentle grey; Gidyon.

The city with the rot. The corpse city. The meatmart.

For the freighters carried cargoes of men, criminals and derelicts and troublemakers from a dozen worlds bought with hard Vendalian cash (and there were darker rumors, of liners that had vanished mysteriously on routine tourist hops). And the soaring towers were hospitals and corpseyards, where men and women died and deadmen were born to walk anew. And all along the ironspike boardwalks were corpse-seller's shops and meathouses.

The meathouses of Vendalia were far-famed. The corpses were guaranteed beautiful.

Trager sat across from one, on the other side of the wide grey avenue, under the umbrella of an outdoor cafe. He sipped a bittersweet wine, thought about how his leave had evaporated too quickly, and tried to keep his eyes from wandering across the street. The wine was warm on his tongue, and his eyes were very restless.

Up and down the avenue, between him and the meathouse, strangers moved. Dark-faced corpse handlers from Vendalia, Skrakky, Slagg, pudgy merchants, gawking tourists from the Clean Worlds like Old Earth and Zephyr, and dozens of question-marks whose names and occupations and errands Trager would never know. Sitting there, drinking his wine and watching, Trager felt utterly cut off. He could not touch these people, could not reach them; he didn't know how, it wasn't possible, it wouldn't work. He could rise and walk out into the street and grab one, and still they would not touch. The stranger would only pull free and run. All his leave like that, all of it; he'd run through all the bars of Gidyon, forced a thousand contacts, and nothing had clicked.

His wine was gone. Trager looked at the glass dully, turning it in his hands, blinking. Then, abruptly, he stood up and paid his bill. His hands trembled.

It had been so many years, he thought as he started across the street. Josie, he thought, forgive me.

Trager returned to the wilderness camp, and his corpses flew their buzztrucks like men gone wild. But he was strangely silent around the campfire, and he did not talk to Donelly at night. Until finally, hurt and puzzled, Donelly followed him into the forest. And found him by a lanquid death-dark stream, sitting on the bank with a pile of throwing stones at his feet.

T: . . . *went in . . . after all I said, all I promised . . . still I went in . . .*
D: . . . *nothing to worry . . . remember what you told me . . . keep on believing . . .*
T: . . . *did believe, DID . . . no difficulties . . . Josie . . .*
D: . . . *you say I shouldn't give up, you better not . . . repeat everything you told me, everything Josie told you . . . everybody finds someone . . . if they keep looking . . . give up, dead . . . all you need . . . openess . . . courage to look . . . stop feeling sorry for*

yourself . . . told me that a hundred times . . .
T: *. . . fucking lot easier to tell you than do it myself . . .*
D: *. . . Greg . . . not a meathouse man . . . a dreamer . . . better than they are . . .*
T: (*sighing*) *. . . yeah . . . hard, though . . . why do I do this to myself? . . .*
D: *. . . rather be like you were? . . . not hurting, not living? . . . like me? . . .*
T: *. . . no . . . no . . . you're right . . .*

(2) The Pilgrim, Up and Down

Her name was Laurel. She was nothing like Josie, save in one thing alone. Trager loved her.

"Pretty? Trager didn't think so, not at first. She was too tall, a half-foot taller than he was, and she was a bit on the heavy side, and more than a bit on the awkward side. Her hair was her best feature, her hair that was red-brown in winter and glowing blond in summer, that fell long and straight down past her shoulders and did wild beautiful things in the wind. But she was not beautiful, not the way Josie had been beautiful. Although, oddly, she grew more beautiful with time, and maybe that was because she was losing weight, and maybe that was because Trager was falling in love with her and seeing her though kinder eyes, and maybe that was because he *told* her she was pretty and the very telling made it so. Just as Laurel told him he was wise, and her belief gave him wisdom. Whatever the reason, Laurel was very beautiful indeed after he had known her for a time.

She was five years younger than he, clean scrubbed and innocent, shy where Josie had been assertive. She was intelligent, romantic, a dreamer, she was wonderously fresh and eager, she was painfully insecure, and full of hungry need.

She was new to Gidyon, fresh from the Vendalian outback, a student forester. Trager, on leave again, was visiting the forestry college to say hello to a teacher who'd once worked with his crew. They met in the teacher's office. Trager had two weeks free in a city of strangers and meathouses; Laurel was alone. He showed her the glittering decadence of Gidyon, feeling smooth and sophisticated, and she was suitably impressed.

Two weeks went quickly. They came to the last night. Trager, suddenly afraid, took her to the park by the river that ran through Gidyon and they sat together on the low stone wall by the water's edge. Close, not touching.

"Time runs too fast," he said. He had a stone in his hand. He flicked it out over the water, flat and hard. Thoughtfully, he watched it splash and sink. Then he looked at her. "I'm nervous," he said, laughing. "I—Laurel. I don't want to leave."

Her face was unreadable (wary?). "The city is nice," she agreed.

Trager shook his head violently. "No. *No!* Not the city, you. Laurel, I think I . . . well . . ."

Laurel smiled for him. Her eyes were bright, very happy. "I know," she said.

Trager could hardly believe. He reached out, touched her cheek. She turned her head and kissed his hand. They smiled at each other.

He flew back to the forest camp to quit. "Don, *Don,* you've got to meet her," he shouted. "See, you can do it, *I* did it, just keep believing, keep trying. I feel so goddamn good it's obscene."

Donelly, stiff and logical, smiled for him, at a loss as how to handle such a flood of happiness. "What will you do?," he asked, a little awkwardly. "The arena?"

Trager laughed. "Hardly, you know how I feel. But something like that. There's a theatre near the spaceport, puts on pantomime with corpse actors. I've got a job there. The pay is rotten, but I'll be near Laurel. That's all that matters."

They hardly slept at night. Instead they talked and cuddled and made love. The lovemaking was a joy, a game, a glorious discovery; never as good technically as the meathouse, but Trager hardly cared. He taught her to be open. He told her every secret he had, and wished he had more secrets.

"Poor Josie," Laurel would often say at night, her body warm against his. "She doesn't know what she missed. I'm lucky. There couldn't be anyone else like you."

"No," said Trager, *"I'm* lucky."

They would argue about it, laughing.

Donelly came to Gidyon and joined the theatre. Without Trager, the forest work had been no fun, he said. The three of them spent a lot of time together, and Trager glowed. He wanted to share his friends with Laurel, and he'd already mentioned Donelly a lot. And he wanted Donelly to see how happy he'd become, to see what belief could accomplish.

"I like her," Donelly said, smiling, the first night after Laurel had left.

"Good," Trager replied, nodding.

"No," said Donelly. "Greg, I *really* like her."

They spent a *lot* of time together.

"Greg," Laurel said one night in bed. "I think that Don is . . . well, after me. You know."

Trager rolled over and propped his head up on his elbow. "God," he said. He sounded concerned.

"I don't know how to handle it."

"Carefully," Trager said. "He's very vulnerable. You're probably the first woman he's ever been interested in. Don't be too hard on him. He shouldn't have to go through the stuff I went through, you know?"

The sex was never as good as a meathouse. And, after a while, Laurel began to close. More and more nights now she went to sleep after they made love; the days when they talked till dawn were gone. Perhaps they had nothing left to say. Trager had noticed that she had a tendency to finish his stories for him. It was nearly impossible to come up with one he hadn't already told her.

"He said *that?*" Trager got up out of bed, turned on a light, and sat down frowning. Laurel pulled the covers up to her chin.

"Well, what did *you* say?"

She hesitated. "I can't tell you. It's between Don and me. He said it wasn't fair, the way I turn around and tell you everything that goes on between us, and he's right."

"*Right!* But I tell you everything. Don't you remember what we . . ."

"I know, but . . ."

Trager shook his head. His voice lost some of its anger. "What's going on, Laurel, huh? I'm scared, all of a sudden. I love you, remember? How can everything change so fast?"

Her face softened. She sat up, and held out her arms, and the covers fell back from full soft breasts. "Oh, Greg," she said. "Don't worry. I love you, I always will, but it's just that I love him too, I guess. You know?"

Trager, mollified, came into her arms, and kissed her with fervor. Then, suddenly, he broke off. "Hey," he said, with mock sternness to hide the trembling in his voice, "who do you love *more?*"

"You, of course, always you."

Smiling, he returned to the kiss.

"I know you know," Donelly said. "I guess we have to talk about it."

Trager nodded. They were backstage in the theatre. Three of his corpses walked up behind him, and stood, arms crossed, like a guard. "All right." He looked straight at Donelly, and his face—smiling until the other's words—was suddenly stern. "Laurel asked me to pretend I didn't know anything. She said you felt guilty. But pretending was quite a strain, Don. I guess it's time we got everything out into the open."

Donelly's pale blue eyes shifted to the floor, and he stuck his hands into his pockets. "I don't want to hurt you," he said.

"Then don't."

"But I'm not going to pretend I'm dead, either. I'm not. I love her too."

"You're supposed to be my friend, Don. Love someone else. You're just going to get yourself hurt this way."

"I have more in common with her than you do."

Trager just stared.

Donelly looked up at him. Then, abashed, back down again. "I don't know. Oh, Greg. She loves you more anyway, she said so. I never should have expected anything else. I feel like I've stabbed you in the back. I . . . ."

Trager watched him. Finally, he laughed softly. "Oh, shit, I can't take this. Look, Don, you haven't stabbed me, c'mon, don't talk like that. I guess, if you love her, this is the way it's got to be, you know. I just hope everything comes out all right."

Later that night, in bed with Laurel; "I'm worried about him," he told her.

His face, once tanned, now ashen. "Laurel?," he said. Not believing. "I don't love you anymore. I'm sorry. I don't. It seemed real at the time, but now it's almost like a dream. I don't even know if I ever loved you, really."

"Don," he said woodenly.

Laurel flushed. "Don't say anything bad about Don. I'm tired of hearing you run him down. He never says anything except good about you."

"Oh, Laurel. Don't you *remember?* The things we said, the way we felt? I'm the same person you said those words to."

"But I've grown," Laurel said, hard and tearless, tossing her red-gold hair. "I remember perfectly well, but I just don't feel that way any more."

"Don't," he said. He reached for her.

She stepped back. "Keep your hands off me. I told you, Greg, it's *over.* You have to leave now. Don is coming by."

It was worse than Josie. A thousand times worse.

(III) Wanderings

He tried to keep on at the theatre; he enjoyed the work, he had friends there. But it was impossible. Donelly was there every day, smiling and being friendly, and sometimes Laurel came to meet him after the day's show and they went off together, arm in arm. Trager would stand and watch, try not to notice. While the twisted thing inside him shrieked and clawed.

He quit. He would not see them again. He would keep his pride.

The sky was bright with the lights of Gidyon and full of laughter, but it was dark and quiet in the park.

Trager stood stiff against a tree, his eyes on the river, his hands folded tightly against his chest. He was a statue. He hardly seemed to breathe. Not even his eyes moved.

Kneeling near the low wall, the corpse pounded until the stone was slick with blood and its hands were mangled clots of torn meat. The sounds of the blows were dull and wet, but for the infrequent scraping of bone against rock.

✳ ✳ ✳

They made him pay first, before he could even enter the booth. Then he sat there for an hour while they found her and punched through. Finally, though, finally; "Josie."

"Greg," she said, grinning her distinctive grin. "I should have known. Who else would call all the way from Vendalia? How are you?"

He told her.

Her grin vanished. "Oh, Greg," she said. "I'm sorry. But don't let it get to you. Keep going. The next one will work out better. They always do."

Her words didn't satisfy him. "Josie," he said, "how are things back there? You miss me?"

"Oh, sure. Things are pretty good. It's still Skrakky, though. Stay where you are, you're better off." She looked off screen, then back. "I should go, before your bill gets enormous. Glad you called, love."

"Josie," Trager started. But the screen was already dark.

Sometimes, at night, he couldn't help himself. He would move to his home screen and ring Laurel. Invariably her eyes would narrow when she saw who it was. Then she would hang up.

And Trager would sit in a dark room and recall how once the sound of his voice made her so very, very happy.

The streets of Gidyon are not the best of places for lonely midnight walks. They are brightly lit, even in the darkest hours, and jammed with men and deadmen. And there are meathouses, all up and down the boulevards and the ironspike boardwalks.

Josie's words had lost their power. In the meathouses, Trager abandoned dreams and found cheap solace. The sensuous evenings with Laurel and the fumbling sex of his boyhood were things of yesterday; Trager took his meatmates hard and quick, almost brutally, fucked them with a wordless savage power to the inevitable perfect orgasm. Sometimes, remembering the theatre, he would have them act out short erotic playlets to get him in the mood.

In the night. Agony.

He was in the corridors again, the low dim corridors of the corpse handlers' dorm on Skrakky, but now the corridors were twisted and torturous and Trager had long since lost his way. The air was thick with a rotting grey haze, and growing thicker. Soon, he feared, he would be all but blind.

Around and around he walked, up and down, but always there was more corridor, and all of them led nowhere. The doors were grim black rectangles, knobless, locked to him forever; he passed them by without thinking, most of them. Once or twice, though, he paused, before doors where light leaked around the frame. He would listen, and inside there were sounds, and then he would begin to knock wildly. But no one ever answered.

So he would move on, through the haze that got darker and thicker and seemed to burn his skin, past door after door after door, until he was weeping and his feet were tired and bloody. And then, off aways, down a long long corridor that loomed straight before him, he would see an open door. From it came light so hot and white it hurt the eyes, and music bright and joyful, and the sounds of people laughing. Then Trager would run, though his feet were raw bundles of pain and his lungs burned with the haze he was breathing. He would run and run until he reached the room with the open door.

Only when he got there, it was his room, and it was empty.

Once, in the middle of their brief time together, they'd gone out into the wilderness and made love under the stars. Afterwards she had snuggled hard against him, and he stroked her gently. "What are you thinking?," he asked.

"About us," Laurel said. She shivered. The wind was brisk and cold. "Sometimes I get scared, Greg. I'm so afraid something will happen to us, something that will ruin it. I don't ever want you to leave me."

"Don't worry," he told her. "I won't."

Now, each night before sleep came, he tortured himself with her words. The good memories left him with ashes and tears; the bad ones with a wordless rage.

He slept with a ghost beside him, a supernaturally beautiful ghost, the husk of a dead dream. He woke to her each morning.

He hated them. He hated himself for hating.

***

(3) Duvalier's Dream

Her name does not matter. Her looks are not important. All that counts is that she *was*, that Trager tried again, that he forced himself on and made himself believe and didn't give up. He *tried*.

But something was missing. Magic?

The words were the same.

How many times can you speak them, Trager wondered, *speak them and believe them, like you believed them the first time you said them? Once? Twice? Three times, maybe? Or a hundred? And the people who say it a hundred times, are they really so much better at loving? Or only at fooling themselves? Aren't they really people who long ago abandoned the dream, who use its name for something else?*

He said the words, holding her, cradling her and kissing her. He said the words, with a knowledge that was surer and heavier and more dead than any belief. He said the words and *tried*, but no longer could he mean them.

And she said the words back, and Trager realized that they meant nothing to him. Over and over again they said the things each wanted to hear, and both of them knew they were pretending.

They tried *hard*. But when he reached out, like an actor caught in his role, doomed to play out the same part over and over again, when he reached out his hand and touched her cheek—the skin was smooth and soft and lovely. And wet with tears.

(IV) Echoes

"I don't want to hurt you," said Donelly, shuffling and looking guilty, until Trager felt ashamed for having hurt a friend.

He touched her cheek, and she spun away from him.

"I never wanted to hurt you," Josie said, and Trager was sad. She had given him so much; he'd only made her guilty. Yes, he was hurt, but a stronger man would never have let her know.

He touched her cheek, and she kissed his hand.

"I'm sorry. I don't," Laurel said. And Trager was lost. What had he done, where was his fault, how had he ruined it? She had been so sure. They had had so much.

He touched her cheek, and she wept.

How many times can you speak them, his voice echoed, *speak them and believe them, like you believed them the first time you said them?*

The wind was dark and dust heavy, the sky throbbed painfully with flickering scarlet flame. In the pit, in the darkness, stood a young women with goggles and a filtermask and short brown hair and answers. "It breaks down, it breaks down, it breaks down, and they keep sending it out," she said. "Should realize that something is wrong. After that many failures, it's sheer self-delusion to think the thing's going to work right next time out."

(4) Trager, Come of Age

The enemy corpse is huge and black, its torso rippling with muscle, a product of months of exercise, the biggest thing that Trager has ever faced. It advances across the sawdust in a slow, clumsy crouch, holding the gleaming broadsword in one hand. Trager watches it come from his chair atop one end of the fighting area. The other corpsemaster is careful, cautious.

His own deadman, a wiry blond, stands and waits, a morningstar trailing down in the blood-soaked arena dust. Trager will move him fast enough and well enough when the time is right. The enemy knows it, and the crowd.

The black corpse suddenly lifts its broadsword and scrambles forward in a run, hoping to use reach and speed to get its kill. But Trager's corpse is no longer there when the enemy's measured blow cuts the air where he had been.

Sitting comfortably above the fighting pit/Down in the arena, his feet grimy with blood and sawdust - Trager/the corpse - snaps the command/ swings the morningstar - and the great studded ball drifts up and around, almost lazily, almost gracefully. Into the back of the enemy's head, as he tried to recover and turn. A flower of blood and brain blooms swift and sudden, and the crowd cheers.

Trager walks his corpse from the arena, then stands to receive applause. It is his tenth kill. Soon the championship will be his. He is building such a record that they can no longer deny him a match.

She is beautiful, his lady, his love. Her hair is short and blond, her body very slim, graceful, almost athletic, with trim legs and small hard breasts. Her eyes are bright green, and they always welcome him. And there is a strange erotic innocence in her smile.

She waits for him in bed, waits for his return from the arena, waits for him eager and playful and loving. When he enters, she is sitting up, smiling for him, the covers bunched around her waist. From the door he admires her nipples.

Aware of his eyes, shy, she covers her breasts and blushes. Trager knows it is all false modesty, all playing. He moves to the bedside, sits, reaches out to stroke her cheek. Her skin is very soft; she nuzzles against his hand as it brushes her. Then Trager draws her hands aside, plants one gentle kiss on each breast, and a not-so-gentle kiss on her mouth. She kissed back, with ardor, their tongues dance.

They make love, he and she, slow and senuous, locked together in a loving embrace that goes on and on. Two bodies move flawlessly in perfect rhythm, each knowing the other's needs. Trager thrusts, and his other body meets the thrusts. He reaches, and her hand is there. They come together (always, *always,* both orgasms triggered by the handler's brain), and a bright red flush burns on her breasts and earlobes. They kiss.

Afterwards, he talks to her, his love, his lady. You should always talk afterwards; he learned that long ago.

"You're lucky," he tells her sometimes, and she snuggles up to him and plants tiny kisses all across his chest. "Very lucky. They lie to you out there, love. They teach you a silly shining dream and they tell you to believe and chase it and they tell you that for you, for everyone, there is someone. But it's all wrong. The universe isn't fair, it never has been, so why do they tell you so? You run after the phantom, and lose, and they tell you next time, but it's all rot, all empty rot. Nobody ever finds the dream at all, they just kid themselves, trick themselves so they can go on believing. It's just a clutching lie that desperate people tell each other, hoping to convince themselves."

But then he can't talk anymore, for her kisses have gone lower and lower, and now she takes him in her mouth. And Trager smiles at his love and gently strokes her hair.

Of all the bright cruel lies they tell you, the cruelest is the one called love.

Sandkings

Simon Kress lived alone in a sprawling manor house among the dry, rocky hills fifty kilometers from the city. So, when he was called away unexpectedly on business, he had no neighbors he could conveniently impose on to take his pets. The carrion hawk was no problem; it roosted in the unused belfry and customarily fed itself anyway. The shambler Kress simply shooed outside and left to fend for itself; the little monster would gorge on slugs and birds and rockjocks. But the fish tank, stocked with genuine Earth piranha, posed a difficulty. Kress finally just threw a haunch of beef into the huge tank. The piranha could always eat each other if he were detained longer than expected. They'd done it before. It amused him.

Unfortunately, he was detained *much* longer than expected this time. When he finally returned, all the fish were dead. So was the carrion hawk. The shambler had climbed up to the belfry and eaten it. Simon Kress was vexed.

The next day he flew his skimmer to Asgard, a journey of some two hundred kilometers. Asgard was Baldur's largest city and boasted the oldest and largest starport as well. Kress liked to impress his friends with animals that were unusual, entertaining, and expensive; Asgard was the place to buy them.

This time, though, he had poor luck. Xenopets had closed its doors, t'Etherane the Petseller tried to foist another carrion hawk off on him, and Strange Waters offered nothing more exotic than piranha, glow-sharks, and spidersquids. Kress had had all those; he wanted something new.

Near dusk, he found himself walking down the Rainbow Boulevard, looking for places he had not patronized before. So close to the starport, the street was lined by importers' marts. The big corporate emporiums had impressive long windows, where rare and costly alien artifacts reposed on felt cushions against dark drapes that made the interiors of the stores a mystery. Between them were the junk shops—narrow, nasty little places whose display areas were crammed with all manner of offworld bric-a-brac. Kress tried both kinds of shops, with equal dissatisfaction.

Then he came across a store that was different.

It was quite close to the port. Kress had never been there before. The shop occupied a small, single-story building of moderate size, set between a euphoria bar and a temple-brothel of the Secret Sisterhood. Down this far, the Rainbow Boulevard grew tacky. The shop itself was unusual. Arresting.

The windows were full of mist; now a pale red, now the gray of true fog, now sparkling and golden. The mist swirled and eddied and glowed faintly from within. Kress glimpsed objects in the window—machines, pieces of art, other things he could not recognize—but he could not get a good look at any of them. The mists flowed sensuously around them, displaying a bit of first one thing and then another, then cloaking all. It was intriguing.

As he watched, the mist began to form letters. One word at a time. Kress stood and read:

WO. AND. SHADE. IMPORTERS. ARTIFACTS.
ART. LIFEFORMS. AND MISC.

The letters stopped. Through the fog, Kress saw something moving. That was enough for him, that and the word "Lifeforms" in their advertisement. He swept his walking cloak over his shoulder and entered the store.

Inside, Kress felt disoriented. The interior seemed vast, much larger than he would have guessed from the relatively modest frontage. It was dimly lit, peaceful. The ceiling was a starscape, complete with spiral nebulae, very dark and realistic, very nice. The counters all shone faintly, the better to display the merchandise within. The aisles were carpeted with ground fog. In places, it came almost to his knees and swirled about his feet as he walked.

"Can I help you?"

She seemed almost to have risen from the fog. Tall and gaunt and pale, she wore a practical gray jumpsuit and a strange little cap that rested well back on her head.

"Are you Wo or Shade?" Kress asked. "Or only sales help?"

"Jala Wo, ready to serve you," she replied. "Shade does not see customers. We have no sales help."

"You have quite a large establishment," Kress said. "Odd that I have never heard of you before."

"We have only just opened this shop on Baldur," the woman said. "We have franchises on a number of other worlds, however. What can I sell you? Art, perhaps? You have the look of a collector. We have some fine Nor T'alush crystal carvings."

"No," Simon Kress said. "I own all the crystal carvings I desire. I came to see about a pet."

"A lifeform?"

"Yes."

"Alien?"

"Of course."

"We have a mimic in stock. From Celia's World. A clever little simian. Not only will it learn to speak, but eventually it will mimic your voice, inflections, gestures, even facial expressions."

"Cute," said Kress. "And common. I have no use for either, Wo. I want something exotic. Unusual. And not cute. I detest cute animals. At the moment I own a shambler. Imported from Cotho, at no mean expense. From time to time I feed him a litter of unwanted kittens. That is what I think of *cute*. Do I make myself understood?"

Wo smiled enigmatically. "Have you ever owned an animal that worshiped you?" she asked.

Kress grinned. "Oh, now and again. But I don't require worship, Wo. Just entertainment."

"You misunderstand me," Wo said, still wearing her strange smile. "I meant worship literally."

"What are you talking about?"

"I think I have just the thing for you," Wo said. "Follow me."

She led Kress between the radiant counters and down a long, fog-shrouded aisle beneath false starlight. They passed through a wall of mist into another section of the store, and stopped before a large plastic tank. An aquarium, thought Kress.

Wo beckoned. He stepped closer and saw that he was wrong. It was a terrarium. Within lay a miniature desert about two meters square. Pale sand bleached scarlet by wan red light. Rocks: basalt and quartz and granite. In each corner of the tank stood a castle.

Kress blinked, and peered, and corrected himself; actually only three castles stood. The fourth leaned; a crumbled, broken ruin. The other three were crude but intact, carved of stone and sand. Over their battlements and through their rounded porticoes, tiny creatures climbed and scrambled. Kress pressed his face against the plastic. "Insects?" he asked.

"No," Wo replied. "A much more complex lifeform. More intelligent as well. Considerably smarter than your shambler. They are called sandkings."

"Insects," Kress said, drawing back from the tank. "I don't care how complex they are." He frowned. "And kindly don't try to gull me with this talk of intelligence. These things are far too small to have anything but the most rudimentary brains."

"They share hiveminds," Wo said. "Castle minds, in this case. There are only three organisms in the tank, actually. The fourth died. You see how her castle has fallen."

Kress looked back at the tank. "Hiveminds, eh? Interesting." He frowned again. "Still, it is only an oversized ant farm. I'd hoped for something better."

"They fight wars."

"Wars? Hmmmm." Kress looked again.

"Note the colors, if you will," Wo told him. She pointed to the creatures that swarmed over the nearest castle. One was scrabbling at the tank wall. Kress studied it. It still looked like an insect to his eyes. Barely as long as his fingernail, six-limbed, with six tiny eyes set all around its body. A wicked set of mandibles clacked visibly, while two long, fine antennae wove patterns in the air. Antennae, mandibles, eyes, and legs were sooty black, but the dominant color was the burnt orange of its armor plating. "It's an insect," Kress repeated.

"It is not an insect," Wo insisted calmly. "The armored exo-skeleton is shed when the sandking grows larger. *If* it grows larger. In a tank this size, it won't." She took Kress by the elbow and led him around the tank to the next castle. "Look at the colors here."

He did. They were different. Here the sandkings had bright red armor; antennae, mandibles, eyes, and legs were yellow. Kress glanced across the tank. The denizens of the third live castle were off-white, with red trim. "Hmmm," he said.

"They war, as I said," Wo told him. "They even have truces and alliances. It was an alliance that destroyed the fourth castle in this tank. The blacks were getting too numerous, so the others joined forces to destroy them."

Kress remained unconvinced. "Amusing, no doubt. But insects fight wars too."

"Insects do not worship," Wo said.

"Eh?"

Wo smiled and pointed at the castle. Kress stared. A face had been carved into the wall of the highest tower. He recognized it. It was Jala Wo's face. "How . . .?"

"I projected a holograph of my face into the tank, kept it there for a few days. The face of god, you see? I feed them; I am always close. The sandkings have a rudimentary psionic sense. Proximity telepathy. They sense me, and worship me by using my face to decorate their buildings. All the castles have them, see." They did.

On the castle, the face of Jala Wo was serene and peaceful, and very lifelike. Kress marveled at the workmanship. "How do they do it?"

"The foremost legs double as arms. They even have fingers of a sort; three small, flexible tendrils. And they co-operate well, both in building and in battle. Remember, all the mobiles of one color share a single mind."

"Tell me more," Kress said.

Wo smiled. "The maw lives in the castle. Maw is my name for her. A pun, if you will; the thing is mother and stomach both. Female, large as your fist, immobile. Actually, sandking is a bit of a misnomer. The mobiles are peasants and warriors, the real ruler is the queen. But that analogy is faulty as well. Considered as a whole, each castle is a single hermaphroditic creature."

"What do they eat?"

"The mobiles eat pap—predigested food obtained inside the castle. They get it from the maw after she has worked on it for several days. Their stomachs can't handle anything else, so if the maw dies, they soon die as well. The maw . . . the maw eats anything. You'll have no special expense there. Table scraps will do excellently."

"Live food?" Kress asked.

Wo shrugged. "Each maw eats mobiles from the other castles, yes."

"I am intrigued," he admitted. "If only they weren't so small."

"Yours can be larger. These sandkings are small because their tank is small. They seem to limit their growth to fit available space. If I moved these to a larger tank, they'd start growing again."

"Hmmmm. My piranha tank is twice this size, and vacant. It could be cleaned out, filled with sand . . . ."

"Wo and Shade would take care of the installation. It would be our pleasure."

"Of course," said Kress, "I would expect four intact castles."

"Certainly," Wo said.
They began to haggle about the price.

Three days later Jala Wo arrived at Simon Kress' estate, with dormant sandkings and a work crew to take charge of the installation. Wo's assistants were aliens unlike any Kress was familiar with—squat, broad bipeds with four arms and bulging, multifaceted eyes. Their skin was thick and leathery, twisted into horns and spines and protrusions at odd spots upon their bodies. But they were very strong, and good workers. Wo ordered them about in a musical tongue that Kress had never heard.

In a day it was done. They moved his piranha tank to the center of his spacious living room, arranged couches on either side of it for better viewing, scrubbed it clean, and filled it two-thirds of the way up with sand and rock. Then they installed a special lighting system, both to provide the dim red illumination the sandkings preferred and to project holographic images into the tank. On top they mounted a sturdy plastic cover, with a feeder mechanism built in. "This way you can feed your sandkings without removing the top of the tank," Wo explained. "You would not want to take any chances on the mobiles escaping."

The cover also included climate control devices, to condense just the right amount of moisture from the air. "You want it dry, but not too dry," Wo said.

Finally one of the four-armed workers climbed into the tank and dug deep pits in the four corners. One of his companions handed the dormant maws over to him, removing them one by one from their frosted cryonic traveling cases. They were nothing to look at. Kress decided they resembled nothing so much as a mottled, half-spoiled chunk of raw meat. With a mouth.

The alien buried them, one in each corner of the tank. Then they sealed it all up and took their leave.

"The heat will bring the maws out of dormancy," Wo said. "In less than a week, mobiles will begin to hatch and burrow to the surface. Be certain to give them plenty of food. They will need all their strength until they are well established. I would estimate that you will have castles rising in about three weeks."

"And my face? When will they carve my face?"

"Turn on the hologram after about a month," she advised him. "And be patient. If you have any questions, please call. Wo and Shade are at your service." She bowed and left.

Kress wandered back to the tank and lit a joy-stick. The desert was still and empty. He drummed his fingers impatiently against the plastic, and frowned.

On the fourth day, Kress thought he glimpsed motion beneath the sand, subtle subterranean stirrings.

On the fifth day, he saw his first mobile, a lone white.

On the sixth day, he counted a dozen of them, whites and reds and blacks. The oranges were tardy. He cycled through a bowl of half-decayed table-scraps. The mobiles sensed it at once, rushed to it, and began to drag pieces back to their respective corners. Each color group was very organized. They did not fight. Kress was a bit disappointed, but he decided to give them time.

The oranges made their appearance on the eighth day. By then the other sandkings had begun to carry small stones and erect crude fortifications. They still did not war. At the moment they were only half the size of those he had seen at Wo and Shade's, but Kress thought they were growing rapidly.

The castles began to rise midway through the second week. Organized battalions of mobiles dragged heavy chunks of sandstone and granite back to their corners, where other mobiles were pushing sand into place with mandibles and tendrils. Kress had purchased a pair of magnifying goggles so he could watch them work, wherever they might go in the tank. He wandered around and around the tall plastic walls, observing. It was fascinating. The castles were a bit plainer than Kress would have liked, but he had an idea about that. The next day he cycled through some obsidian and flakes of colored glass along with the food. Within hours, they had been incorporated into the castle walls.

The black castle was the first completed, followed by the white and red fortresses. The oranges were last, as usual. Kress took his meals into the living room and ate seated on the couch, so he could watch. He expected the first war to break out any hour now.

He was disappointed. Days passed; the castles grew taller and more grand, and Kress seldom left the tank except to attend to his sanitary needs and answer critical business calls. But the sandkings did not war. He was getting upset.

Finally, he stopped feeding them.

Two days after the table scraps had ceased to fall from their desert sky, four black mobiles surrounded an orange and dragged it back to their maw. They maimed it first, ripping off its mandibles and antennae and limbs, and carried it through the shadowed main gate of their miniature castle. It never emerged. Within an hour, more than forty orange mobiles marched across the sand and attacked the blacks' corner. They were outnumbered by the blacks that came rushing up from the depths. When the fighting was over, the attackers had been slaughtered. The dead and dying were taken down to feed the black maw.

Kress, delighted, congratulated himself on his genius.

When he put food into the tank the following day, a three-cornered battle broke out over is possession. The whites were the big winners.

After that, war followed war.

Almost a month to the day after Jala Wo had delivered the sandkings, Kress turned on the holographic projector, and his face materialized in the tank. It turned, slowly, around and around, so his gaze fell on all four castles equally. Kress thought it rather a good likeness—it had his impish grin, wide mouth, full cheeks. His blue eyes sparkled, his gray hair was carefully arrayed in a fashionable sidesweep, his eyebrows were thin and sophisticated.

Soon enough, the sandkings set to work. Kress fed them lavishly while his image beamed down at them from their sky. Temporarily, the wars stopped. All activity was directed towards worship.

His face emerged on the castle walls.

At first all four carvings looked alike to him, but as the work continued and Kress studied the reproductions, he began to detect subtle differences in technique and execution. The reds were the most creative, using tiny flakes of slate to put the gray in his hair. The white idol seemed young and mischievous to him, while the face shaped by the blacks—although virtually the same, line for line—struck him as wise and beneficent. The orange sandkings, as ever, were last and least. The wars had not gone well for them, and their castle was sad compared to the others. The image they carved was crude and cartoonish, and they seemed to intend to leave it that way. When they stopped work on the face, Kress grew quite piqued with them, but there was really nothing he could do.

When all the sandkings had finished their Kress-faces, he turned off the holograph and decided that it was time to have a party. His friends would be impressed. He could even stage a war for them, he thought. Humming happily to himself, he began to draw up a guest list.

*** *** ***

The party was a wild success.

Kress invited thirty people: a handful of close friends who shared his amusements, a few former lovers, and a collection of business and social rivals who could not afford to ignore his summons. He knew some of them would be discomfited and even offended by his sandkings. He counted on it. Simon Kress customarily considered his parties a failure unless at least one guest walked out in high dudgeon.

On impulse he added Jala Wo's name to his list. "Bring Shade if you like," he added when dictating her invitation.

Her acceptance surprised him just a bit. "Shade, alas, will be unable to attend. He does not go to social functions," Wo added. "As for myself, I look forward to the chance to see how your sandkings are doing."

Kress ordered them up a sumptuous meal. And when at last the conversation had died down, and most of his guests had gotten silly on wine and joy-sticks, he shocked them by personally scraping their table leavings into a large bowl. "Come, all of you," he told them. "I want to introduce you to my newest pets." Carrying the bowl, he conducted them into his living room.

The sandkings lived up to his fondest expectations. He had starved them for two days in preparation, and they were in a fighting mood. While the guests ringed the tank, looking through the magnifying glasses Kress had thoughtfully provided, the sandkings waged a glorious battle over the scraps. He counted almost sixty dead mobiles when the struggle was over. The reds and whites, who had recently formed an alliance, emerged with most of the food.

"Kress, you're disgusting," Cath m'Lane told him. She had lived with him for a short time two years before, until her soppy sentimentality almost drove him mad. "I was a fool to come back here. I thought perhaps you'd changed, wanted to apologize." She had never forgiven him for the time his shambler had eaten an excessively cute puppy of which she had been fond. "Don't *ever* invite me here again, Simon." She strode out, accompanied by her current lover and a chorus of laughter.

His other guests were full of questions.

Where did the sandkings come from?, they wanted to know. "From Wo and Shade, Importers," he replied, with a polite gesture towards Jala Wo, who had remained quiet and apart through most of the evening.

Why did they decorate their castles with his likeness? "Because I am the source of all good things. Surely you know that?" That brought round of chuckles.

Will they fight again? "Of course, but not tonight. Don't worry. There will be other parties."

Jad Rakkis, who was an amateur xenologist, began talking about other social insects and the wars they fought. "These sandkings are amusing, but nothing really. You ought to read about Terran soldier ants, for instance."

"Sandkings are not insects," Jala Wo said sharply, but Jad was off and running, and no one paid her the slightest attention. Kress smiled at her and shrugged.

Malada Blane suggested a betting pool the next time they got together to watch a war, and everyone was taken with the idea. An animated discussion about rules and odds ensued. It lasted for almost an hour. Finally the guests began to take their leave.

Jala Wo was the last to depart. "So," Kress said to her when they were alone, "it appears my sandkings are a hit."

"They are doing well," Wo said. "Already they are larger than my own."

"Yes," Kress said, "except for the oranges."

"I had noticed that," Wo replied. "They seem few in number, and their castle is shabby."

"Well, someone must lose," Kress said. "The oranges were late to emerge and get established. They have suffered for it."

"Pardon," said Wo, "but might I ask if you are feeding your sandkings sufficiently?"

Kress shrugged. "They diet from time to time. It makes them fiercer."

She frowned. "There is no need to starve them. Let them war in their own time, for their own reasons. It is their nature, and you will witness conflicts that are delightfully subtle and complex. The constant war brought on by hunger is artless and degrading."

Simon Kress repaid Wo's frown with interest. "You are in my house, Wo, and here I am the judge of what is degrading. I fed the sandkings as you advised, and they did not fight."

"You must have patience."

"No," Kress said. "I am their master and their god, after all. Why should I wait on their impulses? They did not war often enough to suit me. I corrected the situation."

"I see," said Wo. "I will discuss the matter with Shade."

"It is none of your concern, or his," Kress snapped.

"I must bid you good night, then," Wo said with resignation. But as she slipped into her coat to depart, she fixed him with a final disapproving stare. "Look to your faces, Simon Kress," she warned him. "Look to your faces."

Puzzled, he wandered back to the tank and stared at the castles after she had taken her departure. His faces were still there, as ever. Except— he snatched up his magnifying goggles and slipped them on. Even then it was hard to make out. But it seemed to him that the expression on the face of his images had changed slightly, that his smile was somehow twisted so that it seemed a touch malicious. But it was a very subtle change, if it was a change at all. Kress finally put it down to his suggestibility, and resolved not to invite Jala Wo to any more of his gatherings.

Over the next few months, Kress and about a dozen of his favorites got together weekly for what he liked to call his "war games." Now that his initial fascination with the sandkings was past, Kress spent less time around his tank and more on his business affairs and his social life, but he still enjoyed having a few friends over for a war or two. He kept the combatants sharp on a constant edge of hunger. It had severe effects on the orange sandkings, who dwindled visibly until Kress began to wonder if their maw was dead. But the others did well enough.

Sometimes at night, when he could not sleep, Kress would take a bottle of wine into the darkened living room, where the red gloom of his miniature desert was the only light. He would drink and watch for hours, alone. There was usually a fight going on somewhere, and when there was not he could easily start one by dropping in some small morsel of food.

They took to betting on the weekly battles, as Malada Blane had suggested. Kress won a good amount by betting on the whites, who had become the most powerful and numerous colony in the tank, with the grandest castle. One week he slid the corner of the tank top aside, and dropped the food close to the white castle instead of on the central battle ground as usual, so that the others had to attack the whites in their stronghold to get any food at all. They tried. The whites were brilliant in defense. Kress won a hundred standards from Jad Rakkis.

Rakkis, in fact, lost heavily on the sandkings almost every week. He pretended to a vast knowledge of them and their ways, claiming that he had studied them after the first party, but he had no luck when it came to placing his bets. Kress suspected that Jad's claims were empty boasting. He had tried to study the sandkings a bit himself, in a moment of idle curiosity, tying in to the library to find out to what world his pets were native. But there was no listing for them. He wanted to get in touch with

Wo and ask her about it, but he had other concerns, and the matter kept slipping his mind.

Finally, after a month in which his losses totalled more than a thousand standards, Jad Rakkis arrived at the war games carrying a small plastic case under his arm. Inside was a spiderlike thing covered with fine golden hair.

"A sand spider," Rakkis announced. "From Cathaday. I got it this afternoon from t'Etherane the Petseller. Usually they remove the poison sacs, but this one is intact. Are you game, Simon? I want my money back. I'll bet a thousand standards, sand spider against sandkings."

Kress studied the spider in its plastic prison. His sandkings had grown—they were twice as large as Wo's, as she'd predicted—but they were still dwarfed by this thing. It was venomed, and they were not. Still, there were an awful lot of them. Besides, the endless sandking wars had begun to grow tiresome lately. The novelty of the match intrigued him. "Done," Kress said. "Jad, you are a fool. The sandkings will just keep coming until this ugly creature of yours is dead."

"You are the fool, Simon," Rakkis replied, smiling. "The Cathadayn sand spider customarily feeds on burrowers that hide in nooks and crevices and—well, watch—it will go straight into those castles, and eat the maws."

Kress scowled amid general laughter. He hadn't counted on that. "Get on with it," he said irritably. He went to freshen his drink.

The spider was too large to cycle conveniently through the food chamber. Two of the others helped Rakkis slide the tank top slightly to one side, and Malada Blane handed him up his case. He shook the spider out. It landed lightly on a miniature dune in front of the red castle, and stood confused for a moment, mouth working, legs twitching menacingly.

"Come on," Rakkis urged. They all gathered round the tank. Simon Kress found his magnifiers and slipped them on. If he was going to lose a thousand standards, at least he wanted a good view of the action.

The sandkings had seen the invader. All over the castle, activity had ceased. The small scarlet mobiles were frozen, watching.

The spider began to move toward the dark promise of the gate. On the tower above, Simon Kress' countenance stared down impassively.

At once there was a flurry of activity. The nearest red mobiles formed themselves into two wedges and streamed over the sand toward the spider. More warriors erupted from inside the castle and assembled in a triple line to guard the approach to the underground chamber where the maw lived. Scouts came scuttling over the dunes, recalled to fight.

Battle was joined.

The attacking sandkings washed over the spider. Mandibles snapped shut on legs and abdomen, and clung. Reds raced up the golden legs to the invader's back. They bit and tore. One of them found an eye, and ripped it loose with tiny yellow tendrils. Kress smiled and pointed.

But they were *small*, and they had no venom, and the spider did not stop. Its legs flicked sandkings off to either side. Its dripping jaws found others, and left them broken and stiffening. Already a dozen of the reds lay dying. The sand spider came on and on. It strode straight through the triple line of guardians before the castle. The lines closed around it, covered it, waging desperate battle. A team of sandkings had bitten off one of the spider's legs, Kress saw. Defenders leaped from atop the towers to land on the twitching, heaving mass.

Lost beneath the sandkings, the spider somehow lurched down into the darkess and vanished.

Jad Rakkis let out a long breath. He looked pale. "Wonderful," someone else said. Malada Blane chuckled deep in her throat.

"Look," said Idi Noreddian, tugging Kress by the arm.

They had been so intent on the struggle in the corner that none of them had noticed the activity elsewhere in the tank. But now the castle was still, the sands empty save for dead red mobiles, and now they saw.

Three armies were drawn up before the red castle. They stood quite still, in perfect array, rank after rank of sandkings, orange and white and black. Waiting to see what emerged from the depths.

Simon Kress smiled. "A *cordon sanitaire*," he said. "And glance at the other castles, if you will, Jad."

Rakkis did, and swore. Teams of mobiles were sealing up the gates with sand and stone. If the spider somehow survived this encounter, it would find no easy entrance at the other castles. "I should have brought four spiders," Jad Rakkis said. "Still, I've won. My spider is down there right now, eating your damned maw."

Kress did not reply. He waited. There was motion in the shadows.

All at once, red mobiles began pouring out of the gate. They took their positions on the castle, and began repairing the damage the spider had wrought. The other armies dissolved and began to retreat to their respective corners.

"Jad," said Simon Kress, "I think you are a bit confused about who is eating who."

The following week Rakkis brought four slim silver snakes. The sandkings dispatched them without much trouble.

Next he tried a large black bird. It ate more than thirty white mobiles, and its thrashing and blundering virtually destroyed their castle, but ultimately its wings grew tired, and the sandkings attacked in force wherever it landed.

After that it was a case of insects, armored beetles not too unlike the sandkings themselves. But stupid, stupid. An allied force of oranges and blacks broke their formation, divided them, and butchered them.

Rakkis began giving Kress promissory notes.

It was around that time that Kress met Cath m'Lane again, one evening when he was dining in Asgard at his favorite restaurant. He stopped at her table briefly and told her about the war games, inviting her to join them. She flushed, then regained control of herself and grew icy. "Someone has to put a stop to you, Simon. I guess it's going to be me," she said. Kress shrugged and enjoyed a lovely meal and thought no more about her threat.

Until a week later, when a small, stout woman arrived at his door and showed him a police wristband. "We've had complaints," she said. "Do you keep a tank full of dangerous insects, Kress?"

"Not insects," he said, furious. "Come, I'll show you."

When she had seen the sandkings, she shook her head. "This will never do. What do you know about these creatures, anyway? Do you know what world they're from? Have they been cleared by the ecological board? Do you have a license for these things? We have a report that they're carnivores, possibly dangerous. We also have a report that they are semi-sentient. Where did you get these creatures, anyway?"

"From Wo and Shade," Kress replied.

"Never heard of them," the woman said. "Probably smuggled them in, knowing our ecologists would never approve them. No, Kress, this won't do. I'm going to confiscate this tank and have it destroyed. And you're going to have to expect a few fines as well."

Kress offered her a hundred standards to forget all about him and his sandkings.

She *tsked.* "Now I'll have to add attempted bribery to the charges against you."

Not until he raised the figure to two thousand standards was she willing to be persuaded. "It's not going to be easy, you know," she said. "There are forms to be altered, records to be wiped. And getting a forged license from the ecologists will be time consuming. Not to mention dealing with the complainant. What if she calls again?"

"Leave her to me," Kress said. "Leave her to me."

***

He thought about it for a while. That night he made some calls.

First he got t' Etherane the Petseller. "I want to buy a dog," he said, "A puppy."

The round-faced merchant gawked at him. "A puppy? That is not like you, Simon. Why don't you come in? I have a lovely choice."

"I want a very specific *kind* of puppy," Kress said. "Take notes, I'll describe to you what it must look like."

Afterward he punched for Idi Noreddian. "Idi," he said, "I want you out here tonight with your holo equipment. I have a notion to record a sandking battle. A present for one of my friends."

The night after they made the recording, Simon Kress stayed up late. He absorbed a controversial new drama in his sensorium, fixed himself a small snack, smoked a joy-stick or two, and broke out a bottle of wine. Feeling very happy with himself, he wandered into the living room, glass in hand.

The lights were out. The red glow of the terrarium made the shadows flushed and feverish. He walked over to look at his domain, curious as to how the blacks were doing in the repairs on their castle. The puppy had left it in ruins.

The restoration went well. But as Kress inspected the work through his magnifiers, he chanced to glance closely at the face. It startled him.

He drew back, blinked, took a healthy gulp of wine, and looked again.

The face on the walls was still his. But it was all wrong, all *twisted.* His cheeks were bloated and piggish, his smile was a crooked leer. He looked impossibly malevolent.

Uneasy, he moved around the tank to inspect the other castles. They were each a bit different, but ultimately all the same.

The oranges had left out most of the fine detail, but the result still seemed monstrous, crude— a brutal mouth and mindless eyes.

The reds gave him a satanic, twitching kind of smile. His mouth did odd, unlovely things at its corners.

The whites, his favorites, had carved a cruel idiot god.

Simon Kress flung his wine across the room in rage. "You *dare,"* he said under his breath. "Now you won't eat for a week, you damned . . ." His voice was shrill. "I'll teach you." He had an idea. He strode out of the room, and returned a moment later with an antique iron throwing-sword in his hand. It was a meter long, and the point was still sharp. Kress smiled, climbed up and moved the tank cover aside just enough to give him working room, opening one corner of the desert. He leaned down, and jabbed the sword at the white castle below him. He waved it back and forth, smashing towers and ramparts and walls. Sand and stone collapsed, burying the scrambling mobiles. A flick of his wrist obliterated the features of the insolent, insulting caricature the sandkings had made of his face. Then he poised the point of the sword above the dark mouth that opened down into the maw's chamber, and thrust with all his strength. He heard a soft, squishing sound, and met resistance. All of the mobiles trembled and collapsed. Satisfied, Kress pulled back.

He watched for a moment, wondering whether he'd killed the maw. The point of the throwing-sword was wet and slimy. But finally the white sandkings began to move again. Feebly, slowly, but they moved.

He was preparing to slide the cover back in place and move on to a second castle when he felt something crawling on his hand.

He screamed and dropped the sword, and brushed the sandking from his flesh. It fell to the carpet, and he ground it beneath his heel, crushing it thoroughly long after it was dead. It had crunched when he stepped on it. After that, trembling, he hurried to seal the tank up again, and rushed off to shower and inspect himself carefully. He boiled his clothing.

Later, after several fresh glasses of wine, he returned to the living room. He was a bit ashamed of the way the sandking had terrified him. But he was not about to open the tank again. From now on, the cover stayed sealed permanently. Still, he had to punish the others.

Kress decided to lubricate his mental processes with another glass of wine. As he finished it, an inspiration came to him. He went to the tank smiling, and made a few adjustments to the humidity controls.

By the time he fell asleep on the couch, his wine glass still in his hand, the sand castles were melting in the rain.

Kress woke to angry pounding on his door.

He sat up, groggy, his head throbbing. Wine hangovers were always the worst, he thought. He lurched to the entry chamber.

Cath m'Lane was outside. "You monster," she said, her face swollen and puffy and streaked by tears. "I cried all night, damn you. But no more, Simon, no more."

"Easy," he said, holding his head. "I've got a hangover."

She swore and shoved him aside and pushed her way into the house. The shambler came peering round a corner to see what the noise was. She spat at it and stalked into the living room, Kress trailing ineffectually after her. "Hold on," he said, "where do you . . . you can't . . ." He stopped, suddenly horrorstruck. She was carrying a heavy sledge-hammer in her left hand. "No," he said.

She went directly to the sandking tank. "You like the little charmers so much, Simon? Then you can live with them."

"*Cath!*" he shrieked.

Gripping the hammer with both hands, she swung as hard as she could against the side of the tank. The sound of the impact set his head to screaming, and Kress made a low blubbering sound of despair. But the plastic held.

She swung again. This time there was a *crack*, and a network of thin lines sprang into being.

Kress threw himself at her as she drew back her hammer for a third swing. They went down flailing, and rolled. She lost her grip on the hammer and tried to throttle him, but Kress wrenched free and bit her on the arm, drawing blood. They both staggered to their feet, panting.

"You should see yourself, Simon," she said grimly. "Blood dripping from your mouth. You look like one of your pets. How do you like the taste?"

"Get out," he said. He saw the throwing-sword where it had fallen the night before, and snatched it up. "Get out," he repeated, waving the sword for emphasis. "Don't go near that tank again."

She laughed at him. "You wouldn't dare," she said. She bent to pick up her hammer.

Kress shrieked at her, and lunged. Before he quite knew what was happening, the iron blade had gone clear through her abdomen. Cath m'Lane looked at him wonderingly, and down at the sword. Kress fell back whimpering. "I didn't mean . . . I only wanted . . ."

She was transfixed, bleeding, dead, but somehow she did not fall. "You monster," she managed to say, though her mouth was full of blood. And she whirled, impossibly, the sword in her, and swung with her last strength at the tank. The tortured wall shattered, and Cath m'Lane was buried beneath an avalanche of plastic and sand and mud.

Kress made small hysterical noises and scrambled up on the couch.

Sandkings were emerging from the muck on his living room floor. They were crawling across Cath's body. A few of them ventured tentatively out across the carpet. More followed.

He watched as a column took shape, a living, writhing square of sandkings, bearing something, something slimy and featureless, a piece of raw meat big as a man's head. They began to carry it away from the tank. It pulsed.

That was when Kress broke and ran.

It was late afternoon before he found the courage to return.

He had run to his skimmer and flown to the nearest city, some fifty kilometers away, almost sick with fear. But once safely away, he found a small restaurant, put down several mugs of coffee and two anti-hangover tabs, eaten a full breakfast, and gradually regained his composure.

It had been a dreadful morning, but dwelling on that would solve nothing. He ordered more coffee and considered his situation with icy rationality.

Cath m'Lane was dead at his hand. Could he report it, plead that it had been an accident? Unlikely. He had run her through, after all, and he had already told that policer to leave her to him. He would have to get rid of the evidence, and hope that she had not told anyone where she was going this morning. That was probable. She could only have gotten his gift late last night. She said that she had cried all night, and she had been alone when she arrived. Very well; he had one body and one skimmer to dispose of.

That left the sandkings. They might prove more of a difficulty. No doubt they had all escaped by now. The thought of them around his house, in his bed and his clothes, infesting his food—it made his flesh crawl. He shuddered and overcame his revulsion. It really shouldn't be too hard to kill them, he reminded himself. He didn't have to account for every mobile. Just the four maws, that was all. He could do that. They were large, as he'd seen. He would find them and kill them.

Simon Kress went shopping before he flew back to his home. He bought a set of skinthins that would cover him from head to foot, several bags of poison pellets for rockjock control, and a spray cannister of illegally strong pesticide. He also bought a magnalock towing device.

When he landed, he went about things methodically. First he hooked Cath's skimmer to his own with the magnalock. Searching it, he had his first piece of luck. The crystal chip with Idi Noreddian's holo of the sandking fight was on the front seat. He had worried about that.

When the skimmers were ready, he slipped into his skinthins and went inside for Cath's body.

It wasn't there.

He poked through the fast-drying sand carefully, but there was no doubt of it; the body was gone. Could she have dragged herself away? Unlikely, but Kress searched. A cursory inspection of his house turned up neither the body nor any sign of the sandkings. He did not have time for a more thorough investigation, not with the incriminating skimmer outside his front door. He resolved to try later.

Some seventy kilometers north of Kress' estate was a range of active volcanoes. He flew there, Cath's skimmer in tow. Above the glowering cone of the largest, he released the magnalock and watched it vanish in the lava below.

It was dusk when he returned to his house. That gave him pause. Briefly he considered flying back to the city and spending the night there. He put the thought aside. There was work to do. He wasn't safe yet.

He scattered the poison pellets around the exterior of his house. No one would find that suspicious. He'd always had a rockjock problem. When that task was completed, he primed the cannister of pesticide and ventured back inside.

Kress went through the house room by room, turning on lights everywhere he went until he was surrounded by a blaze of artificial illumination. He paused to clean up in the living room, shoveling sand and plastic fragments back into the broken tank. The sandkings were all gone, as he'd feared. The castles were shrunken and distorted, slagged by the watery bombardment Kress had visited upon them, and what little remained was crumbling as it dried.

He frowned and searched on, the cannister of pest spray strapped across his shoulders.

Down in his deepest wine cellar, he came upon Cathm' Lane's corpse.

It sprawled at the foot of a steep flight of stairs, the limbs twisted as if by a fall. White mobiles were swarming all over it, and as Kress watched, the body moved jerkily across the hard-packed dirt floor.

He laughed, and twisted the illumination up to maximum. In the far corner, a squat little earthen castle and a dark hole were visible between two wine racks. Kress could make out a rough outline of his face on the cellar wall.

The body shifted once again, moving a few centimeters towards the castle. Kress had a sudden vision of the white maw waiting hungrily. It might be able to get Cath's foot in its mouth, but no more. It was too absurd. He laughed again, and started down into the cellar, finger poised on the trigger of the hose that snaked down his right arm. The sandkings— hundreds of them moving as one—deserted the body and formed up battle lines, a field of white between him and their maw.

Suddenly Kress had another inspiration. He smiled and lowered his firing hand. "Cath was always hard to swallow," he said, delighted at his wit. "Especially for one your size. Here, let me give you some help. What are gods for, after all?"

He retreated upstairs, returning shortly with a cleaver. The sandkings, patient, waited and watched while Kress chopped Cath m'Lane into small, easily digestible pieces.

* * *

Simon Kress slept in his skinthins that night, the pesticide close at hand, but he did not need it. The whites, sated, remained in the cellar, and he saw no sign of the others.

In the morning he finished the clean-up of the living room. After he was through, no trace of the struggle remained except for the broken tank.

He ate a light lunch, and resumed his hunt for the missing sandkings. In full daylight, it was not too difficult. The blacks had located in his rock garden, and built a castle heavy with obsidian and quartz. The reds he found at the bottom of his long-disused swimming pool, which had partially filled with wind-blown sand over the years. He saw mobiles of both colors ranging about his grounds, many of them carrying poison pellets back to their maws. Kress decided his pesticide was unnecessary. No use risking a fight when he could just let the poison do its work. Both maws should be dead by evening.

That left only the burnt orange sandkings unaccounted for. Kress circled his estate several times, in ever-widening spirals, but found no trace of them. When he began to sweat in his skinthins—it was a hot, dry day—he decided it was not important. If they were out here, they were probably eating the poison pellets along with the reds and blacks.

He crunched several sandkings underfoot, with a certain degree of satisfaction, as he walked back to the house. Inside, he removed his skinthins, settled down to a delicious meal, and finally began to relax. Everything was under control. Two of the maws would soon be defunct, the third was safely located where he could dispose of it after it had served his purposes, and he had no doubt that he would find the fourth. As for Cath, all trace of her visit had been obliterated.

His reverie was interrupted when his viewscreen began to blink at him. It was Jad Rakkis, calling to brag about some cannibal worms he was bringing to the war games tonight.

Kress had forgotten about that, but he recovered quickly. "Oh, Jad, my pardons. I neglected to tell you. I grew bored with all that, and got rid of the sandkings. Ugly little things. Sorry, but there'll be no party tonight."

Rakkis was indignant. "But what will I do with my worms?"

"Put them in a basket of fruit and send them to a loved one," Kress said, signing off. Quickly he began calling the others. He did not need anyone arriving at his doorstep now, with the sandkings alive and infesting the estate.

As he was calling Idi Noreddian, Kress became aware of an annoying oversight. The screen began to clear, indicating that someone had answered at the other end. Kress flicked off.

Idi arrived on schedule an hour later. She was surprised to find the party cancelled, but perfectly happy to share an evening alone with Kress. He delighted her with his story of Cath's reaction to the holo they had made together. While telling it, he managed to ascertain that she had not mentioned the prank to anyone. He nodded, satisfied, and refilled their wine glasses. Only a trickle was left. "I'll have to get a fresh bottle," he said. "Come with me to my wine cellar, and help me pick out a good vintage. You've always had a better palate than I."

She came along willingly enough, but balked at the top of the stairs when Kress opened the door and gestured for her to precede him. "Where are the lights?" she said. "And that smell—what's that peculiar smell, Simon?"

When he shoved her, she looked briefly startled. She screamed as she tumbled down the stairs. Kress closed the door and began to nail it shut with the boards and airhammer he had left for that purpose. As he was finishing, he heard Idi groan. "I'm hurt," she called. "Simon, what is this?" Suddenly she squealed, and shortly after that the screaming started.

It did not cease for hours. Kress went to his sensorium and dialed up a saucy comedy to blot it out of his mind.

When he was sure she was dead, Kress flew her skimmer north to the volcanoes and discarded it. The magnalock was proving a good investment.

Odd scrabbling noises were coming from beyond the wine cellar door the next morning when Kress went down to check it out. He listened for several uneasy moments, wondering if Idi Noreddian could possibly have survived, and was now scratching to get out. It seemed unlikely; it had to be the sandkings. Kress did not like the implications of that. He decided that he would keep the door sealed, at least for the moment, and went outside with a shovel to bury the red and black maws in their own castles.

He found them very much alive.

The black castle was glittering with volcanic glass, and sandkings were all over it, repairing and improving. The highest tower was up to his waist, and on it was a hideous caricature of his face. When he approached, the blacks halted in their labors, and formed up into two threatening phalanxes. Kress glanced behind him and saw others closing off his escape. Startled, he dropped the shovel and sprinted out of the trap, crushing several mobiles beneath his boots.

The red castle was creeping up the walls of the swimming pool. The maw was safely settled in a pit, surrounded by sand and concrete and battlements. The reds crept all over the bottom of the pool. Kress watched them carry a rockjock and a large lizard into the castle. He stepped back from the poolside, horrified, and felt something crunch. Looking down, he saw three mobiles climbing up his leg. He brushed them off and stamped them to death, but others were approaching quickly. They were larger than he remembered. Some were almost as big as his thumb.

He ran. By the time he reached the safety of the house, his heart was racing and he was short of breath. The door closed behind him, and Kress hurried to lock it. His house was supposed to be pest-proof. He'd be safe in here.

A stiff drink steadied his nerve. So poison doesn't faze them, he thought. He should have known. Wo had warned him that the maw could eat anything. He would have to use the pesticide. Kress took another drink for good measure, donned his skinthins, and strapped the cannister to his back. He unlocked the door.

Outside, the sandkings were waiting.

Two armies confronted him, allied against the common threat. More than he could have guessed. The damned maws must be breeding like rockjocks. They were everywhere, a creeping sea of them.

Kress brought up the hose and flicked the trigger. A gray mist washed over the nearest rank of sandkings. He moved his hand from side to side.

Where the mist fell, the sandkings twitched violently and died in sudden spasms. Kress smiled. They were no match for him. He sprayed in a wide arc before him and stepped forward confidently over a litter of black and red bodies. The armies fell back. Kress advanced, intent on cutting through them to their maws.

All at once the retreat stopped. A thousand sandkings surged toward him.

Kress had been expecting the counterattack. He stood his ground, sweeping his misty sword before him in great looping strokes. They came at him and died. A few got through; he could not spray everywhere at once. He felt them climbing up his legs, sensed their mandibles biting futilely at the reinforced plastic of his skinthins. He ignored them, and kept spraying.

Then he began to feel soft impacts on his head and shoulders.

Kress trembled and spun and looked up above him. The front of his house was alive with sandkings. Blacks and reds, hundreds of them. They were launching themselves into the air, raining down on him. They fell all around him. One landed on his faceplate, its mandibles scraping at his eyes for a terrible second before he plucked it away.

He swung up his hose and sprayed the air, sprayed the house, sprayed until the airborne sandkings were all dead and dying. The mist settled back on him, making him cough. He coughed, and kept spraying. Only when the front of the house was clean did Kress turn his attention back to the ground.

They were all around him, on him, dozens of them scurrying over his body, hundreds of others hurrying to join them. He turned the mist on them. The hose went dead. Kress heard a loud *hiss*, and the deadly fog rose in a great cloud from between his shoulders, cloaking him, choking him, making his eyes burn and blur. He felt for the hose, and his hand came away covered with dying sandkings. The hose was severed; they'd eaten it through. He was surrounded by a shroud of pesticide, blinded. He stumbled and screamed, and began to run back to the house, pulling sandkings from his body as he went.

Inside, he sealed the door and collapsed on the carpet, rolling back and forth until he was sure he had crushed them all. The cannister was empty by then, hissing feebly. Kress stripped off his skinthins and showered. The hot spray scalded him and left his skin reddened and sensitive, but it made his flesh stop crawling.

He dressed in his heaviest clothing, thick workpants and leathers, after shaking them out nervously. "Damn," he kept muttering, "damn." His throat was dry. After searching the entry hall thoroughly to make certain it was clean, he allowed himself to sit and pour a drink. "Damn," he repeated. His hand shook as he poured, slopping liquor on the carpet.

The alcohol settled him, but it did not wash away the fear. He had a second drink, and went to the window furtively. Sandkings were moving across the thick plastic pane. He shuddered and retreated to his communications console. He had to get help, he thought wildly. He would punch through a call to the authorities, and policers would come out with flamethrowers and . . .

Simon Kress stopped in mid-call, and groaned. He couldn't call in the police. He would have to tell them about the whites in his cellar, and they'd find the bodies there. Perhaps the maw might have finished Cath m'Lane by now, but certainly not Idi Noreddian. He hadn't even cut her up. Besides, there would be bones. No, the police could be called in only as a last resort.

He sat the console, frowning. His communications equipment filled a whole wall; from here he could reach anyone on Baldur. He had plenty of money, and his cunning—he had always prided himself on his cunning. He would handle this somehow.

He briefly considered calling Wo, but soon dismissed the idea. Wo knew too much, and she would ask questions, and he did not trust her.

No, he needed someone who would do as he asked *without* questions.

His frown faded, and slowly turned into a smile. Simon Kress had contacts. He put through a call to a number he had not used in a long time.

A woman's face took shape on his viewscreen: white-haired, bland of expression, with a long hook nose. Her voice was brisk and efficient. "Simon," she said. "How is business?"

"Business is fine, Lissandra," Kress replied. "I have a job for you."

"A removal? My price has gone up since last time, Simon. It has been ten years, after all."

"You will be well paid," Kress said. "You know I'm generous. I want you for a bit of pest control."

She smiled a thin smile. "No need to use euphemisms, Simon. The call is shielded."

"No, I'm serious. I have a pest problem. Dangerous pests. Take care of them for me. No questions. Understood?"

"Understood."

"Good. You'll need . . . oh, three or four operatives. Wear heat-resistant skinthins, and equip them with flame-throwers, or lasers, something on that order. Come out to my place. You'll see the problem. Bugs, lots and lots of them. In my rock garden and the old swimming pool you'll find castles. Destroy them, kill everything inside them. Then knock on the door, and I'll show you what else needs to be done. Can you get out here quickly?"

Her face was impassive. "We'll leave within the hour."

Lissandra was true to her word. She arrived in a lean black skimmer with three operatives. Kress watched them from the safety of a second-story window. They were all faceless in dark plastic skinthins. Two of them wore portable flamethrowers, a third carried lasercannon and explosives. Lissandra carried nothing; Kress recognized her by the way she gave orders.

Their skimmer passed low overhead first, checking out the situation. The sandkings went mad. Scarlet and ebon mobiles ran everywhere, frenetic. Kress could see the castle in the rock garden from his vantage point. It stood tall as a man. Its ramparts were crawling with black defenders, and a steady stream of mobiles flowed down into its depths.

Lissandra's skimmer came down next to Kress' and the operatives vaulted out and unlimbered their weapons. They looked inhuman, deadly.

The black army drew up between them and the castle. The reds—Kress suddenly realized that he could not see the reds. He blinked. Where had they gone?

Lissandra pointed and shouted, and her two flamethrowers spread out and opened up on the black sandkings. Their weapons coughed dully and began to roar, long tongues of blue-and-scarlet fire licking out before them. Sandkings crisped and blackened and died. The operatives began to play the fire back and forth in an efficient, interlocking pattern. They advanced with careful, measured steps.

The black army burned and disintegrated, the mobiles fleeing in a thousand different directions, some back toward the castle, others toward the enemy. None reached the operatives with the flame throwers. Lissandra's people were very professional.

Then one of them stumbled.

Or seemed to stumble. Kress looked again, and saw that the ground had given way beneath the man. Tunnels, he thought with a tremor of fear—tunnels, pits, traps. The flamer was sunk in sand up to his waist, and suddenly the ground around him seemed to erupt, and he was covered with scarlet sandkings. He dropped the flamethrower and began to claw wildly at his own body. His screams were horrible to hear.

His companion hesitated, then swung and fired. A blast of flame swallowed human and sandkings both. The screaming stopped abruptly. Satisfied, the second flamer turned back to the castle and took another step forward, and recoiled as his foot broke through the ground and vanished up to the ankle. He tried to pull it back and retreat, and the sand all around him gave way. He lost his balance and stumbled, flailing, and the sandkings were everywhere, a boiling mass of them, covered him as he writhed and rolled. His flamethrower was useless and forgotten.

Kress pounded wildly on the window, shouting for attention. "The castle! Get the castle!"

Lissandra, standing back by her skimmer, heard and gestured. Her third operative sighted with the lasercannon and fired. The beam throbbed across the grounds and sliced off the top of the castle. He brought it down sharply, hacking at the sand and stone parapets. Towers fell. Kress' face disintegrated. The laser bit into the ground, searching round and about. The castle crumbled; now it was only a heap of sand. But the black mobiles continued to move. The maw was buried too deeply; they hadn't touched her.

Lissandra gave another order. Her operative discarded the laser, primed an explosive, and darted forward. He leaped over the smoking corpse of the first flamer, landed on solid ground within Kress' rock garden, and heaved. The explosive ball landed square atop the ruins of the black castle. White-hot light seared Kress' eyes, and there was a tremendous gout of sand and rock and mobiles. For a moment dust obscured everything. It was raining sandkings and pieces of sandkings.

Kress saw that the black mobiles were dead and unmoving.

"The pool," he shouted down through the window. "Get the castle in the pool."

Lissandra understood quickly; the ground was littered with motionless blacks, but the reds were pulling back hurriedly and re-forming. Her operative stood uncertain, then reached down and pulled out another explosive ball. He took one step forward, but Lissandra called him and he sprinted back in her direction.

It was all so simple then. He reached the skimmer, and Lissandra took him aloft. Kress rushed to another window in another room to watch. They came swooping in just over the pool, and the operative pitched his bombs down at the red castle from the safety of the skimmer. After the fourth run, the castle was unrecognizable, and the sandkings stopped moving.

Lissandra was thorough. She had him bomb each castle several additional times. Then he used the lasercannon, crisscrossing methodically until it was certain that nothing living could remain intact beneath those small patches of ground.

Finally they came knocking at his door. Kress was grinning manically when he let them in. "Lovely," he said, "lovely."

Lissandra pulled off the mask of her skinthins. "This will cost you, Simon. Two operatives gone, not to mention the danger to my own life."

"Of course," Kress blurted. "You'll be well paid, Lissandra. Whatever you ask, just so you finish the job."

"What remains to be done?"

"You have to clean out my wine cellar," Kress said. "There's another castle down there. And you'll have to do it without explosives. I don't want my house coming down around me."

Lissandra motioned to her operative. "Go outside and get Rajk's flamethrower. It should be intact."

He returned armed, ready, silent. Kress led them down to the wine cellar.

The heavy door was still nailed shut, as he had left it. But it bulged outward slightly, as if warped by some tremendous pressure. That made Kress uneasy, as did the silence that held reign about them. He stood well away from the door as Lissandra's operative removed his nails and planks. "Is that safe in here?" he found himself muttering, pointing at the flamethrower. "I don't want a fire, either, you know."

"I have the laser," Lissandra said. "We'll use that for the kill. The flamethrower probably won't be needed. But I want it here just in case. There are worse things than fire, Simon."

He nodded.

The last plank came free of the cellar door. There was still no sound from below. Lissandra snapped an order, and her underling fell back, took up a position behind her, and leveled the flamethrower square at the door. She slipped her mask back on, hefted the laser, stepped forward, and pulled open the door.

No motion. No sound. It was dark down there.

"Is there a light?" Lissandra asked.

"Just inside the door," Kress said. "On the right hand side. Mind the stairs, they're quite steep."

She stepped into the door, shifted the laser to her left hand, and reached up with her right, fumbling inside for the light panel. Nothing happened. "I feel it," Lissandra said, "but it doesn't seem to . . ."

Then she was screaming, and she stumbled backward. A great white sandking had clamped itself around her wrist. Blood welled through her skinthins where its mandibles had sunk in. It was fully as large as her hand.

Lissandra did a horrible little jig across the room and began to smash her hand against the nearest wall. Again and again and again. It landed with a heavy, meaty thud. Finally the sandking fell away. She whimpered and fell to her knees. "I think my fingers are broken," she said softly. The blood was still flowing freely. She had dropped the laser near the cellar door.

"I'm not going down there," her operative announced in clear firm tones.

Lissandra looked up at him. "No," she said. "Stand in the door and flame it all. Cinder it. Do you understand?"

He nodded.

Simon Kress moaned. "My *house*," he said. His stomach churned. The white sandking had been so *large*. How many more were down there? "Don't," he continued. "Leave it alone. I've changed my mind. Leave it alone."

Lissandra misunderstood. She held out her hand. It was covered with blood and greenish-black ichor. "Your little friend bit clean through my glove, and you saw what it took to get it off. I don't care about your house, Simon. Whatever is down there is going to die."

Kress hardly heard her. He thought he could see movement in the shadows beyond the cellar door. He imagined a white army bursting forth, all as large as the sandking that had attacked Lissandra. He saw himself being lifted by a hundred tiny arms, and dragged down into the

darkness where the maw waited hungrily. He was afraid. "Don't," he said.
They ignored him.

Kress darted forward, and his shoulder slammed into the back of
Lissandra's operative just as the man was bracing to fire. He grunted and
unbalanced and pitched forward into the black. Kress listened to him fall
down the stairs. Afterward there were other noises— scuttlings and snaps
and soft squishing sounds.

Kress swung around to face Lissandra. He was drenched in cold
sweat, but a sickly kind of excitement was on him. It was almost sexual.

Lissandra's calm cold eyes regarded him through her mask. "What are
you doing?" she demanded as Kress picked up the laser she had dropped.
"Simon!"

"Making a peace," he said, giggling. "They won't hurt god, no, not so
long as god is good and generous. I was cruel. Starved them. I have to
make up for it now, you see."

"You're insane," Lissandra said. It was the last thing she said. Kress
burned a hole in her chest big enough to put his arm through. He dragged
the body across the floor and rolled it down the cellar stairs. The noises
were louder—chitinous clackings and scrapings and echoes that were
thick and liquid. Kress nailed up the door once again.

As he fled, he was filled with a deep sense of contentment that coated
his fear like a layer of syrup. He suspected it was not his own.

He planned to leave his home, to fly to the city and take a room for a
night, or perhaps for a year. Instead Kress started drinking. He was not
quite sure why. He drank steadily for hours, and retched it all up violently
on his living room carpet. At some point he fell asleep. When he woke, it
was pitch dark in the house.

He cowered against the couch. He could hear *noises.* Things were
moving in the walls. They were all around him. His hearing was
extraordinarily acute. Every little creak was the footstep of a sandking.
He closed his eyes and waited, expecting to feel their terrible touch,
afraid to move lest he brush against one.

Kress sobbed, and was very still for a while, but nothing happened.

He opened his eyes again. He trembled. Slowly the shadows began to
soften and dissolve. Moonlight was filtering through the high windows.
His eyes adjusted.

The living room was empty. Nothing there, nothing, nothing. Only his
drunken fears.

Simon Kress steeled himself, and rose, and went to a light.

Nothing there. The room was quiet, deserted.

He listened. Nothing. No sound. Nothing in the walls. It had all been his imagination, his fear.

The memories of Lissandra and the thing in the cellar returned to him unbidden. Shame and anger washed over him. Why had he done that? He could have helped her burn it out, kill it. *Why*... he knew why. The maw had done it to him, put fear in him. Wo had said it was psionic, even when it was small. And now it was large, so large. It had feasted on Cath, and Idi, and now it had two more bodies down there. It would keep growing. And it had learned to like the taste of human flesh, he thought.

He began to shake, but he took control of himself again and stopped. It wouldn't hurt him. He was god. The whites had always been his favorites.

He remembered how he had stabbed it with his throwing-sword. That was before Cath came. Damn her anyway.

He couldn't stay here. The maw would grow hungry again. Large as it was, it wouldn't take long. Its appetite would be terrible. What would it do then? He had to get away, back to the safety of the city while it was still contained in his wine cellar. It was only plaster and hard-packed earth down there, and the mobiles could dig and tunnel. When they got free.... Kress didn't want to think about it.

He went to his bedroom and packed. He took three bags. Just a single change of clothing, that was all he needed; the rest of the space he filled with his valuables, with jewelry and art and other things he could not bear to lose. He did not expect to return.

His shambler followed him down the stairs, staring at him from its baleful glowing eyes. It was gaunt. Kress realized that it had been ages since he had fed it. Normally it could take care of itself, but no doubt the pickings had grown lean of late. When it tried to clutch at his leg, he snarled at it and kicked it away, and it scurried off, offended.

Kress slipped outside, carrying his bags awkwardly, and shut the door behind him.

For a moment he stood pressed against the house, his heart thudding in his chest. Only a few meters between him and his skimmer. He was afraid to cross them. The moonlight was bright, and the front of his house was a scene of carnage. The bodies of Lissandra's two flamers lay where they had fallen, one twisted and burned, the other swollen beneath a mass of dead sandkings. And the mobiles, the black and red mobiles, they were all around him. It was an effort to remember that they were dead. It was almost as if they were simply waiting, as they had waited so often before.

Nonsense, Kress told himself. More drunken fears. He had seen the castles blown apart. They were dead, and the white maw was trapped in his cellar. He took several deep and deliberate breaths, and stepped forward onto the sandkings. They crunched. He ground them into the sand savagely. They did not move.

Kress smiled, and walked slowly across the battleground, listening to the sounds, the sounds of safety.

Crunch. Crackle. Crunch.

He lowered his bags to the ground and opened the door to his skimmer.

Something moved from shadow into light. A pale shape on the seat of his skimmer. It was as long as his forearm. Its mandibles clacked together softly, and it looked up at him from six small eyes set all around its body.

Kress wet his pants and backed away slowly.

There was more motion from inside the skimmer. He had left the door open. The sandking emerged and came toward him, cautiously. Others followed. They had been hiding beneath his seats, burrowed into the upholstery. But now they emerged. They formed a ragged ring around the skimmer.

Kress licked his lips, turned, and moved quickly to Lissandra's skimmer.

He stopped before he was halfway there. Things were moving inside that one too. Great maggoty things, half-seen by the light of the moon.

Kress whimpered and retreated back toward the house. Near the front door, he looked up.

He counted a dozen long white shapes creeping back and forth across the walls of the building. Four of them were clustered close together near the top of the unused belfry where the carrion hawk had once roosted. They were carving something. A face. A very recognizable face.

Simon Kress shrieked and ran back inside.

A sufficient quality of drink brought him the easy oblivion he sought. But he woke. Despite everything, he woke. He had a terrific headache, and he smelled, and he was hungry. Oh so very hungry. He had never been so hungry.

Kress knew it was not his *own* stomach hurting.

A white sandking watched him from atop the dresser in his bedroom, its antennae moving faintly. It was as big as the one in the skimmer the night before. He tried not to shrink away. "I'll... I'll feed you," he said to it. "I'll feed you." His mouth was horribly dry, sandpaper dry. He licked his lips and fled from the room.

The house was full of sandkings; he had to be careful where he put his feet. They all seemed busy on errands of their own. They were making modifications in his house, burrowing into or out of his walls, carving things. Twice he saw his own likeness staring out at him from unexpected places. The faces were warped, twisted, livid with fear.

He went outside to get the bodies that had been rotting in the yard, hoping to appease the white maw's hunger. They were gone, both of them. Kress remembered how easily the mobiles could carry things many times their own weight.

It was terrible to think that the maw was *still* hungry after all of that.

When Kress re-entered the house, a column of sandkings was wending its way down the stairs. Each carried a piece of his shambler. The head seemed to look at him reproachfully as it went by.

Kress emptied his freezers, his cabinets, everything, piling all the food in the house in the center of his kitchen floor. A dozen whites waited to take it away. They avoided the frozen food, leaving it to thaw in a great puddle, but they carried off everything else.

When all the food was gone, Kress felt his own hunger pangs abate just a bit, though he had not eaten a thing. But he knew the respite would be short-lived. Soon the maw would be hungry again. He had to feed it.

Kress knew what to do. He went to his communicator. "Malada," he began casually when the first of his friends answered, "I'm having a small party tonight. I realize this is terribly short notice, but I hope you can make it. I really do."

He called Jad Rakkis next, and then the others. By the time he had finished, nine of them had accepted his invitation. Kress hoped that would be enough.

Kress met his guests outside—the mobiles had cleaned up remarkably quickly, and the grounds looked almost as they had before the battle— and walked them to his front door. He let them enter first. He did not follow.

When four of them had gone through, Kress finally worked up his courage. He closed the door behind his latest guest, ignoring the startled exclamations that soon turned into shrill gibbering, and sprinted for the skimmer the man had arrived in. He slid in safely, thumbed the startplate, and swore. It was programmed to lift only in response to its owner's thumbprint, of course.

Jad Rakkis was the next to arrive. Kress ran to his skimmer as it set down, and seized Rakkis by the arm as he was climbing out. "Get back in, quickly," he said, pushing. "Take me to the city. Hurry, Jad. *Get out of here.*"

But Rakkis only stared at him, and would not move. "Why, what's wrong, Simon? I don't understand. What about your party?"

And then it was too late, because the loose sand all around them was stirring, and the red eyes were staring at them, and the mandibles were clacking. Rakkis made a choking sound, and moved to get back in his skimmer, but a pair of mandibles snapped shut about his ankle, and suddenly he was on his knees. The sand seemed to boil with subterranean activity. Jad thrashed and cried terribly as they tore him apart. Kress could hardly bear to watch.

After that, he did not try to escape again. When it was all over, he cleaned out what remained in his liquor cabinet, and got extremely drunk. It would be the last time he would enjoy that luxury, he knew. The only alcohol remaining in the house was stored down in the wine cellar.

Kress did not touch a bit of food the entire day, but he fell asleep feeling bloated, sated at last, the awful hunger vanquished. His last thoughts before the nightmares took him were of whom he could ask out tomorrow.

Morning was hot and dry. Kress opened his eyes to see the white sandkings on his dresser again. He shut them again quickly, hoping the dream would leave him. It did not, and he could not go back to sleep. Soon he found himself staring at the thing.

He stared for almost five minutes before the strangeness of it dawned on him; the sandking was not moving.

The mobiles could be preternaturally still, to be sure. He had seen them wait and watch a thousand times. But always there was some motion about them—the mandibles clacked, the legs twitched, the long fine antennae stirred and swayed.

But the sandking on his dresser was completely still.

Kress rose, holding his breath, not daring to hope. Could it be dead? Could something have killed it? He walked across the room.

The eyes were glassy and black. The creature seemed swollen, somehow, as if it were soft and rotting inside, filling up with gas that pushed outward at the plates of white armor.

Kress reached out a trembling hand and touched it.

It was warm—hot even—and growing hotter. But it did not move.

He pulled his hand back, and as he did, a segment of the sandking's white exoskeleton fell away from it. The flesh beneath was the same color, but softer-looking, swollen and feverish. And it almost seemed to throb.

Kress backed away, and ran to the door.

Three more white mobiles lay in his hall. They were all like the one in his bedroom.

He ran down the stairs, jumping over sandkings. None of them moved. The house was full of them, all dead, dying, comatose, whatever. Kress did not care what was wrong with them. Just so they could not move.

He found four of them inside his skimmer. He picked them up one by one, and threw them as far as he could. Damned monsters. He slid back in, on the ruined half-eaten seats, and thumbed the starplate.

Nothing happened.

Kress tried again, and again. Nothing. It wasn't fair. This was *his* skimmer, it ought to start, why wouldn't it lift, he didn't understand.

Finally he got out and checked, expecting the worst. He found it. The sandkings had torn apart his gravity grid. He was trapped. He was still trapped.

Grimly, Kress marched back into the house. He went to his gallery and found the antique axe that had hung next to the throwing-sword he had used on Cath m'Lane. He set to work. The sandkings did not stir even as he chopped them to pieces. But they splattered when he made the first cut, the bodies almost bursting. Inside was awful; strange half-formed organs, a viscous reddish ooze that looked almost like human blood, and the yellow ichor.

Kress destroyed twenty of them before he realized the futility of what he was doing. The mobiles were nothing, really. Besides, there were so *many* of them. He could work for a day and night and still not kill them all.

He had to go down into the wine cellar and use the axe on the maw.

Resolute, he started down. He got within sight of the door, and stopped.

It was not a door any more. The walls had been eaten away, so that the hole was twice the size it had been, and round. A pit, that was all. There was no sign that there had ever been a door nailed shut over that black abyss.

A ghastly, choking, fetid odor seemed to come from below.

And the walls were wet and bloody and covered with patches of white fungus.

And worst, it was *breathing*.

Kress stood across the room and felt the warm wind wash over him as it exhaled, and he tried not to choke, and when the wind reversed direction, he fled.

Back in the living room, he destroyed three more mobiles, and collapsed. What was *happening?* He didn't understand.

Then he remembered the only person who might understand. Kress went to his communicator again, stepping on a sandking in his haste, and prayed feverently that the device still worked.

When Jala Wo answered, he broke down and told her everything.

She let him talk without interruption, no expression save for a slight frown on her gaunt, pale face. When Kress had finished, she said only, "I ought to leave you there."

Kress began to blubber. "You can't. Help me. I'll pay. . . ."

"I ought to," Wo repeated, "but I won't."

"Thank you," Kress said. "Oh, thank. . . ."

"Quiet," said Wo. "Listen to me. This is your own doing. Keep your sandkings well, and they are courtly ritual warriors. You turned yours into something else, with starvation and torture. You were their god. You made them what they are. That maw in your cellar is sick, still suffering from the wound you gave it. It is probably insane. Its behavior is . . . unusual.

"You have to get out of there quickly. The mobiles are not dead, Kress. They are dormant. I told you the exoskeleton falls off when they grow larger. Normally, in fact, it falls off much earlier. I have never heard of sandkings growing as large as yours while still in the insectoid stage. It is another result of crippling the white maw, I would say. That does not matter.

"What matters is the metamorphosis your sandkings are now undergoing. As the maw grows, you see, it gets progressively more intelligent. Its psionic powers strengthen, and its mind becomes more sophisticated, more ambitious. The armored mobiles are useful enough when the maw is tiny and only semi-sentient, but now it needs better servants, bodies with more capabilities. Do you understand? The mobiles are all going to give birth to a new breed of sandking. I can't say exactly what it will look like. Each maw designs its own, to fit its perceived needs and desires. But it will be biped, with four arms, and opposable thumbs. It will be able to construct and operate advanced machinery. The individual sandkings will not be sentient. But the maws will be very sentient indeed."

Simon Kress was gaping at Wo's image on the viewscreen. "Your workers," he said, with an effort. "The ones who came out here . . . who installed the tank. . . ."

Jala Wo managed a faint smile. "Shade," she said.

"Shade is a sandking," Kress repeated numbly. "And you sold me a tank of . . . of . . . infants, ah. . . ."

"Do not be absurd," Wo said. "A first-stage sandking is more like a sperm than an infant. The wars temper and control them in nature. Only one in a hundred reaches second stage. Only one in a thousand achieves the third and final plateau, and becomes like Shade. Adult sandkings are not sentimental about the small maws. There are too many of them, and their mobiles are pests." She sighed. "And all this talk wastes time. That white sandking is going to waken to full sentience soon. It is not going to need you any longer, and it hates you, and it will be very hungry. The transformation is taxing. The maw must eat enormous amounts both before and after. So you have to get out of there. Do you understand?"

"I can't," Kress said. "My skimmer is destroyed, and I can't get any of the others to start. I don't know how to reprogram them. Can you come out for me?"

"Yes," said Wo. "Shade and I will leave at once, but it is more than two hundred kilometers from Asgard to you, and there is equipment we will need to deal with the deranged sandking you've created. You cannot wait there. You have two feet. Walk. Go due east, as near as you can determine, as quickly as you can. The land out there is pretty desolate. We can find you easily with an aerial search, and you'll be safely away from the sandking. Do you understand?"

"Yes," said Simon Kress. "Yes, oh, yes."

They signed off, and he walked quickly toward the door. He was halfway there when he heard the noise—a sound halfway between a pop and a crack.

One of the sandkings had split open. Four tiny hands covered with pinkish-yellow blood came up out of the gap and began to push the dead skin aside.

Kress began to run.

He had not counted on the heat.

The hills were dry and rocky. Kress ran from the house as quickly as he could, ran until his ribs ached and his breath was coming in gasps. Then he walked, but as soon as he had recovered he began to run again. For almost an hour he ran and walked, ran and walked, beneath the fierce hot sun. He sweated freely, and wished that he had thought to bring some water. He watched the sky in hopes of seeing Wo and Shade.

He was not made for this. It was too hot, and too dry, and he was in no condition. But he kept himself going with the memory of the way the maw had breathed, and the thought of the wriggling little things that by now were surely crawling all over his house. He hoped Wo and Shade would know how to deal with them.

He had his own plans for Wo and Shade. It was all their fault, Kress had decided, and they would suffer for it. Lissandra was dead, but he knew others in her profession. He would have his revenge. He promised himself that a hundred times as he struggled and sweated his way east.

At least he hoped it was east. He was not that good at directions, and he wasn't certain which way he had run in his initial panic, but since then he had made an effort to bear due east, as Wo had suggested.

When he had been running for several hours, with no sign of rescue, Kress began to grow certain that he had gone wrong.

When several more hours passed, he began to grow afraid. What if Wo and Shade could not find him? He would die out here. He hadn't eaten in two days; he was weak and frightened; his throat was raw for want of water. He couldn't keep going. The sun was sinking now, and he'd be completely lost in the dark. What was wrong? Had the sandkings eaten Wo and Shade? The fear was on him again, filling him, and with it a great thirst and a terrible hunger. But Kress kept going. He stumbled now when he tried to run, and twice he fell. The second time he scraped his hand on a rock, and it came away bloody. He sucked at it as he walked, and worried about infection.

The sun was on the horizon behind him. The ground grew a little cooler, for which Kress was grateful. He decided to walk until last light and settle in for the night. Surely he was far enough from the sandkings to be safe, and Wo and Shade would find him come morning.

When he topped the next rise, he saw the outline of a house in front of him.

It wasn't as big as his own house, but it was big enough. It was habitation, safety. Kress shouted and began to run toward it. Food and drink, he had to have nourishment, he could taste the meal now. He was aching with hunger. He ran down the hill towards the house, waving his arms and shouting to the inhabitants. The light was almost gone now, but he could still make out a half-dozen children playing in the twilight. "Hey there," he shouted. "Help, help."

They came running toward him.

Kress stopped suddenly. "No," he said, "oh, no. Oh, no." He back-pedaled, slipped on the sand, got up and tried to run again. They caught him easily. They were ghastly little things with bulging eyes and dusky orange skin. He struggled, but it was useless. Small as they were, each of them had four arms, and Kress had only two.

They carried him toward the house. It was a sad, shabby house built of crumbling sand, but the door was quite large, and dark, and it breathed.

That was terrible, but it was not the thing that set Simon Kress to screaming. He screamed because of the others, the little orange children who came crawling out from the castle, and watched impassive as he passed.

All of them had his face.

Nightflyers

When Jesus of Nazareth hung dying on his cross, the *volcryn* passed within a year of his agony, headed outward.

When the Fire Wars raged on Earth, the *volcryn* sailed near Old Poseidon, where the seas were still unnamed and unfished. By the time the stardrive had transformed the Federated Nations of Earth into the Federal Empire, the *volcryne* had moved into the fringes of Hrangan space. The Hrangans never knew it. Like us, they were children of the small bright worlds that circled their scattered suns, with little interest in and less knowledge of the things that moved in the gulfs between.

War flamed for a thousand years and the *volcryn* passed through it, unknowing and untouched, safe in a place where no fires could ever burn. Afterward the Federal Empire was shattered and gone, and the Hrangans vanished in the dark of the Collapse, but it was no darker for the *volcryn.*

When Kleronomas took his survey ship out from Avalon, the *volcryn* came within ten light years of him. Kleronomas found many things, but he did not find the *volcryn.* Not then and not on his return to Avalon a lifetime later.

When I was a child of three, Kleronomas was dust, as distant and dead as Jesus of Nazareth, and the *volycryn* passed close to Daronne. That season all the Crey sensitives grew strange and sat staring at the stars with luminous, flickering eyes.

When I was grown, the *volcryn* had sailed beyond Tara, past the range of even the Crey, still heading outward.

And now I am old and growing older and the *volcryn* will soon pierce the Tempter's Veil where it hangs like a black mist between the stars. And we follow, we follow. Through the dark gulfs where no one goes, through the emptiness, through the silence that goes on and on, my *Nightflyer* and I give chase.

They made their way slowly down the length of the transparent tube that linked the orbital docks to the waiting starship ahead, pulling themselves hand over hand through weightlessness.

Melantha Jhirl, the only one among them who did not seem clumsy and ill at ease in free-fall, paused briefly to look at the dappled globe of Avalon below, a stately vastness in jade and amber. She smiled and moved swiftly down the tube, passing her companions with an easy grace. They had boarded starships before, all of them, but never like this. Most ships docked flush against the station, but the craft that Karoly d'Branin had chartered for his mission was too large, and of too singular a design. It loomed ahead; three small eggs side by side, two larger spheres beneath and at right angles, the cylinder of the driveroom between, lengths of tube connecting it all. The ship was white and austere.

Melantha Jhirl was the first one through the airlock. The others straggled up one by one until they had all boarded; five women and four men, each an Academy scholar, their backgrounds as diverse as their fields of study. The frail young telepath, Thale Lasamer, was the last to enter. He glanced about nervously as the others chatted and waited for the entry procedure to be completed. "We're being watched," he said.

The outer door was closed behind them, the tube had fallen away; now the inner door slid open. "Welcome to my *Nightflyer*," said a mellow voice from within.

But there was no one there.

Melantha Jhirl stepped into the corridor. "Hello," she said, looking about quizzically. Karoly d'Branin followed her.

"Hello," the mellow voice replied. It was coming from a communicator grill beneath a darkened viewscreen. "This is a Royd Eris, master of the *Nightflyer*. I'm pleased to see you again, Karoly, and pleased to welcome the rest of you."

"Where are you?" someone demanded.

"In my quarters, which occupy half of this life-support sphere," the voice of Royd Eris replied amiably. "The other half is comprised of a lounge-library-kitchen, two sanitary stations, one double cabin, and a rather small single. The rest of you will have to rig sleepwebs in the cargo spheres, I'm afraid. The *Nightflyer* was designed as a trader, not a passenger vessel. However, I've opened all the appropriate passageways and locks, so the holds have air and heat and water. I thought you'd find it more comfortable that way. Your equipment and computer system have been stowed in the holds, but there is still plenty of space, I assure you. I suggest you settle in, and then meet in the lounge for a meal."

"Will you join us?" asked the psipsych, a querulous, hatched-faced woman named Agatha Marij-Black.

"In a fashion," Royd Eris said, "in a fashion."

The ghost appeared at the banquet.

They found the lounge easily enough, after they had rigged their sleepwebs and arranged their personal belongings around their sleeping quarters. It was the largest room in this section of the ship. One end of it was a fully equipped kitchen, well stocked with provisions. The opposite end offered several comfortable chairs, two readers, a holotank, and a wall of books and tapes and crystal chips. In the center was a long table with places set for ten.

A light meal was hot and waiting. The academicians helped themselves and took seats at the table, laughing and talking to each other, more at ease now than when they had boarded. The ship's gravity grid was on, which went a long way toward making them more comfortable; the queasy awkwardness of their weightless transit was soon forgotten.

Finally all the seats were occupied except for one at the head of the table.

The ghost materialized there.

All conversation stopped.

"Hello," said the specter, the bright shade of a lithe, pale-eyed young man with white hair. He was dressed in clothing twenty years out of date: a loose blue pastel shirt that ballooned at his wrists; clinging white trousers with built-in boots. They could see through him, and his own eyes did not see them at all.

"A holograph," said Alys Northwind, the short, stout xenotech.

"Royd, Royd, I do not understand," said Karoly d'Branin, staring at the ghost. "What is this? Why do you send us a projection? Will you not join us in person?"

The ghost smiled faintly and lifted an arm. "My quarters are on the other side of that wall," he said. "I'm afraid there is no door or lock between the two halves of the sphere. I spend most of my time by myself and I value my privacy. I hope you will all understand, and respect my wishes. I will be a gracious host nonetheless. Here in the lounge my projection can join you. Elsewhere, if you have anything you need, if you want to talk to me, just use a communicator. Now please resume your meal, and your conversations. I'll gladly listen. It's been a long time since I had passengers."

They tried. But the ghost at the head of the table cast a long shadow and the meal was strained and hurried.

From the hour the *Nightflyer* slipped into stardrive, Royd Eris watched his passengers.

Within a few days most of the academicians had grown accustomed to the disembodied voice from the communicators and the holographic specter in the lounge, but only Melantha Jhirl and Karoly d'Branin ever seemed really comfortable in his presence. The others would have been even more uncomfortable if they had known that Royd was always with them. Always and everywhere, he watched. Even in the sanitary stations, Royd had eyes and ears.

He watched them work, eat, sleep, copulate; he listened untiringly to their talk. Within a week he knew them, all nine, and had begun to ferret out their tawdry little secrets.

The cyberneticist, Lommie Thorne, talked to her computers and seemed to prefer their company to that of humans. She was bright and quick, with a mobile, expressive face and a small hard boyish body; most of the others found her attractive, but she did not like to be touched. She sexed only once, with Melantha Jhirl. Lommie Thorne wore shirts of softly woven metal and had an implant in her left wrist that let her interface directly with her computers.

The xenobiologist, Rojan Christopheris, was a surly, argumentative man, a cynic whose contempt for his colleagues was barely kept in check, a solitary drinker. He was tall and stooped and ugly.

The two linguists, Dannel and Lindran, were lovers in public, constantly holding hands and supporting each other. In private they quarreled bitterly, Lindran had a mordant wit and liked to wound Dannel where it hurt the most, with jokes about his professional competence. They sexed often, both of them, but not with each other.

Agatha Marij-Black, the psipsych, was a hypochondriac given to black depressions which worsened in the close confines of the *Nightflyer.*

Xenotech Alys Northwind ate constantly and never washed. Her stubby fingernails were always caked with black dirt, and she wore the same jumpsuit for the first two weeks of the voyage, taking it off only for sex, and then only briefly.

Telepath Thale Lasamer was nervous and temperamental, afraid of everyone around him, yet given to bouts of arrogance in which he taunted his companions with thoughts he had snatched from their minds.

Royd Eris watched them all, studied them, lived with them and through them. He neglected none, not even the ones he found the most distasteful. But by the time the *Nightflyer* had been lost in the roiling flux of stardrive for two weeks, two of his riders had come to engage the bulk of his attention.

"Most of all, I want to know the *why* of them," Karoly d'Branin told him one false night the second week out from Avalon.

Royd's luminescent ghost sat close to d'Branin in the darkened lounge, watching him drink bittersweet chocolate. The others were all asleep. Night and day are meaningless on a starship, but the *Nightflyer* kept the usual cycles and most of the passengers followed them. Old d'Branin, administrator, generalist, and mission leader, was the exception; he kept his own hours, preferred work to sleep, and liked nothing better than to talk about his pet obsession, the *volcryn* he hunted.

"The *if* of them is important as well, Karoly," Royd answered. "Can you truly be certain these aliens of yours exist?"

"*I* can be certain," Karoly d'Branin said, with a broad wink. He was a compact man, short and slender, iron-gray hair carefully styled and tunic almost fussily neat, but the expansiveness of his gestures and the giddy enthusiasms to which he was prone belied his sober appearance. "That is enough. If everyone else were certain as well, we would have a fleet of research ships instead of your little *Nightflyer.*" He sipped at his chocolate and sighed with satisfaction. "Do you know the Nor T'alush, Royd?"

The name was strange, but it took Royd only a moment to consult his library computer. "An alien race on the other side of human space, past the Fyndii worlds and the Damoosh. Possibly legendary."

D'Branin chuckled. "No, no, no! Your library is out of date, my friend, you must supplement it the next time you visit Avalon. Not legends, no; real enough, though far away. We have little information about the Nor

T'alush, but we are sure they exist, though you and I may never meet one. They were the start of it all."

"Tell me," Royd said. "I am interested in your work, Karoly."

"I was coding some information into the Academy computers, a packet newly arrived from Dam Tullian after twenty standard years in transit. Part of it was Nor T'alush forklore. I had no idea how long that had taken to get to Dam Tullian, or by what route it had come, but it did not matter—forklore is timeless anyway, and this was fascinating material. Did you know that my first degree was in xenomythology?"

"I did not. Please continue."

"The *volcryn* story was among the Nor T'alush myths. It awed me; a race of sentients moving out from some mysterious origin in the core of the galaxy, sailing toward the galactic edge and, it was alleged, eventually bound for intergalactic space itself, meanwhile always keeping to the interstellar depths, no planetfalls, seldom coming within a light-year of a star." D'Branin's gray eyes sparkled, and as he spoke, his hands swept enthusiastically to either side as if they could encompass the galaxy. "And doing it all *without a stardrive*, Royd, that is the real wonder! Doing it in ships moving only a fraction of the speed of light! That was the detail that obsessed me! How different they must be, my *volcryn*— wise and patient, long-lived and long-viewed, with none of the terrible haste and passion that consume the lesser races. Think how *old* they must be, those *volcryn* ships!"

"Old," Royd agreed. "Karoly, you said *ships*. More than one?"

"Oh, yes," d'Branin said. "According to the Nor T'alush, one or two appeared first, on the innermost edges of their trading sphere, but others followed. Hundreds of them, each solitary, moving by itself, bound outward, always outward. The direction was always the same. For fifteen thousand standard years they moved among the Nor T'alush stars, and then they began to pass out from among them. The myth said that the last *volcryn* ship was gone three thousand years ago."

"Eighteen thousand years," Royd said, adding. "Are the Nor T'alush that old?"

"Not as star-travelers, no," d'Branin said, smiling."According to their own histories, the Nor T'alush have only been civilized for about half that long. That bothered me for a while. It seemed to make the *volcryn* story clearly a legend. A wonderful legend, true, but nothing more.

"Ultimately, however, I could not let it alone. In my spare time I investigated, cross-checking with other alien cosmologies to see whether this particular myth was shared by any races other than the Nor T'alush. I thought perhaps I could get a thesis out of it. It seemed a fruitful line of inquiry.

"I was startled by what I found. Nothing from the Hrangans, or the Hrangan slaveraces, but that made sense, you see. They were *out* from human space; the *volcryn* would not reach them until after they had passed through our own sphere. When I looked *in*, however, the *volcryn* story was everywhere." D'Branin leaned forward eagerly. "Ah, Royd, the stories, the *stories!*"

"Tell me," Royd said.

"The Fyndii call them *iy-wivii*, which translates to something like void-horde or dark-horde. Each Fyndii horde tells the same story; only the mindmutes disbelieve. The ships are said to be vast, much larger than any known in their history or ours. Warships, they say. There is a story of a lost Fyndii horde, three hundred ships under *rala-fyn*, all destroyed utterly when they encountered an *iy-wivii*. This was many thousands of years ago, of course, so the details are unclear.

"The Damoosh have a different story, but they accept it as literal truth—and the Damoosh, you know, are the oldest race we've yet encountered. The people of the gulf, they call my *volcryn*. Lovely stories, Royd, lovely! Ships like great dark cities, still and silent, moving at a slower pace than the universe around them. Damoosh legends say the *volcryn* are refugees from some unimaginable war deep in the core of the galaxy, at the very beginning of time. They abandoned the worlds and stars on which they had evolved, sought true peace in the emptiness between.

"The gethsoids of Aath have a similar story, but in their tale that war destroyed all life in our galaxy, and the *volcryn* are gods of a sort, reseeding the worlds as they pass. Other races see them as God's messengers, or shadows out of hell warning us all to flee some terror soon to emerge from the core."

"Your stories contradict each other, Karoly."

"Yes, yes, of course, but they all agree on the essentials—the *volcryn* sailing out, passing through our short-lived empires and transient glories in their ancient eternal sublight ships. *That* is what matters! The rest is frippery, ornamentation; we will soon know the truth of it. I checked what little was known about the races said to flourish further in still, beyond even the Nor T'alush—civilizations and peoples half-legendary themselves, like the Dan'lai and the Ullish and the Rohenna'kh—and where I could find anything at all, I found the *volcryn* story once again."

"The legend of the legends," Royd suggested. The specter's wide mouth turned up in a smile.

"Exactly, exactly," d'Branin agreed. "At that point I called in the experts, specialists from the Institute for the Study of Non-Human Intelligence. We researched for two years. It was all there, in the libraries and memories and matrices of the Academy. No one had ever looked before, or bothered to put it together.

"The *volcryn* have been moving through the man-realm for most of human history, since before the dawn of spaceflight. While we twist the fabric of space itself to cheat relativity, they have been sailing their great ships right through the heart of our alleged civilization, past our most populous worlds, at stately slow sublight speeds, bound for the Fringe and the dark between the galaxies. Marvelous, Royd, marvelous!"

"Marvelous," Royd agreed.

Karoly d'Branin drained his chocolate cup with a swig and reached out to catch Royd's arm, but his hand passed through empty light. He seemed disconcerted for a moment, before he began to laugh at himself. "Ah, my *volcryn*. I grow overenthused, Royd. I am so close now. They have preyed on my mind for a dozen years, and within the month I will have them, will behold their splendor with my own weary eyes. Then, *then*, if only I can open communication, if only my people can reach ones so great and strange as they, so different from us—I have hopes, Royd, hopes that at last I will know the *why* of it!"

The ghost of Royd Eris smiled for him, and looked on through calm transparent eyes.

Passengers soon grow restless on a starship under drive, sooner on one as small and spare as the *Nightflyer*. Late in the second week the speculation began in deadly earnest.

"Who is this Royd Eris, really?" the xenobiologist, Rojan Christopheris, complained one night when four of them were playing cards. "Why doesn't he come out? What's the purpose of keeping himself sealed off from the rest of us?"

"Ask him," suggested Dannel, the male linguist.

"What if he's a criminal of some sort?" Christopheris said. "Do we know anything about him? No, of course not. D'Branin engaged him, and d'Branin is a senile old fool, we all know that."

"It's your play," Lommie Thorne said.

Christopheris snapped down a card. "Setback," he declared, "you have to draw again." He grinned. "As for this Eris, who knows that he isn't planning to kill us all."

"For our vast wealth, no doubt," said Lindran, the female linguist. She played a card on top of the one Christopheris had laid down. "Ricochet," she called softly. She smiled.

So did Royd Eris, watching.

Melantha Jhirl was good to watch.

Young, healthy, active, Melantha Jhirl had a vibrancy about her the others could not match. She was big in every way; a head taller than anyone else on board, large-framed, large-breasted, long-legged, strong muscles moving fluidly beneath shiny coal-black skin. Her appetites were big as well. She ate twice as much as any of her colleagues, drank heavily without ever seeming drunk, exercised for hours every day on equipment she had brought with her and set up in one of the cargo holds. By the third week out she had sexed with all four of the men on board and two of the other women. Even in bed she was always active, exhausting most of her partners. Royd watched her with consuming interest.

"I am an improved model," she told him once as she worked out on her parallel bars, sweat glistening on her bare skin, her long black hair confined in a net.

"Improved?" Royd said. He could not send his projection down to the holds, but Melantha had summoned him with the communicator to talk while she exercised, not knowing he would have been there anyway.

She paused in her routine, holding her body straight and aloft with the strength of her arms and her back. "Altered, captain," she said. She had taken to calling him captain. "Born on Prometheus among the elite, child of two genetic wizards. Improved, captain. I require twice the energy you do, but I use it all. A more efficient metabolism, a stronger and more durable body, an expected life span half again the normal human's. My people have made some terrible mistakes when they try to radically redesign humanity, but the small improvements they do well."

She resumed her exercises, moving quickly and easily, silent until she had finished. When she was done, she vaulted away from the bars and stood breathing heavily for a moment, then crossed her arms and cocked her head and grinned. "Now you know my life story, captain," she said. She pulled off the net to shake free her hair.

"Surely there is more," said the voice from the communicator.

Melantha Jhirl laughed. "Surely," she said. "Do you want to hear about my defection to Avalon, the whys and wherefores of it, the trouble it caused my family on Prometheus? Or are you more interested in my extraordinary work in cultural xenology? Do you want to hear about that?"

"Perhaps some other time," Royd said politely. "What is that crystal you wear?"

It hung between her breasts, ordinarily; she had removed it when she stripped for her exercises. She picked it up again and slipped it over her head; a small green gem laced with traceries of black, on a silver chain. When it touched her, Melantha closed her eyes briefly, then opened them again, grinning. "It's alive," she said. "Haven't you ever seen one? A whisperjewel, captain. Resonant crystal, etched psionically to hold a memory, a sensation. The touch brings it back, for a time."

"I am familiar with the principle," Royd said, "but not this use. Yours contains some treasured memory, then? Of your family, perhaps?"

Melantha Jhirl snatched up a towel and began to dry the sweat from her body. "Mine contains the sensations of a particularly satisfying session in bed, captain. It arouses me. Or it did. Whisperjewels fade in time, and this isn't as potent as it once was. But sometimes—often when I've come from lovemaking or strenuous exercise—it comes alive on me again, like it did just then."

"Oh," said Royd's voice. "It has made you aroused, then? Are you going off to copulate now?"

Melantha grinned. "I know what part of my life *you* want to hear about, captain—my tumultuous and passionate love life. Well you won't have it. Not until I hear your life story, anyway. Among my modest attributes is an insatiable curiosity. Who are you, captain? Really?"

"One as improved as you," Royd replied, "should certainly be able to guess."

Melantha laughed and tossed her towel at the communicator grill.

Loomie Thorne spent more of her days in the cargo hold they had designated the computer room, setting up the system they would use to analyze the *volcryn.* As often as not, the xenotech Alys Northwind came with her to lend a hand. The cyberneticist whistled as she worked; Northwind obeyed her orders in a sullen silence. Occasionally they talked.

"Eris isn't human," Lommie Thorne said one day as she supervised the installation of a display viewscreen.

Alys Northwind grunted. "What?" A frown broke across her square, flat features. Christopheris and his talk had made her nervous about Eris. She clicked another component into position and turned.

"He talks to us, but he can't be seen," the cyberneticist said. "This ship is uncrewed, seemingly all automated except for him. Why not entirely automated, then? I'd wager this Royd Eris is a fairly sophisticated computer system, perhaps a genuine Artificial Intelligence. Even a modest program can carry on a blind conversation indistinguishable from a human's. This one could fool you, I'd bet, once it's up and running."

The xenotech grunted and turned back to her work. "Why fake being human, then?"

"Because," said Lommie Thorne, "most legal systems give AIs no rights. A ship can't own itself, even on Avalon. The *Nightflyer* is probably afraid of being seized and disconnected." She whistled. "Death, Alys, the end of self-awareness and conscious thought."

"I work with machines every day," Alys Northwind said stubbornly. "Turn them off, turn them on, makes no difference. They don't mind. Why should this machine care?"

Lommie Thorne smiled. "A computer is different, Alys," she said. "Mind, thought, life, the big systems have all of that." Her right hand curled around her left wrist, and her thumb began idly rubbing the nubs of her implant. "Sensation, too. I know. No one wants the end of sensation. They are not so different from you and I, really."

The xenotech glanced back and shook her head. "Really," she repeated, in a flat, disbelieving voice.

Royd Eris listened and watched, unsmiling.

Thale Lasamer was a frail young thing, nervous, sensitive, with limp flaxen hair that fell to his shoulders, and watery blue eyes. Normally he dressed like a peacock, favoring the lacy V-neck shirts and cod-pieces that were still the fashion among the lower classes of his homeworld. But on the day he sought out Karoly d'Branin in his cramped, private cabin, Lasamer was dressed almost somberly, in an austere gray jumpsuit.

"I feel it," he said, clutching d'Branin by the arm, his long fingernails digging in painfully. "Something is wrong, Karoly, something is very wrong. I'm beginning to get frightened."

The telepath's nails bit, and d'Branin pulled away hard. "You are hurting me," he protested. "My friend, what is it? Frightened? Of what, of who? I do not understand. What could there be to fear?"

Lasamer raised pale hands to his face. "I don't know, I don't *know*," he wailed. "Yet it's *there*; I feel it. Karoly, I'm picking up something. You know I'm good. I am, that's why you picked me. Just a moment ago, when my nails dug into you, I felt it. I can read you now, in flashes. You're thinking I'm too excitable, that it's the confinement, that I've got to be calmed down." The young man laughed a thin hysterical laugh that died as quickly as it had begun. "No, you see, I am good. Class one, tested, and I tell you I'm afraid. I sense it. Feel it. Dream of it. I felt it even as we were boarding, and it's gotten worst. Something dangerous. Something volatile. And alien, Karoly, *alien!*"

"The *volcryn?*" d'Branin said.

"No, impossible. We're in drive, they're light-years away." The edgy laughter sounded again. "I'm not that good, Karoly. I've heard your Crey story, but I'm only a human. No, this is close. On the ship."

"One of us?"

"Maybe," Lasamer said. He rubbed his cheek absently. "I can't sort it out."

D'Branin put a fatherly hand on his shoulder. "Thale, this feeling of yours—could it be that you are just tired? All of us have been under strain. Inactivity can be taxing."

"Get your hand off me," Lasamer snapped.

D'Branin drew back his hand quickly.

"This is *real,*" the telepath insisted, "and I don't need you thinking that maybe you shouldn't have taken me, all that crap. I'm as stable as anyone on this . . . this . . . how *dare* you think I'm unstable. You ought to look inside some of these others— Christopheris with his bottle and his dirty little fantasies, Dannel half-sick with fear, Lommie and her machines, with her it's all metal and lights and cool circuits, sick, I tell you, and Jhirl's arrogant and Agatha whines even in her head to herself all the time, and Alys is empty, like a cow. You, you don't touch them, see into them, what do you know of *stable?* Losers, d'Branin, they've given you a bunch of losers, and I'm one of your best, so don't you go thinking that I'm not stable, not sane, you hear." His blue eyes were fevered. "Do you *hear?*"

"Easy," d'Branin said. "Easy, Thale, you're getting excited."

The telepath blinked, and suddenly the wildness was gone. "Excited?" he said. "Yes." He looked around guiltily. "It's hard, Karoly, but listen to me. You must; I'm warning you. We're in danger."

"I will listen," d'Branin said, "but I cannot act without more definite information. You must use your talent to get it for me, yes? You can do that."

Lasamer nodded. "Yes," he said. "Yes." They talked quietly for more than an hour, and finally the telepath left peacefully.

Afterward d'Branin went straight to the psipsych, who was lying in her sleepweb surrounded by medicines, complaining bitterly of aches. "Interesting," she said when d'Branin told her. "I've felt something, too, a sense of threat, very vague, diffuse. I thought it was me, the confinement, the boredom, the way I feel. My moods betray me at times. Did he say anything more specific?"

"No."

"I'll make an effort to move around, read him, read the others, see what I can pick up. Although, if this is real, he should know it first. He's a one, I'm only a three."

D'Branin nodded. "He seems very receptive," he said. "He told me all kinds of things about the others."

"Means nothing. Sometimes, when a telepath insists he is picking up everything, what it means is that he's picking up nothing at all. He imagines feelings, readings, to make up for those that will not come. I'll keep careful watch on him, d'Branin. Sometimes a talent can crack, slip into a kind of hysteria, and begin to broadcast instead of receive. In a closed environment that's very dangerous."

Karoly d'Branin nodded. "Of course, of course."

In another part of the ship, Royd Eris frowned.

"Have you noticed the clothing on that holograph he sends us?" Rojan Christopheris asked Alys Northwind. They were alone in one of the holds, reclining on a mat, trying to avoid the wet spot. The xenobiologist had lit a joystick. He offered it to his companion, but Northwind waved it away. "A decade out of style, maybe more. My father wore shirts like that when he was a boy on Old Poseidon."

"Eris has old-fashioned taste," Alys Northwind said. "So? I don't care what he wears. Me, I like my jumpsuits. They're comfortable. Don't care what people think."

"You don't, do you?" Christopheris said, wrinkling his huge nose. She did not see the gesture. "Well, you miss the point. What if that isn't really Eris? A projection can be anything, can be made up out of whole cloth. I don't think he really looks like that."

"No?" Now her voice was curious. She rolled over and curled up beneath his arm, her heavy white breasts against his chest.

"What if he's sick, deformed, ashamed to be seen the way he really looks?" Christopheris said. "Perhaps he has some disease. The Slow Plague can waste a person terribly, but it takes decades to kill, and there are other contagions—manthrax, new leprosy, the melt, Langamen's Disease, lots of them. Could be that Royd's self-imposed quarantine is just that. A quarantine. Think about it."

Alys Northwind frowned. "All this talk of Eris," she said, "is making me edgy."

The xenobiologist sucked on his joystick and laughed. "Welcome to the *Nightflyer,* then. The rest of us are already there."

In the fifth week out Melantha Jhirl pushed her pawn to the sixth rank and Royd saw that it was unstoppable and resigned. It was his eighth straight defeat at her hands in as many days. She was sitting cross-legged on the floor of the lounge, the chessmen spread out before her in front of a darkened viewscreen. Laughing, she swept them all away. "Don't feel bad, Royd," she told him. "I'm an improved model. Always three moves ahead."

"I should tie in my computer," he replied. "You'd never know." His holographic ghost materialized suddenly, standing in front of the viewscreen, and smiled at her.

"I'd know within three moves," Melantha Jhirl said. "Try it."

They were the last victims of a chess fever that had swept the *Nightflyer* for more than a week. Initially it had been Christopheris who produced the set and urged people to play, but the others had lost interest quickly when Thale Lasamer sat down and beat them all, one by one. Everyone was certain that he'd done it by reading their minds, but the telepath was in a volatile, nasty mood, and no one dared voice the accusation. Melantha, however, had been able to defeat Lasamer without very much trouble. "He isn't that good a player," she told Royd afterward, "and if he's trying to lift ideas from me, he's getting gibberish. The improved model knows certain mental disciplines. I can shield myself well enough, thank you." Christopheris and a few of the others then tried a game or two against Melantha and were routed for their troubles. Finally Royd asked if he might play. Only Melantha and Karoly were willing to sit down with him over the board, and since Karoly could barely recall how the pieces moved from one moment to the next, that left Melantha and Royd as regular opponents. They both seemed to thrive on the games, though Melantha always won.

Melantha stood up and walked to the kitchen, stepping right through Royd's ghostly form, which she steadfastly refused to pretend was real. "The rest of them walk around me," Royd complained.

She shrugged and found a bulb of beer in a storage compartment. "When are you going to break down and let me behind your wall for a visit, captain?" she asked. "Don't you get lonely back there? Sexually frustrated? Claustrophobic?"

"I have flown the *Nightflyer* all my life, Melantha," Royd said. His projection ignored, winked out. "If I were subject to claustrophobia, sexual frustration, or loneliness, such a life would have been impossible. Surely that should be obvious to you, being as improved a model as you are?"

She took a squeeze of her beer and laughed her mellow, musical laugh at him. "I'll solve you yet, captain," she warned.

"Meanwhile," he said, "tell me some more lies about your life."

"Have you ever heard of Jupiter?" the xenotech demanded of the others. She was drunk, lolling in her sleepweb in the cargo hold.

"Something to do with Earth," said Lindran. "The same myth system originated both names, I believe."

"Jupiter," the xenotech announced loudly, "is a gas giant in the same solar system as Old Earth. Didn't know that, did you?"

"I've got more important things to occupy my mind than such trivia, Alys," Lindran said.

Alys Northwind smiled down smugly. "Listen, I'm talking to you. They were on the verge of exploring this Jupiter when the stardrive was discovered, oh, way back. After that, course, no one bothered with gas giants. Just slip into drive and find the habitable worlds, settle them, ignore the comets and the rocks and the gas giants—there's another star just a few light-years away, and it has *more* habitable planets. But there were people who thought those Jupiters might have life, you know. Do you see?"

"I see that you're blind drunk," Lindran said.

Christopheris looked annoyed. "If there is intelligent life on the gas giants, it shows no interest in leaving them," he snapped. "All of the sentient species we have met up to now have originated on worlds similar to Earth, and most of them are oxygen breathers. Unless you're suggesting that the *volcryn* are from a gas giant?"

The xenotech pushed up to a sitting position and smiled conspiratorially. "Not the *volcryn*," she said. "Royd Eris. Crack that forward bulkhead in the lounge, and watch the methane and ammonia come smoking out." Her hand made a sensuous waving motion through the air, and she convulsed with giddy laughter.

The system was up and running. Cyberneticist Lommie Thorne sat at the master console, a featureless black plastic plate upon which the phantom images of a hundred keyboard configurations came and went in holographic display, vanishing and shifting even as she used them.

Around her rose crystalline data grids, ranks of viewscreens and readout panels upon which columns of figures marched and geometric shapes did stately whirling dances, dark columns of seamless metal that contained the mind and soul of her system. She sat in the semi-darkness happily, whistling as she ran the computer through several simple routines, her fingers moving across the flickering keys with blind speed and quickening tempo. "Ah," she said once, smiling. Later, only, "Good."

Then it was time for the final run-through. Lommie Thorne slid back the metallic fabric of her left sleeve, pushed her wrist beneath the console, found the prongs, jacked herself in. Interface.

Ecstasy.

Inkblot shapes in a dozen glowing colors twisted and melded and broke apart on the readout screens.

In an instant it was over.

Lommie Thorne pulled free her wrist. The smile on her face was shy and satisfied, but across it lay another expression, the merest hint of puzzlement. She touched her thumb to the holes of her wrist jack and found them warm to the touch, tingling. Lommie shivered.

The system was running perfectly, hardware in good condition, all software systems functioning according to plan, interface meshing well. It had been a delight, as it always was. When she joined with the system, she was wise beyond her years, and powerful, and full of light and electricity and the stuff of life, cool and clean and exciting to touch, and never alone, never small or weak. That was what it was always like when she interfaced and let herself expand.

But this time something had been different. Something cold had touched her, only for a moment. Something very cold and very frightening, and together she and the system had seen it cleanly for a brief moment, and then it had been gone again.

The cyberneticist shook her head and drove the nonsense out. She went back to work. After a time she began to whistle.

During the sixth week Alys Northwind cut herself badly while preparing a snack. She was standing in the kitchen, slicing a spiced meatstick with a long knife, when suddenly she screamed.

Dannel and Lindran rushed to her and found her staring down in horror at the chopping block in front of her. The knife had taken off the first joint of the index finger on her left hand, and the blood was spreading in ragged spurts. "The ship lurched," Alys said numbly, staring up at

Dannel. "Didn't you feel it jerk? It pushed the knife to the side."

"Get something to stop the bleeding," Lindran said. Dannel looked around in panic.

"Oh, I'll do it myself," Lindran finally said, and she did.

The psipsych, Agatha Marij-Black, gave Northwind a tranquilizer, then looked at the two linguists. "Did you see it happen?"

"She did it herself, with the knife," Dannel said.

From somewhere down the corridor there came the sound of wild, hysterical laughter.

"I dampened him," Marij-Black reported to Karoly d'Branin later the same day. "Psionine-4. It will blunt his receptivity for several days, and I have more if he needs it."

D'Branin wore a stricken look. "We talked several times, and I could see that Thale was becoming ever more fearful, but he could never tell me the *why* of it. Did you have to shut him off?"

The psipsych shrugged. "He was edging into the irrational. Given his level of talent, if he'd gone over the edge, he might have taken us all with him. You should never have taken a class-one telepath, d'Branin. Too unstable."

"We must communicate with an alien race. I remind you that is no easy task. The *volcryn* will be more alien than any sentients we have yet encountered. We needed class-one skills if we were to have any hope of reaching them. And they have so much to teach us, my friend!"

"Glib," she said, "but you might have no working skills at all, given the condition of your class one. Half the time he's curled up into the fetal position in his sleepweb, half the time he's strutting and crowing and half-mad with fear. He insists we're all in real physical danger, but he doesn't know why or from what. The worst of it is that I can't tell if he's really sensing something or simply having an acute attack of paranoia. He certainly displays some classic paranoid symptoms. Among other things he insists that he's being watched. Perhaps his condition is completely unrelated to us, the *volcryn*, and his talent. I can't be sure."

"What of your own talent?" d'Branin said. "You are an empath, are you not?"

"Don't tell me my job," she said sharply. "I sexed with him last week. You don't get more proximity or better rapport for esping than that. Even under those conditions I couldn't be sure of anything. His mind is a chaos, and his fear is so rank it stank up the sheets. I don't read anything from the others either, besides the ordinary tensions and frustrations. But I'm only a three, so that doesn't mean much. My abilities are limited. You know I haven't been feeling well, d'Branin. I can barely breathe on this ship. The air seems thick and heavy to me; my head throbs. Ought to stay in bed."

"Yes, of course," d'Branin said hastily. "I did not mean to criticize. You have been doing all you can under difficult circumstances. How long will it be until Thale is with us again?"

The psipsych rubbed her temple wearily. "I'm recommending we keep him dampened until the mission is over, d'Branin. I warn you, an insane or hysterical telepath is dangerous. That business with Northwind and the knife might have been his doing, you know. He started screaming not long after, remember. Maybe he'd touched her, for just an instant—oh, it's a wild idea, but it's possible. The point is, we don't take chances. I have enough psionine-4 to keep him numb and functional until we're back on Avalon."

"*But*—Royd will take us out of drive soon, and we will make contact with the *volcryn*. We will need Thale—his mind, his talent. Is it vital to keep him dampened? Is there no other way?"

Marij-Black grimaced. "My other option was an injection of esperon. It would have opened him up completely, increased his psionic receptivity tenfold for a few hours. Then, I'd hope, he could focus in on this danger he's feeling. Exorcise it if it's false, deal with it if it's real. But psionine-4 is a lot safer. Esperon is a hell of a drug, with devastating side effects. It raises the blood pressure dramatically, sometimes brings on hyperventilation or seizures, has even been known to stop the heart. Lasamer is young enough so that I'm not worried about that, but I don't think he has the emotional stability to deal with that kind of power. The psionine should tell us something. If his paranoia persists, I'll know it has nothing to do with his telepathy."

"And if it does not persist?" Karoly d'Branin said.

Agatha Marij-Black smiled wickedly at him. "If Lasamer becomes quiescent and stops babbling about danger? Why, that would mean he was no longer picking up anything, wouldn't it? And *that* would mean there had been something to pick up, that he'd been right all along."

At dinner that night Thale Lasamer was quiet and distracted, eating in a rhythmic, mechanical sort of way, with a cloudy look in his blue eyes. Afterward he excused himself and went straight to bed, falling into exhausted slumber almost immediately.

"What did you do to him?" Lommie Thorne asked Marij-Black.

"I shut off that prying mind of his," she replied.

"You should have done it two weeks ago," Lindran said. "Docile, he's a lot easier to take."

Karoly d'Branin hardly touched his food.

False night came, and Royd's wraith materialized while Karoly d'Branin sat brooding over his chocolate. "Karoly," the apparition said, "would it be possible to tie in the computer your team brought on board with my shipboard system? Your *volcryn* stories fascinate me, and I would like to be able to study them further at my leisure. I assume the details of your investigation are in storage."

"Certainly," d'Branin replied in an offhand, distracted manner. "Our system is up now. Patching it into the *Nightflyer* should present no problem. I will tell Lommie to attend to it tomorrow."

Silence hung in the room heavily. Karoly d'Branin sipped at his chocolate and stared off into the darkness, almost unaware of Royd.

"You are troubled," Royd said after a time.

"Eh? Oh, yes." D'Branin looked up. "Forgive me, my friend. I have much on my mind."

"It concerns Thale Lasamer, does it not?"

Karoly d'Branin looked at the pale, luminescent figure across from him for a long time before he finally managed a stiff nod. "Yes. Might I ask how you knew that?"

"I know everything that occurs on the *Nightflyer*," Royd said.

"You have been watching us," d'Branin said gravely, accusation in his tone. "Then it is so, what Thale says, about us being watched. Royd, how could you? Spying is beneath you."

The ghost's transparent eyes had no life in them, did not see. "Do not tell the others," Royd warned. "Karoly, my friend—if I may call you my friend—I have my own reasons for watching, reasons it would not profit you to know. I mean you no harm. Believe that. You have hired me to take you safely to the *volcryn* and safely back, and I mean to do just that."

"You are being evasive, Royd," d'Branin said. "Why do you spy on us? Do you watch everything? Are you a voyeur, some enemy—is that why you do not mix with us? Is watching all you intend to do?"

"Your suspicions hurt me, Karoly."

"Your deception hurts me. Will you now answer me?"

"I have eyes and ears everywhere," Royd said. "There is no place to
hide from me on the *Nightflyer*. Do I see everything? No, not always. I am
only human, no matter what your colleagues might think. I sleep. The
monitors remain on, but there is no one to observe them. I can only pay
attention to one or two scenes or inputs at once. Sometimes I grow
distracted, unobservant. I watch everything, Karoly, but I do not see
everything."

"*Why?*" D'Branin poured himself a fresh cup of chocolate, steadying
his hand with an effort.

"I do not have to answer that question. The *Nightflyer* is my ship."

D'Branin sipped chocolate, blinked, nodded to himself. "You grieve
me, my friend. You give me no choice. Thale said we were being
watched, and he was right, I now learn. He says also that we are in
danger. Something alien, he says. You?"

The projection was still and silent.

D'Branin clucked. "You do not answer. Ah, Royd, what am I to do? I
must believe him, then. We are in danger, perhaps from you. I must abort
our mission, then. Return us to Avalon, Royd. That is my decision."

The ghost smiled wanly. "So close, Karoly? Soon now we will be
dropping out of drive."

Karoly d'Branin made a small, sad noise deep in his throat. "My
volcryn," he said, sighing. "So close—ah, it pains me to desert them. But I
cannot do otherwise, I cannot."

"You can," said the voice of Royd Eris. "Trust me. That is all I ask,
Karoly. Believe me when I tell you that I have no sinister intentions.
Thale Lasamer may speak of danger, but no one has been harmed so far,
have they?"

"No," admitted d'Branin. "No, unless you count Alys, cutting herself
this afternoon."

"What?" Royd hesitated briefly. "Cutting herself? I did not see,
Karoly. When did this happen?"

"Oh, early—just before Lasamer began to scream and rant, I believe."

"I see." Royd's voice was thoughtful. "I was watching Melantha go
through her exercises," he said finally, "and talking to her. I did not
notice. Tell me how it happened."

D'Branin told him.

"Listen to me," Royd said. "Trust me, Karoly, and I will give you your
volcryn. Calm your people. Assure them that I am no threat. And keep
Lasamer drugged and quiescent, do you understand? That is very
important. He is the problem."

"Agatha advises much the same thing."

"I know," said Royd. "I agree with her. Will you do as I ask?"

"I do not know," d'Branin said. "You make it hard for me. I do not understand what is going wrong, my friend. Will you not tell me more?"

Royd Eris did not answer. His ghost waited.

"Well," d'Branin said at last, "you do not talk. How difficult you make it. How soon, Royd? How soon will we see my *volcryn?*"

"Quite soon," Royd replied. "We will drop out of drive in approximately seventy hours."

"Seventy hours," d'Branin said. "Such a short time. Going back would gain us nothing." He moistened his lips, lifted his cup, found it empty. "Go on, then. I will do as you bid. I will trust you, keep Lasamer drugged; I will not tell the others of your spying. Is that enough, then? Give me my *volcryn.* I have waited so long!"

"I know," said Royd Eris. "I know."

Then the ghost was gone, and Karoly d'Branin sat alone in the darkened lounge. He tried to refill his cup, but his hand began to tremble unaccountably, and he poured the chocolate over his fingers and dropped the cup, swearing, wondering, hurting.

The next day was a day of rising tensions and a hundred small irritations. Lindran and Dannel had a "private" arguement that could be overheard through half the ship. A three-handed war game in the lounge ended in disaster when Christopheris accused Melantha Jhirl of cheating. Lommie Thorne complained of unusual difficulties in tying her system into the shipboard computers. Alys Northwind sat in the lounge for hours, staring at her bandaged finger with a look of sullen hatred on her face. Agatha Marij-Black prowled through the corridors, complaining that the ship was too hot, that her joints throbbed, that the air was thick and full of smoke, that the ship was too cold. Even Karoly d'Branin was despondent and on edge.

Only the telepath seemed content. Shot full of psionine-4, Thale Lasamer was often sluggish and lethargic, but at least he no longer flinched at shadows.

Royd Eris made no appearance, either by voice or holographic projection.

He was still absent at dinner. The academicians ate uneasily, expecting him to materialize at any moment, take his accustomed place, and join in the mealtime conversation. Their expectations were still unfulfilled when the afterdinner pots of chocolate and spiced tea and coffee were set on the table.

"Our captain seems to be occupied," Melantha Jhirl observed, leaning back in her chair and swirling a snifter of brandy.

"We will be shifting out of drive soon," Karoly d'Branin said. "Undoubtedly there are preparations to make." Secretly he fretted over Royd's absence and wondered if they were being watched even now.

Rojan Christopheris cleared his throat. "Since we're all here and he's not, perhaps this is a good time to discuss certain things. I'm not concerned about him missing dinner. He doesn't eat. He's a damned holograph. What does it matter? Maybe it's just as well; we need to talk about this. Karoly, a lot of us have been getting uneasy about Royd Eris. What do you know about this mystery man, anyway?"

"Know, my friend?" D'Branin refilled his cup with the thick bitter-sweet chocolate and sipped at it slowly, trying to give himself a moment to think. "What is there to know?"

"Surely you've noticed that he never comes out to play with us," Lindran said dryly. "Before you engaged his ship, did anyone remark on this quirk of his?"

"I'd like to know the answer to that one, too," said Dannel, the other linguist. "A lot of traffic comes and goes through Avalon. How did you come to choose Eris? What were you told about him?"

"Told about him? Very little, I must admit. I spoke to a few port officials and charter companies, but none of them was acquainted with Royd. He had not traded out of Avalon originally, you see."

"How convenient," said Lindran.

"How suspicious," added Dannel.

"Where *is* he from, then?" Lindran demanded. "Dannel and I have listened to him pretty carefully. He speaks standard very flatly, with no discernible accent, no idiosyncrasies to betray his origins."

"Sometimes he sounds a bit archaic," Dannel put in, "and from time to time one of his constructions will give me an association. Only it's a different one each time. He's traveled a lot."

"Such a deduction," Lindran said, patting his hand. "Traders frequently do, love. Comes of owning a starship."

Dannel glared at her, but Lindran just went on. "Seriously, though, do you know anything about him? Where did this nightflyer of ours come from?"

"I do not know," d'Branin admitted. "I—I never thought to ask."

The members of his research team glanced at each other incredulously. "You never thought to *ask?*" Christopheris said. "How did you come to select this ship?"

"It was available. The administrative council approved my project and assigned me personnel, but they could not spare an Academy ship.

There were budgetary constraints as well."

Agatha Marij-Black laughed sourly. "What d'Branin is telling those of you who haven't figured it out is that the Academy was pleased with his studies in xenomyth, with the discovery of the *volcryn* legend, but less than enthusiastic about his plan to seek them out. So they gave him a small budget to keep him happy and productive, assuming this little mission would be fruitless, and they assigned him people who wouldn't be missed back on Avalon." She looked around. "Look at the lot of you. None of us had worked with d'Branin in the early stages, but we were all available for this jaunt. And not a one of us is a first-rate scholar."

"Speak for yourself," Melantha Jhirl said. "I volunteered for this mission."

"I won't argue the point," the psipsych said. "The crux is that the choice of the *Nightflyer* is no large enigma. You just engaged the cheapest charter you could find, didn't you, d'Branin?"

"Some of the available ships would not consider my proposition," d'Branin said. "The sound of it is odd, we must admit. And many shipmasters have an almost superstitious fear of dropping out of drive in interstellar space, without a planet near. Of those who would agree to the conditions, Royd Eris offered the best terms, and he was able to leave at once."

"And we *had* to leave at once," said Lindran. "Otherwise the *volcryn* might get away. They've only been passing through this region for ten thousand years, give or take a few thousand."

Someone laughed. D'Branin was nonplussed. "Friends, no doubt I could have postponed departure. I admit I was eager to meet my *volcryn*, to see their great ships and ask them all the questions that have haunted me, to discover the why of them. But I admit also that a delay would have been no great hardship. But why? Royd has been a gracious host, a good pilot. We have been treated well."

"Did you meet him?" Alys Northwind asked. "When you were making your arrangements, did you ever see him?"

"We spoke many times, but I was on Avalon, and Royd in orbit. I saw his face on my viewscreen."

"A projection, a computer simulation, could be anything," Lommie Thorne said. "I can have my system conjure up all sorts of faces for your viewscreen, Karoly."

"No one has ever seen this Royd Eris," Christopheris said. "He has made himself a cipher from the start."

"Our host wishes his privacy to remain inviolate," d'Branin said.

"Evasions," Lindran said. "What is he hiding?"

Melantha Jhirl laughed. When all eyes had moved to her, she grinned and shook her head. "Captain Royd is perfect—a strange man for a strange mission. Don't any of you love a mystery? Here we are flying light-years to intercept a hypothetical alien starship from the core of the galaxy, that has been outward bound for longer than humanity has been having wars, and all of you are upset because you can't count the warts on Royd's nose." She leaned across the table to refill her brandy snifter. "My mother was right," she said lightly. "Normals are subnormal."

"Maybe we should listen to Melantha," Lommie Thorne said thoughtfully. "Royd's foibles and neuroses are his business, if he does not impose them on us."

"It makes me uncomfortable," Dannel complained weakly.

"For all we know," said Alys Northwind, "we might be traveling with a criminal or an alien."

"*Jupiter*," someone muttered. The xenotech flushed red and there was sniggering around the long table.

But Thale Lasamer looked up furtively from his plate and giggled. "An *alien*," he said. His blue eyes flicked back and forth in his skull as if seeking escape. They were bright and wild.

Marij-Black swore. "The drug is wearing off," she said quickly to d'Branin. "I'll have to go back to my cabin to get some more."

"What drug?" Lommie Thorne demanded. D'Branin had been careful not to tell the others too much about Lasamer's ravings, for fear of inflaming the shipboard tensions. "What's going on?"

"Danger," Lasamer said. He turned to Lommie, sitting next to him, and grasped her forearm hard, his long painted fingernails clawing at the silvery metal of her shirt. "We're in danger, I tell you, I'm reading it. Something *alien*. It means us ill. Blood, I see blood." He laughed. "Can you taste it, Agatha? I can almost taste the blood. *It* can too."

Marij-Black rose. "He's not well," she announced to the others. "I've been dampening him with psionine, trying to hold his delusions in check. I'll get some more." She started toward the door.

"Dampening him?" Christopheris said, horrified. "He's warning us of something. Don't you hear him? I want to know what it *is*."

"Not psionine," said Melantha Jhirl. "Try esperon."

"Don't tell me my job, woman!"

"Sorry," Melantha said. She gave a modest shrug. "I'm one step ahead of you, though. Esperon might exorcise his delusions, no?"

"Yes, but—"

"And it might help him focus on this threat he claims to detect, correct?"

"I know the characteristics of esperon quite well," the psipsych said testily.

Melantha smiled over the rim of her brandy glass. "I'm sure you do. Now listen to me. All of you are anxious about Royd, it seems. You can't stand not knowing whatever it is he's concealing. Rojan has been making up stories for weeks, and he's ready to believe any of them. Alys is so nervous she cut her finger off. We're squabbling constantly. Fears like that won't help us work together as a team. Let's end them. Easy enough." She pointed to Thale. "Here sits a class-one telepath. Boost his power with esperon and he'll be able to recite our captain's life history to us until we're all suitably bored with it. Meanwhile he'll also be vanquishing his personal demons."

"He's watching us," the telepath said in a low, urgent voice.

"No," said Karoly d'Branin, "we must keep Thale dampened."

"Karoly," Christopheris said, "this has gone too far. Several of us are nervous, and this boy is terrified. I believe we all need an end to the mystery of Royd Eris. For once Melantha is right."

"We have no right," d'Branin said.

"We have the need," said Lommie Thorne. "I agree with Melantha."

"Yes," echoed Alys Northwind. The two linguists were nodding.

D'Branin thought regretfully of his promise to Royd. They were not giving him any choice. His eyes met those of the psipsych and he signed. "Do it, then," he said. "Get him the esperon."

"He's going to kill me!" Thale Lasamer screamed. He leaped to his feet, and when Lommie Thorne tried to calm him with a hand on his arm, he seized a cup of coffee, and threw it square in her face. It took three of them to hold him down.

"Hurry," Christopheris barked as the telepath struggled.

Marij-Black shuddered and left the lounge.

When she returned, the others had lifted Lasamer to the table and forced him down, pulling aside his long pale hair to bare the arteries in his neck.

Marij-Black moved to his side.

"Stop that," Royd said. "There is no need."

His ghost shimmered into being in its empty chair at the head of the long dinner table. The psipsych froze in the act of slipping an ampule of esperon into her injection gun, and Alys Northwind started visibly and released one of Lasamer's arms. The captive did not pull free. He lay on the table, breathing heavily, his pale blue eyes fixed glassily on Royd's projection, transfixed by the vision of his sudden materialization.

Melantha Jhirl lifted her brandy glass in salute. "Boo," she said. "You've missed dinner, captain."

"Royd," said Karoly d'Branin, "I am sorry."

The ghost stared unseeing at the far wall. "Release him," said the voice from the communicators. "I will tell you my great secrets, if my privacy intimidates you so."

"He *has* been watching us," Dannel said.

"We're listening," Northwind said suspiciously. "What are you?"

"I liked your guess about the gas giants," Royd said. "Sadly, the truth is less dramatic. I am an ordinary *Homo Sapien* in middle age. Sixty-eight standard, if you require precision. The holograph you see before you is the real Royd Eris, or was so some years ago. I am somewhat older now, but I use computer simulation to project a more youthful apperance to my guests."

"Oh?" Lommie Thorne's face was red where the coffee had scalded her. "Then why the secrecy?"

"I will begin the tale with my mother," Royd replied. "The *Nightflyer* was her ship originally, custom-built to her design in the Newholme spaceyards. My mother was a freetrader, a notably successful one. She was born trash on a world called Vess, which is a very long way from here, although perhaps some of you have heard of it. She worked her way up, position by position, until she won her own command. She soon made a fortune through a willingness to accept the unusual consignment, fly off the major trade routes, take her cargo a month or a year or two years beyond where it was customarily transferred. Such practices are riskier but more profitable than flying the mail runs. My mother did not worry about how often she and her crews returned home. Her ships were her home. She forgot about Vess as soon as she left it, and seldom visited the same world twice if she could avoid it."

"Adventurous," Melantha Jhirl said.

"No," said Royd. "Sociopathic. My mother did not like people, you see. Not at all. Her crews had no love for her, nor she for them. Her one great dream was to free herself from the necessity of crew altogether. When she grew rich enough, she had it done. The *Nightflyer* was the result. After she boarded it at Newholme, she never touched a human being again, or walked a planet's surface. She did all her business from the compartments that are now mine, by viewscreen or lasercom. You would call her insane. You would be right." The ghost smiled faintly. "She did have an interesting life, though, even after her isolation. The worlds she saw, Karoly! The things she might have told you would break your heart, but you'll never hear them. She destroyed most of her records for fear that other people might get some use or pleasure from her experiences after her death. She was like that."

"And you?" asked Alys Northwind.

"She must have touched at least *one* other human being," Lindran put in, with a smile.

"I should not call her my mother," Royd said. "I am her cross-sex clone. After thirty years of flying this ship alone, she was bored. I was to be her companion and lover. She could shape me to be a perfect diversion. She had no patience with children, however, and no desire to raise me herself. After she had done the cloning, I was sealed in a nurturant tank, an embryo linked into her computer. It was my teacher. Before birth and after. I had no birth, really. Long after the time a normal child would have been born, I remained in the tank, growing, learning, on slowtime, blind and dreaming and living through tubes. I was to be released when I had attained the age of puberty, at which time she guessed I would be fit company."

"How horrible," Karoly d'Branin said. "Royd, my friend, I did not know."

"I'm sorry, captain." Melantha Jhirl said. "You were robbed of your childhood."

"I never missed it," Royd said. "Nor her. Her plans were all futile, you see. She died a few months after the cloning, when I was still a fetus in the tank. She had programmed the ship for such an eventuality, however. It dropped out of drive and shut down, drifted in interstellar space for eleven standard years while the computer made me—" He stopped, smiling. "I was going to say *while the computer made me a human being.* Well. While the computer made me whatever I am, then. That was how I inherited the *Nightflyer.* When I was born, it took me some months to acquaint myself with the operation of the ship and my own origins."

"Fascinating," said Karoly d'Branin.

"Yes," said the linquist Lindran, "but it doesn't explain why you keep yourself in isolation."

"Ah, but it does," Melantha Jhirl said. "Captain, perhaps you should explain further for the less improved models?"

"My mother hated planets," Royd said. "She hated stinks and dirt and bacteria, the irregularity of the weather, the sight of other people. She engineered for us a flawless environment, as sterile as she could possibly make it. She disliked gravity as well. She was accustomed to weightlessness from years of service on ancient freetraders that could not afford gravity grids, and she preferred it. These were the conditions under which I was born and raised.

"My body has no immune systems, no natural resistance to anything. Contact with any of you would probably kill me, and would certainly make me very sick. My muscles are feeble, in a sense atrophied. The gravity the *Nightflyer* is now generating is for your comfort, not mine. To me it is agony. At this moment the real me is seated in a floating chair that supports my weight. I still hurt, and my internal organs may be suffering damage. It is one reason I do not often take on passengers."

"You share your mother's opinion of the run of humanity?" asked Marij-Black.

"I do not. I like people. I accept what I am, but I did not choose it. I experience human life in the only way I can—vicariously. I am a voracious consumer of books, tapes, holoplays, fictions and drama and histories of all sorts. I have experimented with dreamdust. And infrequently, when I dare, I carry passengers. At those times I drink in as much of their lives as I can."

"If you kept your ship under weightlessness at all times, you could take on more riders," suggested Lommie Thorne.

"True," Royd said politely. "I have found, however, that most planet-born are as uncomfortable weightless as I am under gravity. A ship master who does not have artificial gravity, or elects not to use it, attracts few riders. The exceptions often spend much of the voyage sick or drugged. No. I could also mingle with my passengers, I know, if I kept to my chair and wore a sealed environwear suit. I have done so. I find it lessens my participation instead of increasing it. I become a freak, a maimed thing, one who must be treated differently and kept at a distance. These things do not suit my purpose. I prefer isolation. As often as I dare, I study the aliens I take on as riders."

"Aliens?" Northwind's voice was confused.

"You are all aliens to me," Royd answered.

Silence filled the *Nightflyer's* lounge.

"I am sorry this has happened, my friend," Karoly d'Branin said. "We ought not have intruded on your personal affairs."

"Sorry," muttered Agatha Marij-Black. She frowned and pushed the ampule of esperon into the injection chamber. "Well, it's glib enough, but is it the truth? We still have no proof, just a new bedtime story. The holograph could have claimed it was a creature from Jupiter, a computer, or a diseased war criminal just as easily. We have no way of verifying anything that he's said. No—we have *one* way, rather." She took two quick steps forward to where Thale Lasamer lay on the table. "He still needs treatment and we still need confirmation, and I don't see any sense in stopping now after we've gone this far. Why should we live with all this anxiety if we can end it all now?" Her hand pushed the telepath's unresisting head to one side. She found the artery and pressed the gun to it.

"Agatha," said Karoly d'Branin. "Don't you think . . . perhaps we should forego this, now that Royd . . .?"

"No," Royd said. "Stop. I order it. This is my ship. Stop, or . . ."

" . . . or what?" The gun hissed loudly, and there was a red mark on the telepath's neck when she lifted it away.

Lasamer raised himself to a half-sitting position, supported by his elbows, and Marij-Black moved close to him. "Thale," she said in her best professional tones, "focus on Royd. You can do it; we all know how good you are. Wait just a moment. The esperon will open it all up for you."

His pale blue eyes were clouded. "Not close enough," he muttered. "One, I'm one, tested. Good, you know I'm good, but I got to be *close.*" He trembled.

The psipsych put an arm around him, stroked him, coaxed him. "The esperon will give you range, Thale," she said. "Feel it, feel yourself grow stronger. Can you feel it? Everything's getting clear, isn't it?" Her voice was a reassuring drone. "You can hear what I'm thinking, I know you can, but never mind that. The others, too, push them aside, all that chatter, thoughts, desires, fear. Push it all aside. Remember the danger now? Remember? Go find it, Thale, go find the danger. Look beyond the wall there, tell us what it's like beyond the wall. Tell us about Royd. Was he telling the truth? Tell us. You're good, we all know that, you can tell us." The phrases were almost an incantation.

He shrugged off her support and sat upright by himself. "I can feel it," he said. His eyes were suddenly clearer. "Something—my head hurts— I'm *afraid!*"

"Don't be afraid," said Marij-Black. "The esperson won't make your head hurt; it just makes you better. We're all here with you. Nothing to fear." She stroked his brow. "Tell us what you see."

Thale Lasamer looked at Royd's ghost with terrified little-boy eyes, and his tongue flicked across his lower lips. "He's—"

Then his skull exploded.

Hysteria and confusion.

The telepath's head had burst with awful force, splattering them all with blood and bits of bone and flesh. His body thrashed madly on the tabletop for a long instant, blood spurting from the arteries in his neck in a crimson stream, his limbs twitching in a macabre dance. His head had simply ceased to exist, but he would not be still.

Agatha Marij-Black, who had been standing closest to him, dropped her injection gun and stood slack-mouthed. She was drenched with his blood, covered with pieces of flesh and brain. Beneath her right eye a long sliver of bone had penetrated her skin, and her own blood was mingling with his. She did not seem to notice.

Rojan Christopheris fell over backward, scrambled to his feet, and pressed himself hard against the wall.

Dannel screamed, and screamed, and screamed, until Lindran slapped him hard across a blood-smeared check and told him to be quiet.

Alys Northwind dropped to her knees and began to mumble a prayer in a strange tongue.

Karoly d'Branin sat very still, staring, blinking, his chocolate cup forgotten in his hand.

"Do something," Lommie Thorne moaned. "Somebody *do* something." One of Lasamer's arms moved feebly and brushed against her. She shrieked and pulled away.

Melantha Jhirl pushed aside her brandy snifter.

"Control yourself," she snapped. "He's dead; he can't hurt you."

They all looked at her, but for d'Branin and Marij-Black, both of whom seemed frozen in shock. Royd's projection had vanished at some point, Melantha realized suddenly. She began to give orders. "Dannel, Lindran, Rojan—find a sheet or something to wrap him in, and get him out of here. Alys, you and Lommie get some water and sponges. We've got to clean up." Melantha moved to d'Branin's side as the others rushed to do as she had told them. "Karoly," she said, putting a gentle hand on his shoulder, "are you all right, Karoly?"

He looked up at here, gray eyes blinking. "I—yes, yes, I am —I told her not to go ahead, Melantha. I told her."

"Yes, you did," Melantha Jhirl said. She gave him a reassuring pat and moved around the table to Agatha Marij-Black. "Agatha," she called. But the psipsych did not respond, not even when Melantha shook her bodily by the shoulders. Her eyes were empty. "She's in shock," Melantha announced. She frowned at the sliver of bone protruding from Marij-Black's cheek. Sponging off her face with a napkin, she carefully removed the splinter.

"What do we do with the body?" asked Lindran. They had found a sheet and wrapped it up. It had finally stopped twitching, although blood continued to seep out, turning the concealing sheet red.

"Put it in a cargo hold," suggested Christopheris.

"No," Melantha said, "not sanitary. It will rot." She thought for a moment. "Suit up and take it down to the driveroom. Cycle it through and lash it in place somehow. Tear up the sheet if you have to. That section of the ship is vacuum. It will be best there."

Christopheris nodded, and the three of them moved off, the dead weight of Lasamer's corpse supported between them. Melantha turned back to Marij-Black, but only for an instant. Lommie Thorne, who was mopping the blood from the tabletop with a piece of cloth, suddenly began to retch violently. Melantha swore. "Someone help her," she snapped.

Karoly d'Branin finally seemed to stir. He rose and took the blood-soaked cloth from Lommie's hand and led her away back to his cabin.

"I can't do this alone," whined Alys Northwind, turning away in disgust.

"Help me, then," Melantha said. Together she and Northwind half-led and half-carried the psipsych from the lounge, cleaned her and undressed her, and put her to sleep with a shot of one of her own drugs. Afterward Melantha took the injection gun and made the rounds. Northwind and Lommie Thorne required mild tranquilizers, Dannel a somewhat stronger one.

It was three hours before they met again.

The survivors assembled in the largest of the cargo holds, where three of them hung their sleepwebs. Seven of eight attended. Agatha Marij-Black was still unconscious, sleeping or in a coma or deep shock; none of them was sure. The rest seemed to have recovered, though their faces were pale and drawn. All of them had changed clothes, even Alys Northwind, who had slipped into a new jumpsuit identical to the old one.

"I do not understand," Karoly d'Branin said. "I do not understand what . . ."

"Royd killed him, is all," Northwind said bitterly. "His secret was endangered, so he just—just blew him apart. We all saw it."

"I cannot believe that," Karoly d'Branin said in an anguished voice. "I cannot. Royd and I, we have talked many a night when the rest of you were sleeping. He is gentle, inquisitive, sensitive. A dreamer. He understands about the *volcryn.* He would not do such a thing, could not."

"His projection certainly winked out quick enough when it happened," Lindran said. "And you'll notice he hasn't had much to say since."

"The rest of us haven't been unusually talkative either," said Melantha Jhirl. "I don't know what to think, but my impulse is to side with Karoly. We have no proof that the captain was responsible for Thale's death. There's something here none of us understands yet."

Alys Northwind grunted. "Proof," she said disdainfully.

"In fact," Melantha continued unperturbed, "I'm not even sure *anyone* is responsible. Nothing happened until he was given the esperon. Could the drug be at fault?"

"Hell of a side effect," Lindran muttered

Rojan Christopheris frowned. "This is not my field, but I would think no. Esperon is extremely potent, with both physical and psionic side effects verging on the extreme, but not *that* extreme."

"What, then?" said Lommie Thorne. "What killed him?"

"The instrument of death was probably his own talent," the xenobiologist said, "undoubtedly augmented by his drug. Besides boosting his principal power, his telepathic sensitivity, esperon would also tend to bring out other psi-talents that might have been latent in him."

"Such as?" Lommie demanded.

"Biocontrol. Telekinesis."

Melantha Jhirl was way ahead of him. "Esperon shoots blood pressure way up anyway. Increase the pressure in his skull even more by rushing all the blood in his body to his brain. Decrease the air pressure around his head simultaneously, using teke to induce a short-lived vacuum. Think about it."

They thought about it, and none of them liked it.

"Who could do such a thing?" Karoly d'Branin said. "It could only have been self-induced, his own talent wild out of control."

"Or turned against him by a greater talent," Alys Northwind said stubbornly.

"No human telepath has talent on that order, to seize control of someone else, body and mind and soul, even for an instant."

"Exactly," the stout xenotech replied. "No *human* telepath."

"Gas-giant people?" Lommie Thorne's tone was mocking.

Alys Northwind stared her down. "I could talk about Crey sensitives or *githyanki* soulsucks, name a half-dozen others off the top of my head, but I don't need to. I'll only name one. A Hrangan Mind."

That was a disquieting thought. All of them fell silent and stirred uneasily, thinking of the vast, inimicable power of a Hrangan Mind hidden in the command chambers of the *Nightflyer*, until Melantha Jhirl broke the spell with a short, derisive laugh. "You're frightening yourself with shadows, Alys," she said. "What you're saying is ridiculous if you stop to think about it. I hope that isn't too much to ask. You're supposed to be xenologists, the lot of you, experts in alien languages, psychology, biology, technology. You don't act the part. We warred with Old Hranga for a thousand years, but we *never* communicated successfully with a Hrangan Mind. If Royd Eris is a Hrangan, they've improved their conversational skills markedly in the centuries since the Colapse."

Alys Northwind flushed. "You're right," she said. "I'm jumpy."

"Friends," said Karoly d'Branin, "we must not let our actions be dictated by panic or hysteria. A terrible thing has happened. One of our colleagues is dead, and we do not know why. Until we do, we can only go on. This is no time for rash actions against the innocent. Perhaps, when we return to Avalon, an investigation will tell us what happened. The body is safe for examination, is it not?"

"We cycled it through the airlock into the driveroom," Dannel said. "It'll keep."

"And it can be studied closely on our return," d'Branin said.

"Which should be immediate," said Northwind. "Tell Eris to turn this ship around!"

D'Branin looked stricken. "But the *volcryn!* A week more and we shall know them, if my figures are correct. To return would take us six weeks. Surely it is worth one additional week to know that they exist? Thale would not have wanted his death to be for nothing."

"Before he died, Thale was raving about aliens, about danger," Northwind insisted. "We're rushing to meet some aliens. What if they're the danger? Maybe these *volcryn* are even more potent than a Hrangan Mind, and maybe they don't want to be met, or investigated, or observed. What about that, Karoly? You ever think about that? Those stories of yours– don't some of them talk about terrible things happening to the races that meet the *volcryn?*"

"Legends," d'Branin said. "Superstition."

"A whole Fyndii horde vanishes in one legend," Rojan Christopheris put in.

"We cannot put credence in these fears of others," d'Branin argued.

"Perhaps there's nothing to the stories," Northwind said, "but do you care to risk it? *I* don't. For what? Your sources may be fictional or exaggerated or wrong, your interpretations and computations may be in error, or they may have changed course—the *volcryn* may not even be within light-years of where we'll drop out."

"Ah," Melantha Jhirl said. "I understand. Then we shouldn't go on because they won't be there, and besides, they might be dangerous."

D'Branin smiled and Lindran laughed. "Not funny," protested Alys Northwind, but she argued no further.

"No," Melantha continued, "any danger we are in will not increase significantly in the time it will take us to drop out of drive and look about for *volcryn.* We have to drop out anyway, to reprogram for the shunt home. Besides, we've come a long way for these *volcryn,* and I admit to being curious." She looked at each of them in turn, but no one spoke. "We continue, then."

"And Royd?" demanded Christopheris. "What do we do about him?"

"What *can* we do?" said Dannel.

"Treat the captain as before," Melantha said decisively. "We should open lines to him and talk. Maybe now we can clear up some of the mysteries that are bothering us, if Royd is willing to discuss things frankly."

"He is probably as shocked and dismayed as we are, my friends," said d'Branin. "Possibly he is fearful that we will blame him, try to hurt him."

"I think we should cut through to his section of the ship and drag him out kicking and screaming," Christopheris said. "We have the tools. That would write a quick end to all our fears."

"It could kill Royd," Melantha said. "Then he'd be justified in anything he did to stop us. He controls this ship. He could do a great deal, if he decided we were his enemies." She shook her head vehemently. "No, Rojan, we can't attack Royd. We've got to reassure him. I'll do it, if no one else wants to talk to him." There were no volunteers. "All right. But I don't want any of you trying any foolish schemes. Go about your business. Act normally."

Karoly d'Branin was nodding agreement. "Let us put Royd and poor Thale from our minds, and concern ourselves with our work, with our preparations. Our sensory instruments must be ready for deployment as soon as we shift out of drive and reenter normal space, so we can find our quarry quickly. We must review everything we know of the *volcryn.*" He turned to the linguists and began discussing some of the preliminaries he expected of them, and in a short time the talk had turned to the *volcryn,* and bit by bit the fear drained out of the group.

Lommie Thorne sat listening quietly, her thumb absently rubbing her wrist implant, but no one noticed the thoughtful look in her eyes.

Not even Royd Eris, watching.

Melantha Jhirl returned to the lounge alone.

Someone had turned out the lights. "Captain?" she said softly.

He appeared to her, pale, glowing softly, with eyes that did not see. His clothes, filmy and out of date, were all shades of white and faded blue. "Hello, Melantha," the mellow voice said from the communicators as the ghost silently mouthed the same words.

"Did you hear, captain?"

"Yes," he said, his voice vaguely tinged by surprise. "I hear and I see everything on my *Nightflyer,* Melantha. Not only in the lounge, and not only when the communicators and viewscreens are on. How long have you known?"

"Known?" She smiled. "Since you praised Alys' gas-giant solution to the Roydian mystery. The communicators were not on that night. You had no way of knowing. Unless . . ."

"I have never made a mistake before," Royd said. "I told Karoly, but that was deliberate. I am sorry. I have been under stress."

"I believe you, captain," she said. "No matter. I'm the improved model, remember? I'd guessed weeks ago."

For a time Royd said nothing. Then: "When do you begin to reassure me?"

"I'm doing so right now. Don't you feel reassured yet?"

The apparition gave a ghostly shrug. "I am pleased that you and Karoly do not think I murdered that man. Otherwise, I am frightened. Things are getting out of control, Melantha. Why didn't she listen to me? I told Karoly to keep him dampened. I told Agatha not to give him that injection. I warned them."

"They were afraid, too," Melantha said. "Afraid that you were only trying to frighten them off, to protect some awful plan. I don't know. It was my fault, in a sense. I was the one who suggested esperon. I thought it would put Thale at ease and tell us something about you. I was curious." She frowned. "A deadly curiosity. Now I have blood on my hands."

Melantha's eyes were adjusting to the darkness in the lounge. By the faint light of the holograph, she could see the table where it had happened, dark streaks of drying blood across its surface among the plates and cups and cold pots of tea and chocolate. She heard a faint dripping as well and could not tell if it was blood or coffee. She shivered. "I don't like it in here."

"If you would like to leave, I can be with you wherever you go."

"No," she said. "I'll stay. Royd, I think it might be better if you were *not* with us wherever we go. If you kept silent and out of sight, so to speak. If I asked you to, would you shut off your monitors throughout the ship? Except for the lounge, perhaps. It would make the others feel better, I'm sure."

"They don't know."

"They will. You made that remark about gas giants in everyone's hearing. Some of them have probably figured it out by now."

"If I told you I had cut myself off, you would have no way of knowing whether it was the truth."

"I could trust you," Melantha Jhirl said.

Silence. The specter stared at her. "As you wish," Royd's voice said finally. "Everything off. Now I see and hear only in here. Now, Melantha, you must promise to control them. No secret schemes or attempts to breach my quarters. Can you do that?"

"I think so," she said.

"Did you believe my story?" Royd asked.

"Ah," she said. "A strange and wondrous story, captain. If it's a lie, I'll swap lies with you anytime. You do it well. If it's true, then you are a strange and wondrous man."

"It's true," the ghost said quietly. "Melantha . . ."

"Yes?"

"Does it bother you that I have . . . watched you? Watched you when you were not aware?"

"A little ," she said, "but I think I can understand it."

"I watched you copulating."

She smiled. "Ah," she said, "I'm good at it."

"I wouldn't know," Royd said. "You're good to watch."

Silence. She tried not to hear the steady, faint dripping off to her right.

"Yes," she said after a long hesitation.

"Yes? What?"

"Yes, Royd," she said, "I would probably sex with you if it were possible."

"How did you know what I was thinking?" Royd's voice was suddenly frightened, full of anxiety and something close to fear.

"Easy," Melantha said, startled. "I'm an improved model. It wasn't so difficult to figure out. I told you, remember? I'm three moves ahead of you."

"You're not a telepath, are you?"

"No," Melantha said. "No."

Royd considered that for a long time. "I believe I'm reassured," he said at last.

"Good," she said.

"Melantha," he added, "one thing. Sometimes it is not wise to be too many moves ahead. Do you understand?"

"Oh? No, not really. You frighten me. Now reassure me. Your turn, Captain Royd."

"Of what?"

"What happened in here? Really?"

Royd said nothing.

"I think you know something," Melantha said. "You gave up your secret to stop us from injecting Lasamer with esperon. Even after your secret was forfeit, you ordered us not to go ahead. Why?"

"Esperon is a dangerous drug," Royd said.

"More than that, captain," Melantha said. "You're evading. Who killed Thale Lasamer? Or is it *who?*"

"I didn't."

"One of us? The *volcryn?*"

Royd said nothing.

"Is there an alien aboard your ship, captain?"

Silence.

"Are we in danger? Am *I* in danger, captain? I'm not afraid. Does that make me a fool?"

"I like people," Royd said at last. "When I can stand it, I like to have passengers. I watch them, yes. It's not so terrible. I like you and Karoly especially. I won't let anything happen to you."

"What might happen?"

Royd said nothing.

"And what about the others, Royd? Christopheris and Northwind, Dannel and Lindran, Lommie Thorne? Are you taking care of them, too? Or only Karoly and me?"

No reply.

"You're not very talkative tonight," Melantha observed.

"I'm under strain," his voice replied. "And certain things you ask are safer not to know. Go to bed, Melantha Jhirl. We've talked long enough."

"All right, captain," she said. She smiled at the ghost and lifted her hand. His own rose to meet it. Warm dark flesh and pale radiance brushed, melded, were one. Melantha Jhirl turned to go. It was not until she was out in the corridor, safe in the light once more, that she began to tremble.

False midnight.

The talks had broken up, and one by one the academicians had gone to bed. Even Karoly d'Branin had retired, his appetite for chocolate quelled by his memories of the lounge.

The linguists had made violent, noisy love before giving themselves up to sleep, as if to reaffirm their life in the face of Thale Lasamer's grisly death. Rojan Christopheris had listened to music. But now they were all still.

The *Nightflyer* was filled with silence.

In the darkness of the largest cargo hold, three sleepwebs hung side by side. Melantha Jhirl twisted occasionally in her sleep, her face feverish, as if in the grip of some nightmare. Alys Northwind lay flat on her back snoring loudly, a reassuring wheeze of noise from her solid, meaty chest.

Lommie Thorne lay awake, thinking.

Finally she rose and dropped to the floor, nude, quiet, light and careful as a cat. She pulled on a tight pair of pants, slipped a wide-sleeved shirt of black metallic cloth over her head, belted it with a silver chain, shook out her short hair. She did not don her boots. Barefoot was quieter. Her feet were small and soft, with no trace of callous.

She moved to the middle sleepweb and shook Alys Northwind by her shoulder. The snoring stopped abruptly. "Huh?" the xenotech said. She grunted in annoyance.

"Come," whispered Lommie Thorne. She beckoned.

Northwind got heavily to her feet, blinking, and followed the cyber-neticist through the door and out into the corridor. She'd been sleeping in her jumpsuit, its seam open nearly to her crotch. She frowned and sealed it. "What the hell," she muttered. She was disarrayed and unhappy.

"There's a way to find out if Royd's story was true," Lommie Thorne said carefully. "Melantha won't like it, though. Are you game to try?"

"What?" Northwind asked. Her face betrayed her interest.

"Come," the cyberneticist said.

They moved silently through the ship to the computer room. The system was up, but dormant. They entered quietly; all empty. Currents of light ran silkily down crystalline channels in the data grids, meeting, joining, splitting apart again; rivers of wan, multihued radiance criss-crossing a black landscape. The chamber was dim, the only noise a buzz at the edge of human hearing, until Lommie Thorne moved through it, touching keys, tripping switches, directing the silent, luminescent currents. Bit by bit the machine woke.

"What are you *doing?*" Alys Northwind said.

"Karoly told me to tie in our system with the ship," Lommie Thorne replied as she worked. "I was told Royd wanted to study the *volcryn* data. Fine, I did it. Do you understand what that means?" Her shirt whispered in soft metallic tones when she moved.

Eagerness broke across the flat features of xenotech Alys Northwind. "The two systems are tied together!"

"Exactly. So Royd can find out about the *volcryn,* and we can find out about Royd." She frowned. "I wish I knew more about the *Nightflyer's* hardware, but I think I can feel my way through. This is a pretty sophisticated system d'Branin requisitioned."

"Can you take over from Eris?"

"Take over?" Lommie sounded puzzled. "You been drinking again, Alys?"

"No, I'm serious. Use your system to break into the ship's control, overwhelm Eris, countermand his orders, make the *Nightflyer* respond to us, down here. Wouldn't you feel safer if we were in control?"

"Maybe," the cyberneticist said doubtfully. "I could try, but why do that?"

"Just in case. We don't have to use the capacity. Just so we have it, if an emergency arises."

Lommie Thorne shrugged. "Emergencies and gas giants. I only want to put my mind at rest about Royd, whether he had anything to do with killing Lasamer." She moved over to a readout panel, where a half-dozen meter-square viewscreens curved around a console, and brought one of them to life. Long fingers ghosted through holographic keys that appeared and disappeared as she used them, the keyboard changing shape again and yet again. The cyberneticist's pretty face grew thoughtful and serious. "We're in," she said. Characters began to flow across a viewscreen, red flickerings in glassy black depths. On a second screen a schematic of the *Nightflyer* appeared, revolved, halved; its spheres shifted size and perspective at the whim of Lommie's fingers, and a line of numerals below gave the specifications. The cyberneticist watched, and finally froze both screens.

"Here," she said, "here's my answer about the hardware. You can dismiss your takeover idea, unless those gas-giant people of yours are going to help. The *Nightflyer's* bigger and smarter than our little system here. Makes sense, when you stop to think about it. Ship's all automated, except for Royd."

Her hands moved again, and two more display screens stirred. Lommie Thorne whistled and coaxed her search program with soft words of encouragement. "It looks as though there *is* a Royd, though. Configurations are all wrong for a robot ship. Damn, I would have bet anything." The characters began to flow again, Lommie watching the figures as they drifted by. "Here's life-support specs, might tell us something." A finger jabbed, and one screen froze yet again.

"Nothing unusual," Alys Northwind said in disappointment.

"Standard waste disposal. Water recycling. Food processor, with protein and vitamin supplements in stores." She began to whistle, "Tanks of Renny's moss and neograss to eat up the CO_2. Oxygen cycle, then. No methane or ammonia. Sorry about that."

"Go sex with a computer!"

The cyberneticist smiled. "Ever tried it?" Her fingers moved again. "What else should I look for? You're the tech—what would be a giveaway? Give me some ideas."

"Check the specs for nurturant tanks, cloning equipment, that sort of thing," the xenotech said. "That would tell us whether he was lying."

"I don't know," Lommie Thorne said. "Long time ago. He might have junked that stuff. No use for it."

"Find Royd's life history," Northwind said. "His mother s. Get a readout on the business they've done, all this alleged trading. They must have records. Account books, profit and loss, cargo invoices, that kind of thing." Her voice grew excited, and she gripped the cyberneticist from behind by her shoulders. "A log, a ship's log! There's got to be a log. Find it!"

"All right." Lommie Thorne whistled, happy, at ease with her system, riding the data winds, curious, in control. Then the screen in front of her turned a bright red and began to blink. She smiled, touched a ghost key, and the keyboard melted away and reformed under her. She tried another tack. Three more screens turned red and began to blink. Her smile faded.

"What is it?"

"Security," said Lommie Thorne. "I'll get through it in a second. Hold on." She changed the keyboard yet again, entered another search program, attached a rider in case it was blocked. Another screen flashed red. She had her machine chew the data she'd gathered, sent out another feeler. More red. Flashing. Blinking. Bright enough to hurt the eyes. All the screens were red now. "A good security program," she said with admiration. "The log is well protected."

Alys Northwind grunted. "Are we blocked?"

"Response time is too slow," Lommie Thorne said, chewing on her lower lip as she thought. "There's a way to fix that." She smiled and rolled back the soft black metal of her sleeve.

"What are you doing?"

"Watch," she said. She slid her arm under the console, found the prongs, jacked in.

"Ah," she said, low in her throat. The flashing red blocks vanished from her readout screens, one after the other, as she sent her mind coursing into the *Nightflyer's* system, easing through all the blocks. "Nothing like slipping past another system's security. Like slipping onto a man." Log entries were flickering past them in a whirling, blurring rush, too fast for Alys Northwind to read. But Lommie read them.

Then she stiffened. "Oh," she said. It was almost a whimper. "Cold," she said. She shook her head and it was gone, but there was a sound in her ears, a terrible whooping sound. "Damn," she said, "that'll wake everyone." She glanced up when she felt Alys's fingers dig painfully into her shoulder, squeezing, hurting.

A gray steel panel slid almost silently across the access to the corridor, cutting off the whooping cry of the alarm. "What?" Lommie Thorne said.

"That's an emergency airseal," said Alys Northwind in a dead voice. She knew starships. "It closes where they're about to load or unload cargo in vacuum."

Their eyes went to the huge curving outer airlock above their heads. The inner lock was almost completely open, and as they watched, it clicked into place, and the seal on the outer door cracked, and now it was open half a meter, sliding, and beyond was twisted nothingness so burning-bright it seared the eyes.

"Oh," said Lommie Thorne, as the cold coursed up her arm. She had stopped whistling.

Alarms were hooting everywhere. The passengers began to stir. Melantha Jhirl tumbled from her sleepweb and darted into the corridor, nude, frantic, alert. Karoly d'Branin sat up drowsily. The psipsych muttered fitfully in drug-induced sleep. Rojan Christopheris cried out in alarm.

Far away, metal crunched and tore, and a violent shudder ran through the ship, throwing the linguists out of their sleepwebs, knocking Melantha from her feet.

In the command quarters of the *Nightflyer* was a spherical room with featureless white walls, a lesser sphere—a suspended control console— floating in its center. The walls were always blank when the ship was in drive; the warped and glaring underside of spacetime was painful to behold.

But now darkness woke in the room, a holoscape coming to life, cold black and stars everywhere, points of icy unwinking brilliance, no up and no down and no direction, the floating control sphere the only feature in the simulated sea of night.

The *Nightflyer* had shifted out of drive.

Melantha Jhirl found her feet again and thumbed on a communicator. The alarms were still hooting, and it was hard to hear. "Captain," she shouted, "what's happening?"

"I don't know," Royd's voice replied. "I'm trying to find out. Wait."

Melantha waited. Karoly d'Branin came staggering out into the corridor, blinking and rubbing his eyes. Rojan Christopheris was not long behind him. "What is it? What's wrong?" he demanded, but Melantha just shook her head. Lindran and Dannel soon appeared as well. There was no sign of Marij-Black, Alys Northwind, or Lommie Thorne. The academicians looked uneasily at the seal that blocked cargo hold three. Finally Melantha told Christopheris to go look. He returned a few minutes later. "Agatha is still unconscious," he said, talking at the top of his voice to be heard over the alarms. "The drugs still have her. She's moving around, though. Crying out."

"Alys and Lommie?"

Christopheris shrugged. "I can't find them. Ask your friend Royd."

The communicator came back to life as the alarms died. "We have returned to normal space," Royd's voice said, "but the ship is damaged. Hold three, your computer room, was breached while we were under drive. It was ripped apart by the flux. The computer dropped us out of drive automatically, fortunately for us, or the drive forces might have torn my entire ship apart."

"Royd," said Melantha, "Northwind and Thorne are missing."

"It appears your computer was in use when the hold was breached," Royd said carefully. "I would presume them dead, although I cannot say that with certainty. At Melantha's request, I have deactivated most of my monitors, retaining only the lounge input. I do not know what transpired. But this is a small ship, and if they are not with you, we must assume the worst." He paused briefly. "If it is any consolation, they died swiftly and painlessly."

"You killed them," Christopheris said, his face red and angry. He started to say more, but Melantha slipped her hand firmly over his mouth. The two linguists exchanged a long, meaningful look.

"Do we know how it happened, captain?" Melantha asked.

"Yes," he said reluctantly.

The xenobiologist had taken the hint, and Melantha took away her hand to let him breathe. "Royd?" she prompted.

"It sounds insane, Melantha," his voice replied, "but it appears your colleagues opened the hold's loading lock. I doubt they did so deliberately, of course. They were using the system interface to gain entry to the *Nightflyer's* data storage and controls, and they shunted aside all the safeties."

"I see," Melantha said. "A terrible tragedy."

"Yes. Perhaps more terrible than you think. I have yet to discover the extent of damage to my ship."

"We should not keep you if you have duties to perform," Melantha said. "All of us are shocked, and it is difficult to talk now. Investigate the condition of your ship, and we'll continue our discussion at a more opportune time. Agreed?"

"Yes," said Royd.

Melantha turned off the communicator. Now, in theory, the device was dead; Royd could neither see nor hear them.

"Do you believe him?" Christopheris snapped.

"I don't know," Melantha Jhirl said, "but I do know that the other three cargo holds can all be flushed just as hold three was. I'm moving my sleepweb into a cabin. I suggest that those of you who are living in hold two do the same."

"Clever," Lindran said with a sharp nod of her head. "We can crowd in. It won't be comfortable, but I doubt that I'd sleep the sleep of angels in the holds after this."

"We should also get our suits out of storage in four," Dannel suggested. "Keep them close at hand. Just in case."

"If you wish," Melantha said. "It's possible that all the locks might pop open simultaneously. Royd can't fault us for taking precautions." She flashed a grim smile. "After today we've earned the right to act irrationally."

"This is no time for your damned jokes, Melantha," Christopheris said. He was still red-faced, and his tone was full of fear and anger. "Three people are dead, Agatha is perhaps deranged or catatonic, the rest of us are endangered—"

"Yes. And we still have no idea what is happening." Melantha pointed out.

"Royd Eris is killing us!" Christopheris shrieked. "I don't know who or what he is and I don't know if that story he gave us is true and I don't *care.* Maybe he's a Hrangan Mind or the avenging angel of the *volcryn* or the second coming of Jesus Christ. What the hell difference does it make? He's *killing* us!" He looked at each of them in turn. "Any one of us could be next," he added. "Any one of us. Unless... we've got to make plans, *do* something, put a stop to this once and for all."

"You realize," Melantha said gently, "that we cannot actually know whether the good captain has turned off his sensory inputs down here. He could be watching and listening to us right now. He isn't, of course. He said he wouldn't and I believe him. But we have only his word on that. Now, Rojan, you don't appear to trust Royd. If that's so, you can hardly put any faith in his promises. It follows, therefore, that from your own point of view, it might not be wise to say the things that you're saying." She smiled slyly. "Do you understand the implications of what I'm saying?"

Christopheris opened his mouth and closed it again, looking very like a tall, ugly fish. He said nothing, but his eyes moved furtively and his flush deepened.

Lindran smiled thinly. "I think he's got it," she said.

"The computer is gone, then," Karoly d'Branin said suddenly in a low voice.

Melantha looked at him. "I'm afraid so, Karoly."

D'Branin ran his fingers through his hair as if half aware of how untidy he looked. "The *volcryn*," he muttered. "How will we work without the computer?" He nodded to himself. "I have a small unit in my cabin, a wrist model, perhaps it will suffice. It *must* suffice; it must. I will get the figures from Royd, learn where we have dropped out. Excuse me, my friends. Pardon, I must go." He wandered away in a distracted haze, talking to himself.

"He hasn't heard a word we've said," Dannel said, incredulous.

"Think how distraught he'd be if *all* of us were dead," added Lindran. "Then he'd have no one to help him look for *volcryn*."

"Let him go," Melantha said. "He is as hurt as any of us, maybe more so. He wears it differently. His obsessions are his defense."

"Ah, And what is *our* defense?"

"Patience, maybe," said Melantha Jhirl. "All of the dead were trying to breach Royd's secret when they died. We haven't tried. Here we are discussing their deaths."

"You don't find that suspicious?" asked Lindran.

"Very," Melantha said. "I even have a method of testing my suspicions. One of us can make yet another attempt to find out whether our captain told us the truth. If he or she dies, we'll know." She shrugged. "Forgive me, however, if I'm not the one who tries. But don't let me stop you if you have the urge. I'll note the results with interest. Until then, I'm going to move out of the cargo hold and get some sleep." She turned and strode off, leaving the others to stare at each other.

"Arrogant bitch," Dannel observed almost conversationally after Melantha had left.

"Do you really think he can hear us?" Christopheris whispered to the two linguists.

"Every pithy word," Lindran said. She smiled at his discomfiture. "Come, Dannel, let's get to a safe area and back to bed."

He nodded.

"But," said Christopheris, "we have to *do* something. Make plans. Defenses."

Lindran gave him a final withering look and pulled Dannel off behind her down the corridor.

"Melantha? Karoly?"

She woke quickly, alert at the mere whisper of her name, fully awake almost at once, and sat up in the narrow single bed. Squeezed in beside her, Karoly d'Branon groaned and rolled over, yawning.

"Royd?" she asked. "Is it morning?"

"We are drifting in interstellar space three light-years from the nearest star, Melantha," replied the soft voice from the walls. "In such a context, the term *morning* has no meaning. But, yes, it is morning."

Melantha laughed. *"Drifting,* you said? How bad is the damage?"

"Serious, but not dangerous. Hold three is a complete ruin, hanging from my ship like half of a broken egg, but the damage was confined. The drives themselves are intact, and the *Nightflyer's* computers did not seem to suffer from your system's destruction. I feared they might. I have heard of phenomena like electronic death traumas."

D'Branin said, "Eh? Royd?"

Melantha stroked him affectionately. "I'll tell you later, Karoly," she said. "Go back to sleep. Royd, you sound serious. Is there more?"

"I am worried about our return flight, Melantha," Royd said. "When I take the *Nightflyer* back into drive, the flux will be playing directly on portions of the ship that were never engineered to withstand it. Our configurations are askew now. I can show you the mathematics of it, but the question of the flux forces is the vital one. The airseal across the access to hold three is a particular concern. I've run some simulations, and I don't know if it can take the stress. If it bursts, my whole ship will split apart in the middle. My engines will go shunting off by themselves, and the rest—Even if the life-supporting sphere remains intact, we will all soon be dead."

"I see. Is there anything we can do?"

"Yes. The exposed areas would be easy enough to reinforce. The outer hull is armored to withstand the warping forces, of course. We could mount it in place—a crude shield, but according to my projections, it would suffice. If we do it correctly, it will help correct our configurations as well. Large portions of the hull were torn loose when the locks opened, but they are still out there, most within a kilometer or two, and could be used."

At some point Karoly d'Branin had finally come awake. "My team has four vacuum sleds," he said. "We can retrieve those pieces for you, my friend."

"Fine, Karoly, but that is not my primary concern. My ship is self-repairing within certain limits, but this exceeds those limits by an order of magnitude. I will have to do this myself."

"You?" D'Branin was startled. "Royd, you said—that is, your muscles, your weakness   this work will be too much for you. Surely we can do this for you!"

Royd's reply was tolerant. "I am only a cripple in a gravity field, Karoly. Weightless, I am in my element, and I will be killing the

Nightflyer's gravity grid momentarily, to try to gather my own strength for the repair work. No, you misunderstand. I am capable of the work. I have the tools, including my own heavy-duty sled."

"I think I know what you are concerned about, captain," Melantha said.

"I'm glad," Royd said. "Perhaps then you can answer my question. If I emerge from the safety of my chambers to do this work, can you keep your colleagues from harming me?"

Karoly d'Branin was shocked. "Oh, Royd, Royd, how could you think such a thing? We are scholars, scientists, not—not criminals, or soldiers, or—or animals. We are human—how can you believe we would threaten you or do you harm?"

"Human," Royd repeated, "but alien to me, suspicious of me. Give me no false assurances, Karoly."

He sputtered. Melantha took him by the hand and bid him be quiet. "Royd," she said, "I won't lie to you. You'd be in some danger. But I'd hope that, by coming out, you'd make our friends joyously happy. They'd be able to see that you told the truth, see that you were only human." She smiled. "They *would* see that, wouldn't they?"

"They would," Royd said, "but would it be enough to offset their suspicions? They believe I am responsible for the deaths of the other three, do they not?"

"Believe is too strong a word. They suspect it, they fear it. They are frightened, captain, and with good cause. *I* am frightened."

"No more than I."

"I would be less frightened if I knew what *did* happen. Will you tell me?"

Silence.

"Royd, if—"

"I have made mistakes, Melantha," Royd said gravely. "But I am not alone in that. I did my best to stop the esperon injection, and I failed. I might have saved Alys and Lommie if I had seen them, heard them, known what they were about. But you made me turn off my monitors, Melantha. I cannot help what I cannot see. Why? If you saw three moves ahead, did you calculate these results?"

Melantha Jhirl felt briefly guilty. "Mea culpa, captain; I share the blame. I know that. Believe me, I know that. It is hard to see three moves ahead when you do not know the rules, however. Tell me the rules."

"I am blind and deaf," Royd said, ignoring her. "It is frustrating. I cannot help if I am blind and deaf. I am going to turn on the monitors again, Melantha. I am sorry if you do not approve. I want your approval, but I must do this with or without it. I have to *see.*"

"Turn them on," Melantha said thoughtfully. "I was wrong, captain. I should never have asked you to blind yourself. I did not understand the situation, and I overestimated my own power to control the others. A failing of mine. Improved models too often think they can do anything." Her mind was racing, and she felt almost sick; she had miscalculated, misled, and there was more blood on her hands. "I think I understand better now."

"Understand what?" Karoly d'Branin said, baffled.

"You do *not* understand," Royd said sternly. "Don't pretend that you do, Melantha Jhirl. Don't! It is not wise or safe to be too many moves ahead." There was something disturbing in his tone.

Melantha understood that, too.

"What?" Karoly said. "I do not understand."

"Neither do I," Melantha said carefully. "Neither do I, Karoly." She kissed him lightly. "None of us understands, do we?"

"Good," said Royd.

She nodded and put a reassuring arm around Karoly. "Royd," she said, "to return to the question of repairs—it seems to me you must do this work, regardless of what promises we can give you. You won't risk your ship by slipping back into drive in your present condition, and the only other option is to drift out here until we all die. What choice do we have?"

"I have a choice," Royd said with deadly seriousness. "I could kill all of you, if that were the only way to save myself and my ship."

"You could try," Melantha said.

"Let us have no more talk of death," d'Branin said.

"You are right, Karoly," Royd said. "I do not wish to kill any of you. But I must be protected."

"You will be," Melantha said. "Karoly can set the others to chasing your hull fragments. I'll be your protection. I'll stay by your side. If anyone tries to attack you, they'll have to deal with me. They won't find that easy. And I can assist you. The work will be done three times as fast."

Royd was polite. "It is my experience that most planet-born are clumsy and easily tired in weightlessness. It would be more efficient if I worked alone, although I will gladly accept your services as a body-guard."

"I remind you that I'm the improved model, captain," Melantha said. "Good in free-fall as well as in bed. I'll help."

"You are stubborn. As you will, then. In a few moments I shall depower the gravity grid. Karoly, go and prepare your people. Unship your vacuum sleds and suit up. I will exit the *Nightflyer* in three standard hours, after I have recovered from the pains of your gravity. I want all of you outside the ship before I leave. Is that condition understood?"

"Yes," said Karoly. "All except Agatha. She has not regained consciousness, friend; she will not be a problem."

"No," said Royd, "I meant *all* of you, including Agatha. Take her outside with you."

"But, Royd!" protested d'Branin.

"You're the captain," Melantha Jhirl said firmly. "It will be as you say; all of us outside. Including Agatha."

Outside. It was as though some vast animal had taken a bite out of the stars.

Melantha Jhirl waited on her sled close by the *Nightflyer* and looked at stars. It was not so very different out here in the depths of interstellar space. The stars were cold, frozen points of light; unwinking, austere, more chill and uncaring somehow than the same suns made to dance and twinkle by an atmosphere. Only the absence of a landmark primary reminded her of where she was: in the places between, where men and women and their ships do not stop, where the *volcryn* sail crafts impossibly ancient. She tried to pick out Avalon's sun, but she did not know where to search. The configurations were strange to her and she had no idea of how she was oriented. Behind her, before her, above, all around, the starfields stretched endlessly. She glanced down, or what seemed like down just then, beyond her feet and her sled and the *Nightflyer,* expecting still more alien stars. And the bite hit her with an almost physical force.

Melantha fought off a wave of vertigo. She was suspended above a pit, a yawning chasm in the universe, black, starless, vast.

Empty.

She remembered then: the Tempter's Veil. Just a cloud of dark gases, nothing really, galactic pollution that obscured the light from the stars of the Fringe. But this close at hand, it seemed immense, terrifying, and she had to break her gaze when she began to feel as if she were falling. It was a gulf beneath her and the frail silver-white shell of the *Nightflyer,* a gulf about to swallow them.

Melantha touched one of the controls on the sled's forked handle, swinging around so the Veil was to her side instead of beneath her. That seemed to help somehow. She concentrated on the *Nightflyer,* ignoring the looming wall of blackness beyond. It was the largest object in her universe, bright amid the darkness, ungainly, its shattered cargo sphere giving the whole craft an unbalanced cast.

She could see the other sleds as they angled through the black, tracking the missing pieces of hull, grappling with them, bringing them back. The linguistic team worked together, as always, sharing a sled. Rojan Christopheris was alone, working in a sullen silence. Melantha had to threaten him with physical violence before he agreed to join them. The xenobiologist was certain that it was all another plot, that once they were outside, the *Nightflyer* would slip into drive without them and leave them to lingering deaths. His suspicions were inflamed by drink, and there had been alcohol on his breath when Melantha and Karoly had finally forced him to suit up. Karoly had a sled, too, and a silent passenger, Agatha Marij-Black, freshly drugged and asleep in her vacuum suit, safely locked into place.

While her colleagues labored, Melantha Jhirl waited for Royd Eris, talking to the others occasionally over the comm link. The two linguists, unaccustomed to weightlessness, were complaining a good deal, and bickering as well. Karoly tried to soothe them frequently. Christopheris said little, and his few comments were edged and biting. He was still angry. Melantha watched him flit across her field of vision, a stick figure in form-fitting black armor standing erect at the controls of his sled.

Finally the circular airlock atop the foremost of the *Nightflyer's* major spheres dilated, and Royd Eris emerged.

She watched him approach, curious, wondering what he would look like. In her mind were a half dozen contradictory pictures. His genteel, cultured, too-formal voice sometimes reminded her of the dark aristocrats of her native Prometheus, the wizards who toyed with human genes and played baroque status games. At other times his naivete made her imagine him as an inexperienced youth. His ghost was a tired looking thin young man, and he was supposed to be considerably older than that pale shadow, but Melantha found it difficult to hear an old man talking when he spoke.

Melantha felt a nervous tingle as he neared. The lines of his sled and his suit were different from theirs, disturbingly so. Alien, she thought, and quickly squelched the thought. Such differences meant nothing. Royd's sled was large, a long oval plate with eight jointed grappling arms bristling from its underside like the legs of a metallic spider. A heavy-duty cutting laser was mounted beneath the controls, its snout jutting threateningly forward. His suit was far more massive than the carefully engineered Academy worksuits they wore, with a bulge between its shoulder blades that was probably a powerpack, and rakish radiant fins atop shoulders and helmet. It made him seem hulking; hunched and deformed.

But when he finally came near enough for Melantha to see his face, it was just a face.

White, very white, that was the predominant impression she got; white hair cropped very short, a white stubble around the sharply chiseled lines of his jaw, almost invisible eyebrows beneath which his eyes moved restlessly. His eyes were large and vividly blue, his best feature. His skin was pale and unlined, scarcely touched by time.

He looked wary, she thought. And perhaps a bit frightened.

Royd stopped his sled close to hers, amid the twisted ruin that had been cargo hold three, and surveyed the damage, the pieces of floating wreckage that had once been flesh, blood, glass, metal, plastic. Hard to distinguish now, all of them fused and burned and frozen together. "We have a good deal of work to do," he said. "Shall we begin?"

"First let's talk," she replied. She shifted her sled closer and reached out to him, but the distance was still too great, the width of the bases of the two vacuum sleds keeping them apart. Melantha backed off and turned herself over completely, so that Royd stood upside down in her world and she upside down in his. She moved to him again, positioning her sled directly over/under his. Their gloved hands met, brushed, parted. Melantha adjusted her altitude. Their helmets touched.

"Now I have touched you," Royd said, with a tremor in his voice. "I have never touched anyone before, or been touched."

"Oh, Royd. This isn't touching, not really. The suits are in the way. But I will touch you, *really* touch you. I promise you that."

"You can't. It's impossible."

"I'll find a way," she said firmly. "Now, turn off your comm. The sound will carry through our helmets."

He blinked and used his tongue controls and it was done.

"Now we can talk," she said. "Privately."

"I do not like this, Melantha," he said. "This is too obvious. This is dangerous."

"There is no other way. Royd, I *do* know."

"Yes," he said. "I knew you did. Three moves ahead, Melantha. I remember the way you play chess. But this is a more serious game, and you are safer if you feign ignorance."

"I understand that, captain. Other things I'm less sure about. Can we talk about them?"

"No. Don't ask me to. Just do as I tell you. You are in peril, all of you, but I can protect you. The less you know, the better I can protect you."

Through the transparent faceplates, his expression was somber.

She stared into his upside-down eyes. "It might be a second crew member, someone else hidden in your quarters, but I don't believe that. It's the ship, isn't it? Your ship is killing us. Not you. It. Only that doesn't make sense. You command the *Nightflyer.* How can it act independently? And why? What motive? And how was Thale Lasamer killed? The business with Alys and Lommie, that was easy, but a psionic murder? A starship with psi? I can't accept that. It can't be the ship. Yet it can't be anything else. Help me, captain."

He blinked, anguish behind his eyes. "I should never have accepted Karoly's charter, not with a telepath among you. It was too risky. But I wanted to see the *volcryn,* and he spoke of them so movingly." He sighed. "You understand too much already, Melantha. I can't tell you more, or I would be powerless to protect you. The ship is malfunctioning; that is all you need to know. It is not safe to push too hard. As long as I am at the controls, I think I can keep you and the others from harm. Trust me."

"Trust is a two-way bond," Melantha said.

Royd lifted his hand and pushed her away, then tongued his communicator back to life. "Enough gossip," he announced. "We have work to do. Come. I want to see just how improved you actually are."

In the solitude of her helmet, Melantha Jhirl swore softly.

With an irregular twist of metal locked beneath him in his sled's magnetic grip, Rojan Christopheris sailed back toward the *Nightflyer.* He was watching from a distance when Royd Eris emerged on his oversized work sled. He was closer when Melantha Jhirl moved to him, inverted her sled, and pressed her faceplate to Royd's. Christopheris listened to their soft exchange, heard Melantha promise to touch him, Eris, the *thing,* the killer. He swallowed his rage. Then they cut him out, cut all of them out, went off the open circuit. But still she hung there, suspended by that cipher in the hunchbacked spacesuit, faces pressed together like two lovers kissing.

Christopheris swept in close, unlocked his captive plate so it would drift toward them. "Here," he announced. "I'm off to get another." He tongued off his own comm and swore, and his sled slid around the spheres and tubes of the *Nightflyer.*

Somehow they were all in it together, Royd and Melantha and possibly old d'Branin as well, he thought sourly. She had protected Eris from the first, stopped them when they might have taken action together, found out who or what he was. He did not trust her. His skin crawled when he remembered that they had been to bed together. She and Eris were the same, whatever they might be. And now poor Alys was dead, and that fool Thorne and even that damned telepath, but still Melantha was with *him,* against them. Rojan Christopheris was deeply afraid, and angry, and half-drunk.

The others were out of sight, off chasing spinning wedges of half-slagged metal. Royd and Melantha were engrossed in each other, the ship abandoned and vulnerable. This was his chance. No wonder Eris had insisted that all of them precede him into the void; outside, isolated from the controls of the *Nightflyer,* he was only a man. A weak one at that.

Smiling a thin hard smile, Christopheris brought his sled curling around the cargo spheres, hidden from sight, and vanished into the gaping maw of the driveroom. It was a long tunnel, everything open to vacuum, safe from the corrosion of an atmosphere. Like most starships, the *Nightflyer* had a triple propulsion system, the gravfield for landing and lifting, useless away from the gravity well, the nukes for deep space sublight maneuverings, and the great stardrives themselves. The lights of his sled flickered past the encircling ring of nukes and sent long bright streaks along the sides of the closed cylinders of the stardrives, the huge engines that bent the stuff of spacetime, encased in webs of metal and crystal.

At the end of the tunnel was a great circular door, reinforced metal, closed: the main airlock.

Christopheris set the sled down, dismounted—pulling his boots free of the sled's magnetic grip with an effort—and moved to the airlock. This was the hardest part, he thought. The headless body of Thale Lasamer was tethered loosely to a massive support strut by the lock, like a grisly guardian of the way. The xenobiologist had to stare at it while he waited for the lock to cycle. Whenever he glanced away, somehow he would find his eyes creeping back to it. The body looked almost natural, as if it had never had a head. Christopheris tried to remember what Lasamer had looked like, but the features would not come to mind. He moved uncomfortably, but then the locked door slid open and he gratefully entered the chamber to cycle through.

He was alone in the *Nightflyer.*

A cautious man, Christopheris kept his suit on, though he collapsed the helmet and yanked loose the suddenly limp metallic fabric so it fell behind his back like a hood. He could snap it in place quickly enough if the need arose. In cargo hold four, where they had stored their equipment, the xenobiologist found what he was looking for: a portable cutting laser, charged and ready. Low power, but it would do.

Slow and clumsy in weightlessness, he pulled himself down the corridor into the darkened lounge.

It was chilly inside, the air cold on his cheeks. He tried not to notice. He braced himself at the door and pushed off across the width of the room, sailing above the furniture, which was all safely bolted into place. As he drifted toward his objective, something wet and cold touched his face. It startled him, but it was gone before he could quite make out what it was.

When it happened again, Christopheris snatched at it, caught it, and felt briefly sick. He had forgotten. No one had cleaned the lounge yet. The—the *remains* were still there, floating now, blood and flesh and bits of bone and brain. All around him.

He reached the far wall, stopped himself with his arms, pulled himself down to where he wanted to go. The bulkhead. The wall. No doorway was visible, but the metal couldn't be very thick. Beyond was the control room, the computer access, safety, power. Rojan Christopheris did not think of himself as a vindictive man. He did not intend to harm Royd Eris; that judgment was not his to make. He would take control of the *Nightflyer,* warn Eris away, make certain the man stayed sealed in his suit. He would take them all back without any more mysteries, any more killings. The Academy arbiters could listen to the story, and probe Eris, and decide the right and wrong of it, guilt and innocence, what should be done.

The cutting laser emitted a thin pencil of scarlet light. Christopheris smiled and applied it to the bulkhead. It was slow work, but he had patience. They would not have missed him, quiet as he'd been, and if they did they would assume he was off sledding after some hunk of salvage. Eris's repairs would take hours, maybe days, to finish. The bright blade of the laser smoked where it touched the metal. Christopheris applied himself diligently.

Something moved on the periphery of his vision, just a little flicker, barely seen. A floating bit of brain, he thought. A sliver of bone. A bloody piece of flesh, hair still hanging from it. Horrible things, but nothing to worry about. He was a biologist; he was used to blood and brains and flesh. And worse, and worse; he had dissected many an alien in his day, cutting through chitin and mucus, pulsing stinking food sacs and poisonous spines; he had seen and touched it all.

Again the motion caught his eye, teased at it. Not wanting to, Christopheris found himself drawn to look. He could not *not* look, somehow, just as he had been unable to ignore the headless corpse near the airlock. He looked.

It was an eye.

Christopheris trembled and the laser slipped sharply off to one side, so he had to wrestle with it to bring it back to the channel he was cutting. His heart raced. He tried to calm himself. Nothing to be frightened of. No one was home, and if Royd should return, well, he had the laser as a weapon and he had his suit on if an airlock blew.

He looked at the eye again, willing away his fear. It was just an eye, Thale Lasamer's eye, pale blue, bloody but intact, the same watery eye the boy had when alive, nothing supernatural. A piece of dead flesh, floating in the lounge amid other pieces of dead flesh. Someone should have cleaned up the lounge, Christopheris thought angrily. It was indecent to leave it like this, it was uncivilized.

The eye did not move. The other grisly bits were drifting on the air currents that flowed across the room, but the eye was still. It neither bobbed nor spun. It was fixed on him. Staring.

He cursed himself and concentrated on the laser, on his cutting. He had burned an almost straight line up the bulkhead for about a meter. He began another at right angles.

The eye watched dispassionately. Christopheris suddenly found he could not stand it. One hand released its grip on the laser, reached out, caught the eye, flung it across the room. The action made him lose balance. He tumbled backward, the laser slipping from his grasp, his arms flapping like the wings of some absurd heavy bird. Finally he caught an edge of the table and stopped himself.

The laser hung in the center of the room, floating amid coffee pots and pieces of human debris, still firing, turning slowly. That did not make sense. It should have ceased fire when he released it. A malfunction, Christopheris thought nervously. Smoke was rising where the thin line of the laser traced a path across the carpet.

With a shiver of fear, Christoperis realized that the laser was turning toward him.

He raised himself, put both hands flat against the table, pushed up out of the way, bobbing toward the ceiling.

The laser was turning more swiftly now.

He pushed away from the ceiling hard, slammed into a wall, grunted in pain, bounced off the floor, kicked. The laser was spinning quickly, chasing him. Christopheris soared, braced himself for another ricochet off the ceiling. The beam swung around, but not fast enough. He'd get it while it was still firing off in the other direction.

He moved close, reached, and saw the eye.

It hung just above the laser. Staring.

Rojan Christopheris made a small whimpering sound low in his throat, and his hand hesitated—not long, but long enough—and the scarlet beam came up and around.

Its touch was a light, hot caress across his neck.

It was more than an hour later before they missed him. Karoly d'Branin noticed his absence first, called for him over the comm link, and got no answer. He discussed it with the others.

Royd Eris moved his sled back from the armor plate he had just mounted, and through his helmet Melantha Jhirl could see the lines around his mouth grow hard.

It was just then that the noises began.

A shrill bleat of pain and fear, followed by moans and sobbing. Terrible wet sounds, like a man choking on his own blood. They all heard. The sounds filled their helmets. And almost clear amid the anguish was something that sounded like a word: "Help."

"That's Christopheris," a woman's voice said. Lindran.

"He's hurt," Dannel added. "He's crying for help. Can't you hear it?"

"Where—?" someone started.

"The ship," Lindran said. "He must have returned to the ship."

Royd Eris said, "the fool. No, I warned—"

"We're going to check," Lindran announced. Dannel cut free the hull fragment they had been bringing in, and it spun away, tumbling. Their sled angled down toward the *Nightflyer*.

"Stop," Royd said. "I'll return to my chambers and check from there, if you wish, but you may not enter the ship. Stay outside until I give you clearance."

The terrible sounds went on and on.

"Go to hell," Lindran snapped at him over the open circuit.

Karoly d'Branin had his sled in motion, too, hastening after the linguists, but he had been further out and it was a long way back to the ship. "Royd, what can you mean? We must help, don't you see? He is hurt—listen to him. Please, my friend."

"No," Royd said. "Karoly, stop! If Rojan went back to the ship alone, he is dead."

"How do you know that?" Dannel demanded. "Did you arrange it? Set traps in case we disobeyed you?"

"No," Royd said. "Listen to me. You can't help him now. Only I could have helped him, and he did not listen to me. Trust me. Stop." His voice was despairing.

In the distance d'Branin's sled slowed. The linguists' did not. "We've already listened to you too damn much, I'd say," Lindran said. She almost had to shout to be heard above the noises, the whimpers and moans, the awful wet sucking sounds, the distorted pleas for help. Agony filled their universe. "Melantha," Lindran continued, "keep Eris right where he is. We'll go carefully, find out what is happening inside, but I don't want him getting back to his controls. Understood?"

Melantha Jhirl hesitated. The sounds beat against her ears. It was hard to think.

Royd swung his sled around to face her, and she could feel the weight of his stare. "Stop them," he said. "Melantha, Karoly, order it. They will not listen to me. They do not know what they are doing." He was clearly in pain.

In his face Melantha found decision. "Go back inside quickly, Royd. Do what you can. I'm going to try to intercept them."

"Whose side are you on?" Lindran demanded.

Royd nodded to her across the gulf, but Melantha was already in motion. Her sled backed clear of the work area, congested with hull fragments and other debris, then accelerated briskly as she raced around the exterior of the *Nightflyer* toward the driveroom.

But even as she approached, she knew it was too late. The linguists were too close and already moving much faster than she was.

"*Don't,*" she said, authority in her tone. "Christopheris is dead."

"His ghost is crying for help, then," Lindran replied. "When they tinkered you together, they must have damaged the genes for hearing, bitch."

"The ship isn't safe."

"Bitch," was all the answer she got.

Karoly's sled pursued vainly. "Friends, you must stop, please, I beg it of you. Let us talk this out together."

The sounds were his only reply.

"I am your superior," he said. "I order you to wait outside. Do you hear me? I order it, I invoke the authority of the Academy of Human Knowledge. Please, my friends, please."

Melantha watched helplessly as Lindran and Dannel vanished down the long tunnel of the driveroom.

A moment later she halted her own sled near the waiting black mouth, debating whether she should follow them on into the *Nightflyer.* She might be able to catch them before the airlock opened.

Royd's voice, hoarse counterpoint to the sounds, answered her unvoiced question. "Stay, Melantha. Proceed no further."

She looked behind her. Royd's sled was approaching.

"What are you doing here? Royd, use your own lock. You have to get back inside!"

"Melantha," he said calmly, "I cannot. The ship will not respond to me. The lock will not dilate. The main lock in the driveroom is the only one with manual override. I am trapped outside. I don't want you or Karoly inside the ship until I can return to my console."

Melantha Jhirl looked down the shadowed barrel of the driveroom, where the linguists had vanished.

"What will—"

"Beg them to come back, Melantha. Plead with them. Perhaps there is still time."

She tried. Karoly d'Branin tried as well. The twisted symphony of pain and pleading went on and on, but they could not raise Dannel or Lindran at all.

"They've cut out their comm," Melantha said furiously. "They don't want to listen to us. Or that . . . that sound."

Royd's sled and d'Branin's reached her at the same time. "I do not understand," Karoly said. "Why can you not enter, Royd? What is happening?"

"It is simple, Karoly," Royd replied, "I am being kept outside until—until—"

"Yes?" prompted Melantha.

"—until mother is done with them."

The linguists left their vacuum sled next to the one that Christopheris had abandoned and cycled through the airlock in unseemly haste, with hardly a glance for the grim headless doorman.

Inside they paused briefly to collapse their helmets. "I can still hear him," Dannel said. The sounds were faint inside the ship.

Lindran nodded. "It's coming from the lounge. Hurry."

They kicked and pulled their way down the corridor in less than a minute. The sounds grew steadily louder, nearer. "He's in there," Lindran said when they reached the doorway.

"Yes," Dannel said, "but is he alone? We need a weapon. What if . . . Royd had to be lying. There *is* someone else on board. We need to defend ourselves."

Lindran would not wait. "There are two of us," she said. "Come *on!*" She launched herself through the doorway, calling Christopheris by name.

It was dark inside. What little light there was spilled through the door from the corridor. Her eyes took a long moment to adjust. Everything was confused; walls and ceilings and floor were all the same, she had no sense of direction. "Rojan," she called, dizzily. "Where are you?" The lounge seemed empty, but maybe it was only the light, or her sense of unease.

"Follow the sound," Dannel suggested. He hung in the door, peering warily about for a minute, and then began to feel his way cautiously down a wall, groping with his hands.

As if in response to his comment, the sobbing sounds grew suddenly louder. But they seemed to come first from one corner of the room, then from another.

Lindran, impatient, propelled herself across the chamber, searching. She brushed against a wall in the kitchen area, and that made her think of weapons, and Dannel's fears. She knew where the utensils were stored. "Here," she said a moment later, turning toward him. "Here, I've got a knife, that should thrill you." She flourished it and brushed against a floating bubble of liquid as big as her fist. It burst and reformed into a hundred smaller globules. One moved past her face, close, and she tasted it. Blood.

But Lasamer had been dead a long time. His blood ought to have dried by now, she thought.

"Oh, merciful god," said Dannel.

"What?" Lindran demanded. "Did you find him?"

Dannel was fumbling his way back toward the door, creeping along the wall like an oversized insect, back the way he had come. "Get out, Lindran," he warned. *"Hurry!"*

"Why?" She trembled despite herself. "What's wrong?"

"The screams," he said. "The wall, Lindran, the wall. The sounds."

"Your not making sense," she snapped. "Get hold of yourself."

He gibbered. "Don't you see? The sounds are coming from the *wall.* The communicator. Faked. Simulated." Dannel reached the door and dove through it, sighing audibly. He did not wait for her. He bolted down the corridor and was gone, pulling himself hand over hand wildly, his feet thrashing and kicking behind him.

Lindran braced herself and moved to follow.

The sounds came from in front of her, from the door. "Help me," it said, in Rojan Christopheris's voice. She heard moaning and that terrible wet choking sound, and she stopped.

From her side came a wheezing ghastly death rattle. "Ahhhh," it moaned, loudly, building in a counterpoint to the other noise. "Help me."

"Help me, help me, help me," said Christopheris from the darkness behind her.

Coughing and a weak groan sounded under her feet.

"Help me," all the voices chorused, "help me, help me, help me." Recordings, she thought, recordings being played back. "Help me, help me, help me, help me." All the voices rose higher and louder, and the words turned into a scream, and the scream ended in wet choking, in wheezes and gasps and death. Then the sounds stopped. Just like that; turned off.

Lindran kicked off, floated toward the door, knife in hand.

Something dark and silent crawled from beneath the dinner table and rose to block her path. She saw it clearly for a moment, as it emerged between her and the light. Rojan Christopheris, still in his vacuum suit, but with the helmet pulled off. He had something in his hand that he raised to point at her. It was a laser, Lindran saw, a simple cutting laser.

She was moving straight toward him, coasting, helpless. She flailed and tried to stop herself, but she could not.

When she got quite close, she saw that Rojan had a second mouth below his chin, a long blackened slash, and it was grinning at her, and little droplets of blood flew from it, wetly, as he moved.

Dannel rushed down the corridor in a frenzy of fear, bruising himself as he smashed off walls and doorways. Panic and weightlessness made him clumsy. He kept glancing over his shoulder as he fled, hoping to see Lindran coming after him, but terrified of what he might see in her stead. Every time he looked back, he lost his sense of balance and went tumbling again.

It took a long, *long* time for the airlock to open. As he waited, trembling, his pulse began to slow. The sounds had dwindled behind him, and there was no sign of pursuit. He steadied himself with an effort. Once inside the lock chamber, with the inner door sealed between him and the lounge, he began to feel safe.

Suddenly Dannel could barely remember why he had been so terrified.

And he was ashamed; he had run, abandoned Lindran. And for what? What had frightened him so? An empty lounge? Noises from the walls? A rational explanation for that forced itself on him all at once. It only meant that poor Christopheris was somewhere else in the ship, that's all, just somewhere else, alive and in pain, spilling his agony into a comm unit.

Dannel shook his head ruefully. He'd hear no end of this, he knew. Lindran liked to taunt him. She would never let him forget it. But at least he would return, and apologize. That would count for something.

Resolute, he reached out and killed the cycle on the airlock, then reversed it. The air that had been partially sucked out came gusting back into the chamber.

As the inner door rolled back, Dannel felt his fear return briefly, an instant of stark terror when he wondered what might have emerged from the lounge to wait for him in the corridors of the *Nightflyer.* He faced the fear and willed it away. He felt strong.

When he stepped out, Lindran was waiting.

He could see neither anger nor disdain in her curiously calm features, but he pushed himself toward her and tried to frame a plea for forgiveness anyway. "I don't know why I—"

With languid grace her hand came out from behind her back. The knife flashed up in a killing arc, and that was when Dannel finally noticed the hole burned in her suit, still smoking, just between her breasts.

"Your *mother?*" Melantha Jhirl said incredulously as they hung helpless in the emptiness beyond the ship.

"She can hear everything we say," Royd replied. "But at this point it no longer makes any difference. Rojan must have done something very foolish, very threatening. Now she is determined to kill you all."

"She, she, what do you mean?" D'Branin's voice was puzzled. "Royd, surely you do not tell us that your mother is still alive. You said she died even before you were born."

"She did, Karoly," Royd said. "I did not lie to you."

"No," Melantha said. "I didn't think so. But you did not tell us the whole truth either."

Royd nodded. "Mother is dead, but her—her spirit still lives, and animates my *Nightflyer.*" He sighed. "Perhaps it would be more fitting to say her *Nightflyer.* My control has been tenuous at best."

"Royd," d'Branin said, "spirits do not exist. They are not real. There is no survival after death. My *volcryn* are more real than any ghosts."

"I don't believe in ghosts either," said Melantha curtly.

"Call it what you will, then," Royd said. "My term is as good as any. The reality is unchanged by the terminology. My mother, or some part of my mother, lives in the *Nightflyer,* and she is killing all of you as she has killed others before."

"Royd, you do not make sense," d'Branin said.

"Quiet, Karoly. Let the captain explain."

"Yes," Royd said. "The *Nightflyer* is very—very advanced, you know.

Automated, self-repairing, large. It had to be, if mother were to be freed from the necessity of crew. It was built on Newholme, you will recall. I have never been there, but I understand that Newholme's technology is quite sophisticated. Avalon could not duplicate this ship, I suspect. There are few worlds that could."

"The point, captain?"

"The point—the point is the computers, Melantha. They had to be extraordinary. They are; believe me, they are. Crystal-matrix cores, lasergrid data retrieval, full sensory extension, and other—features."

"Are you trying to tell us that the *Nightflyer* is an Artificial Intelligence? Lommie Thorne suspected as much."

"She was wrong," Royd said. "My ship is not an Artificial Intelligence; not as I understand it. But it is something close. Mother had a capacity for personality impress built in. She filled the central crystal with her own memories, desires, quirks, her loves and her—her hates. That was why she could trust the computer with my education, you see? She knew it would raise me as she herself would, had she the patience. She programmed it in certain other ways as well."

"And you cannot deprogram, my friend?" Karoly asked.

Royd's voice was despairing. "I have *tried,* Karoly. But I am a weak hand at systems work, and the programs are very complicated, the machines very sophisticated. At least three times I have eradicated her, only to have her surface once again. She is a phantom program, and I cannot track her. She comes and goes as she will. A ghost, do you see? Her memories and her personality are so intertwined with the programs that run the *Nightflyer* that I cannot get rid of her without destroying the central crystal, wiping the entire system. But that would leave me helpless. I could never reprogram, and with the computers down, the entire ship would fail—drives, life support, everything. I would have to leave the *Nightflyer,* and that would kill me."

"You should have told us, my friend," Karoly d'Branin said. "On Avalon we have many cyberneticists, some very great minds. We might have aided you. We could have provided expert help. Lommie Thorne might have helped you."

"Karoly, I have *had* expert help. Twice I have brought systems specialists on board. The first one told me what I have just told you; that it was impossible without wiping the programs completely. The second had trained on Newholme. She thought she might be able to help me. Mother killed her."

"You are still holding something back," Melantha Jhirl said. "I understand how your cybernetic ghost can open and close airlocks at will and arrange other accidents of that nature. But how do you explain what she did to Thale Lasamer?''

"Ultimately I must bear the guilt," Royd replied. "My lonliness led me to a grievous error. I thought I could safeguard you, even with a telepath among you. I have carried other riders safely. I watch them constantly, warn them away from dangerous acts. If mother attempts to interfere, I countermand her directly from the master control console. That usually works. Not always. Usually. Before this trip she had killed only five times, and the first three died when I was quite young. That was how I learned about her, about her presence in my ship. That party included a telepath too.

"I should have known better, Karoly. My hunger for life has doomed you all to death. I overestimated my own abilities, and underestimated her fear of exposure. She strikes out when she is threatened, and telepaths are always a threat. They sense her, you see. A malign, looming presence, they tell me, something cool and hostile and in-human."

"Yes," Karoly d'Branin said, "yes, that was what Thale said. An alien; he was certain of it."

"No doubt she feels alien to a telepath used to the familiar contours of organic minds. Hers is not a human brain, after all. What it is I cannot say—a complex of crystallized memories, a hellish network of interlocking programs, a meld of circuitry and spirit. Yes, I can understand why she might feel alien."

"You still haven't explained how a computer program could explode a man's skull," Melantha said.

"You wear the answer between your breasts, Melantha."

"My whisperjewel?" she said, puzzled. She felt it then, beneath her vacuum suit and her clothing; a touch of cold, a vague hint of eroticism that made her shiver. It was as if his mention had been enough to make the gem come alive.

"I was not familiar with whisperjewels until you told me of yours," Royd said, "but the principle is the same. Esper-etched, you said. Then you know that psionic power can be stored. The central core of my computer is resonant crystal, many times larger than your tiny jewel. I think mother impressed it as she lay dying."

"Only an esper can etch a whisperjewel," Melantha said.

"You never asked the *why* of it, either of you," Royd said. "You never asked why mother hated people so. She was born gifted, you see. On Avalon she might have been a class one, tested and trained and honored, her talent nurtured and rewarded. I think she might have been very famous. She might have been stronger than a class one, but perhaps it is only after death that she acquired such power, linked as she is to the

Nightflyer.

"The point is moot. She was not born on Avalon. On Vess, her ability was seen as a curse, something alien and fearful. So they cured her of it. They used drugs and electroshock and hypnotraining that made her violently ill whenever she tried to use her talent. They used other less savory methods as well. She never lost her power, of course; only the ability to use it effectively, to control it with her conscious mind. It remained part of her, suppressed, erratic, a source of shame and pain, surfacing violently in times of great emotional stress. And half a decade of institutional care almost drove her insane. No wonder she hated people."

"What was her talent? Telepathy?"

"No. Oh, some rudimentary ability, perhaps. I have read that all psi talents have several latent abilities in addition to their one developed strength. But mother could not read minds. She had some empathy, although her cure had twisted it curiously, so that the emotions she felt literally sickened her. But her major strength, the talent they took five years to shatter and destroy, was teke."

Melantha Jhirl swore. "Of *course* she hated gravity! Telekinesis under weightlessness is—"

"Yes," Royd finished, "Keeping the *Nightflyer* under gravity tortures me, but it limits mother."

In the silence that followed that comment, each of them looked down the dark cylinder of the driveroom. Karoly d'Branin moved awkwardly on his sled. "Dannel and Lindran have not returned," he said.

"They are probably dead," Royd said dispassionately.

"What will we do, then? We must plan. We cannot wait here indefinitely."

"The first question is what *I* can do," Royd Eris replied. "I have talked freely, you'll note. You deserved to know. We have passed the point where ignorance was a protection. Obviously things have gone too far. There have been too many deaths and you have been witness to all of them. Mother cannot allow you to return to Avalon alive."

"True," said Melantha. "But what shall she do with you? Is your own status in doubt, captain?"

"The crux of the problem," Royd admitted. "You are still three moves ahead, Melantha. I wonder if it will suffice. Your opponent is four ahead in this game, and most of your pawns are already captured. I fear checkmate is imminent."

"Unless I can persuade my opponent's king to desert, no?"

She could see Royd's wan smile. "She would probably kill me too if I choose to side with you. She does not need me."

Karoly d'Branin was slow to grasp the point. "But—but what else could—"

"My sled has a laser. Yours do not. I could kill you both, right now, and thereby earn my way back into the *Nightflyer's* good graces."

Across the three meters that lay between their sleds, Melantha's eyes met Royd's. Her hands rested easily on the thruster controls. "You could try, captain. Remember, the improved model isn't easy to kill."

"I would not kill you, Melantha Jhirl," Royd said seriously. "I have lived sixty-eight standard years and I have never lived at all. I am tired, and you tell grand gorgeous lies. Will you really touch me?"

"Yes."

"I risk a lot for that touch. Yet in a way it is no risk at all. If we lose we will all die together. If we win, well, I shall die anyway when they destroy the *Nightflyer,* either that or live as a freak in an orbital hospital, and I would prefer death."

"We will build you a new ship, captain," Melantha promised.

"Liar," Royd replied. But his tone was cheerful. "No matter. I have not had much of a life anyway. Death does not frighten me. If we win, you must tell me about your *volcryn* once again, Karoly. And you, Melantha, you must play chess with me, and find a way to touch me, and . . ."

"And sex with you?" she finished, smiling.

"If you would," he said quietly. He shrugged. "Well, mother has heard all of this. Doubtless she will listen carefully to any plans we might make, so there is no sense making them. Now there is no chance that the control lock will admit me, since it is keyed directly into the ship's computer. So we must follow the others through the driveroom, and enter through the main lock, and take what small chances we are given. If I can reach my console and restore gravity, perhaps we can win. If not—"

He was interrupted by a low groan.

For an instant Melantha thought the *Nightflyer* was wailing at them again, and she was surprised that it was so stupid as to try the same tactic twice. Then the groan sounded once more, and in the back of Karoly d'Branin's sled, the forgotten fourth member of their company struggled against the bonds that held her down. D'Branin hastened to free her, and Agatha Marij-Black tried to rise to her feet and almost floated off the sled, until d'Branin caught her hand and pulled her back. "Are you well?" he asked. "Can you hear me? Have you pain?"

Imprisoned beneath a transparent faceplate, wide frightened eyes flicked rapidly from Karoly to Melantha to Royd and then to the broken *Nightflyer.* Melantha wondered whether the woman was insane and started to caution d'Branin, when Marij-Black spoke.

"The *volcryn!*" was all she said. "Oh. The *volcryn!*"

Around the mouth of the driveroom, the ring of nuclear engines took on a faint glow. Melantha Jhirl heard Royd suck in his breath sharply. She gave the thruster controls of her sled a violent twist. "Hurry," she said loudly. "The *Nightflyer* is preparing to move."

A third of the way down the long barrel of the driveroom, Royd pulled abreast of her, stiff and menacing in his black, bulky armor. Side by side they sailed past the cylindrical stardrives and the cyberwebs; ahead, dimly lit, was the main airlock and its ghastly sentinel.

"When we reach the lock, jump over to my sled," Royd said. "I want to stay armed and mounted, and the chamber is not large enough for two sleds."

Melantha Jhirl risked a quick glance behind her. "Karoly," she called. "Where are you?"

"Outside, my love, my friend," the answer came. "I cannot come. Forgive me."

"We have to stay together!"

"No," d'Branin said, "no, I could not risk it, not when we are so close. It would be so tragic, so futile, Melantha. To come so close and fail. Death I do not mind, but I must see them first, finally, after all these years."

"My mother is going to move the ship," Royd cut in. "Karoly, you will be left behind, lost."

"I will wait," d'Branin replied. "My *volcryn* come, and I must wait for them."

Then the time for conversation was gone, for the airlock was almost upon them. Both sleds slowed and stopped, and Royd Eris reached out and began the cycle while Melantha Jhirl moved to the rear of his huge oval worksled. When the outer door moved aside, they glided through into the lock chamber.

"When the inner door opens, it will begin," Royd told her evenly. "The permanent furnishings are either built in or welded or bolted into place, but the things that your team brought on board are not. Mother will use those things as weapons. And beware of doors, airlocks, any equipment tied into the *Nightflyer's* computer. Need I warn you not to unseal your suit?"

"Hardly," she replied.

Royd lowered the sled a little, and its grapplers made a metallic sound as they touched against the floor of the chamber.

The inner door hissed open, and Royd applied his thrusters.

Inside Dannel and Lindran waited, swimming in a haze of blood.
Dannel had been slit from crotch to throat and his intestines moved like a
nest of pale, angry snakes. Lindran still held the knife. They swam closer,
moving with a grace they had never possessed in life.

Royd lifted his foremost grapplers and smashed them to the side as he
surged forward. Dannel caromed off a bulkhead, leaving a wide wet mark
where he struck, and more of his guts came sliding out. Lindran lost
control of the knife. Royd accelerated past them, driving up the corridor
through the cloud of blood.

"I'll watch behind," Melantha said. She turned and put her back to his.
Already the two corpses were safely behind them. The knife was floating
uselessly in the air. She started to tell Royd that they were all right when
the blade abruptly shifted and came after them, gripped by some invisible
force.

"*Swerve!*" she cried.

The sled shot wildly to one side. The knife missed by a full meter and
glanced ringingly off a bulkhead.

But it did not drop. It came at them again.

The lounge loomed ahead. Dark.

"The door is too narrow," Royd said. "We will have to abandon—"
As he spoke, they hit; he wedged the sled squarely into the door frame,
and the sudden impact jarred them loose.

For a moment Melantha floated clumsily in the corridor, her head
whirling, trying to sort up from down. The knife slashed at her, opening
her suit and her shoulder clear through to the bone. She felt sharp pain
and the warm flush of bleeding. "Damn," she shrieked. The knife came
around again, spraying droplets of blood.

Melantha's hand darted out and caught it.

She muttered something under her breath and wrenched the blade free
of the hand that had been gripping it.

Royd had regained the controls of his sled and seemed intent on some
manipulation. Beyond him, in the dimness of the lounge, Melantha
glimpsed a dark semihuman form rise into view.

"*Royd!*" she warned. The thing activated its small laser. The pencil
beam caught Royd square in the chest.

He touched his own firing stud. The sled's heavy-duty laser came
alive, a shaft of sudden brilliance. It cindered Christopheris's weapon
and burned off his right arm and part of his chest. The beam hung in the
air, throbbing, and smoked against the far bulkhead.

Royd made some adjustments and began cutting a hole. "We'll be
through in five minutes or less," he said curtly.

"Are you all right?" Melantha asked.

"I'm uninjured," he replied. "My suit is better armored than yours, and his laser was a low-powered toy."

Melantha turned her attention back to the corridor.

The linguists were pulling themselves toward her, one on each side of the passage, to come at her from two directions at once. She flexed her muscles. Her shoulder stabbed and screamed. Otherwise she felt strong, almost reckless. "The corpses are coming after us again," she told Royd. "I'm going to take them."

"Is that wise?" he asked. "There are two of them."

"I'm an improved model," Melantha said, "and they're dead." She kicked herself free of the sled and sailed toward Dannel in a high, graceful trajectory. He raised his hands to block her. She slapped them aside, bent one arm back and heard it snap, and drove her knife deep into his throat before she realized what a useless gesture that was. Blood oozed from his neck in a spreading cloud, but he continued to flail at her. His teeth snapped grotesquely.

Melantha withdrew her blade, seized him, and with all her considerable strength threw him bodily down the corridor. He tumbled, spinning wildly, and vanished into the haze of his own blood.

Melantha flew in the opposite direction, revolving lazily.

Lindran's hands caught her from behind.

Nails scrabbled against her faceplate until they began to bleed, leaving red streaks on the plastic.

Melantha whirled to face her attacker, grabbed a thrashing arm, and flung the woman down the passageway to crash into her struggling companion. The reaction sent her spinning like a top. She spread her arms and stopped herself, dizzy, gulping.

"I'm through," Royd announced.

Melantha turned to see. A smoking, meter-square opening had been cut through one wall of the lounge. Royd killed the laser, gripped both sides of the door frame, and pushed himself toward it.

A piercing blast of sound drilled through her head. She doubled over in agony. Her tongue flicked out and clicked off the comm; then there was blessed silence.

In the lounge it was raining. Kitchen utensils, glasses and plates, pieces of human bodies all lashed violently across the room and glanced harmlessly off Royd's armored form. Melantha, eager to follow, drew back helplessly. That rain of death would cut her to pieces in her lighter, thinner vacuum suit. Royd reached the far wall and vanished into the secret control section of the ship. She sat alone.

The *Nightflyer* lurched, and sudden acceleration provided a brief semblance of gravity. Melantha was thrown to one side. Her injured shoulder smashed painfully against the sled.

All up and down the corridor doors were opening.

Dannel and Lindran were moving toward her once again.

The *Nightflyer* was a distant star sparked by its nuclear engines. Blackness and cold enveloped them, and below was the unending emptiness of the Tempter's Veil, but Karoly d'Branin did not feel afraid. He felt strangely transformed.

The void was alive with promise.

"They *are* coming," he whispered. "Even I, who have no psi at all, even I can feel it. The Crey story must be so; even from light-years off they can be sensed. Marvelous!"

Agatha Marij-Black seemed small and shrunken. "The *volcryn*," she muttered. "What good can they do us? I hurt. The ship is gone. D'Branin, my head aches." She made a small, frightened noise. "Thale said that, just after I injected him, before—before—you know. He said that his head hurt. It aches so terribly."

"Quiet, Agatha. Do not be afraid. I am here with you. Wait. Think only of what we shall witness, think only of that!"

"I can sense them," the psipsych said.

D'Branin was eager. "Tell me, then. We have our little sled. We shall go to them. Direct me."

"Yes," she agreed. "Yes. Oh, yes."

Gravity returned: in a flicker, the universe became almost normal.

Melantha fell to the deck, landed easily and rolled, and was on her feet cat-quick.

The objects that had been floating ominously through the open doors along the corridor all came clattering down.

The blood was transformed from a fine mist to a slick covering on the corridor floor.

The two corpses dropped heavily from the air and lay still.

Royd spoke to her from the communicators built into the walls. "I made it," he said.

"I noticed," she replied.

"I'm at the main control console. I have restored the gravity with a manual override, and I'm cutting off as many computer functions as possible. We're still not safe, though. She will try to find a way around me. I'm countermanding her by sheer force, as it were. I cannot afford to overlook anything, and if my attention should lapse, even for a moment.. Melantha, was your suit breached?"

"Yes. Cut at the shoulder."

"Change into another one. *Immediately.* I think the counterprogramming I'm doing will keep the locks sealed, but I can't take any chances."

Melantha was already running down the corridor toward the cargo hold where the suits and equipment were stored.

"When you have changed," Royd continued, "dump the corpses into the mass conversion unit. You'll find the appropriate hatch near the driveroom airlock, just to the left of the lock controls. Convert any other loose objects that are not indispensible as well; scientific instruments, books, tapes, tableware—"

"Knives," suggested Melantha.

"By all means."

"Is teke still a threat, captain?"

"Mother is vastly weaker in a gravity field," Royd said. "She has to fight it. Even boosted by the *Nightflyer's* power, she can only move one object at a time, and she has only a fraction of the lifting force she wields under weightless conditions. But the power is still there, remember. Also, it is possible she will find a way to circumvent me and cut out the gravity again. From here I can restore it in an instant, but I don't want any likely weapons lying around even for that brief period of time."

Melantha reached the cargo area. She stripped off her vacuum suit and slipped into another one in record time, wincing at the pain in her shoulder. It was bleeding badly, but she had to ignore it. She gathered up the discarded suit and a double armful of instruments and dumped them into the conversion chamber. Afterward she turned her attention to the bodies. Dannel was no problem. Lindran crawled down the corridor after her as she pushed him through and thrashed weakly when it was her own turn, a grim reminder that the *Nightflyer's* powers were not all gone. Melantha easily overcame her feeble struggles and forced her through.

Christopheris's burned, ruined body writhed in her grasp and snapped its teeth at her, but Melantha had no real trouble with it. While she was cleaning out the lounge, a kitchen knife came spinning at her head. It came slowly, though, and Melantha just batted it aside, then picked it up and added it to the pile for conversion.

She was working through the cabins, carrying Agatha Marij-Black's abandoned drugs and injection gun under her arm, when she heard Royd cry out.

A moment later a force like a giant invisible hand wrapped itself around her chest and squeezed and pulled her, struggling, to the floor.

Something was moving across the stars.

Dimly and far off, d'Branin could see it, though he could not yet make out details. But it was there, that was unmistakable—some vast shape that blocked off a section of the starscape. It was coming at them dead on.

How he wished he had his team with him now, his computer, his telepath, his experts, his instruments.

He pressed harder on the thrusters and rushed to meet his *volcryn.*

Pinned to the floor, hurting, Melantha Jhirl risked opening her suit's comm. She had to talk to Royd. "Are you there?" she asked. "What's happen . . . happening?" The pressure was awful, and it was growing steadily worse. She could barely move.

The answer was pained and slow in coming. ". . . outwitted . . . me," Royd's voice managed. ". . . hurts . . . to . . . talk."

"Royd—"

". . . she . . . teked . . . the . . . dial . . . up . . . two . . . gees . . . three . . . higher . . . right . . . here . . . on . . . the . . . board . . . all . . . I . . . have to . . . to do . . . turn it . . . back . . . let me."

Silence. Then, finally, when Melantha was near despair, Royd's voice again. One word:

". . . can't . . ."

Melantha's chest felt as if it were supporting ten times her own weight. She could imagine the agony Royd must be in; Royd, for whom even one gravity was painful and dangerous. Even if the dial was an arm's length away, she knew his feeble musculature would never let him reach it. "Why," she started. Talking was not as hard for her as it seemed to be for him. "Why would . . . she turn *up* the . . . the gravity . . . it . . . weakens her too . . . yes?"

". . . yes . . . but . . . in a . . . a time . . . hour . . . minute . . . my . . . my heart . . . will burst . . . and . . . and then . . . you alone . . . she . . . will . . . kill gravity . . . kill you . . ."

Painfully Melantha reached out her arm and dragged herself half a length down the corridor. "Royd . . . hold on . . . I'm coming . . ." She dragged herself forward again. Agatha's drug kit was still under her arm, impossibly heavy. She eased it down and started to shove it aside. It felt as if it weighed a hundred kilos. She reconsidered. Instead she opened its lid.

The ampules were all neatly labeled. She glanced over them quickly, searching for adrenaline or synthastim, anything that might give her the strength she needed to reach Royd. She found several stimulants, selected the strongest, and was loading it into the injection gun with awkward, agonized slowness when her eyes chanced on the supply of esperon.

Melantha did not know why she hesitated. Esperon was only one of a half dozen psionic drugs in the kit, none of which could do her any good, but something about seeing it bothered her, reminded her of something she could not quite lay her finger on. She was trying to sort it out when she heard the noise.

"Royd," she said, "your mother . . . could she move . . . she couldn't move anything . . . teke it . . . in this high a gravity . . . could she?"

"Maybe," he answered, ". . . if . . . concentrate . . . all her . . . power . . . hard . . . maybe possible . . . why?"

"Because," Melantha Jhirl said grimly, "because something . . . *someone* . . . is cycling through the airlock."

"It is not truly a ship, not as I thought it would be," Karoly d'Branin was saying. His suit, Academy-designed, had a built-in encoding device, and he was recording his comments for posterity, strangely secure in the certainty of his impending death. "The scale of it is difficult to imagine, difficult to estimate. Vast, vast, I have nothing but my wrist computer, no instruments, I cannot make accurate measurements, but I would say, oh, a hundred kilometers, perhaps as much as three hundred, across. Not solid mass, of course, not at all. It is delicate, airy, no ship as we know ships, no city either. It is—oh, beautiful—it is crystal and gossamer, alive with its own dim lights, a vast intricate kind of spiderwebby craft—it reminds me a bit of the old starsail ships they used once, in the days before drive, but this great construct, it is not solid, it cannot be driven by light. It is no ship at all, really. It is all open to vacuum, it has no sealed cabins or life-support spheres, none visible to me, unless blocked from my line of sight in some fashion, and no, I cannot believe that, it is too open, too fragile. It moves quite rapidly. I would wish for the instrumentation to measure its speed, but it is enough to be here. I am taking the sled at right angles to it, to get clear of its path, but I cannot say that I will make it. It moves so much faster than we. Not at light speed, no, far below light speed, but still faster than the *Nightflyer* and its nuclear engines, I would guess. Only a guess.

"The *volcryn* craft has no visible means of propulsion. In fact, I wonder how—perhaps it is a light-sail, laser-launched millenia ago, now torn and rotted by some unimaginable catastrophe—but no, it is too symetrical, too beautiful—the webbings, the great shimmering veils near the nexus, the beauty of it.

"I must describe it; I must be more accurate, I know. It is difficult; I grow too excited. It is large, as I have said, kilometers across. Roughly—let me count—yes, roughly octagonal in shape. The nexus, the center, is a bright area, a small darkness surrounded by a much greater area of light, but only the dark portion seems entirely solid—the lighted areas are translucent. I can see stars through them, though discolored, shifted toward the purple. Veils, I call those the veils. From the nexus and the veils eight long—oh, vastly long—spurs project, not quite spaced evenly, so it is not a true geometric octagon—ah, I see better now, one of the spurs is shifting, oh, very slowly, the veils are rippling—they are mobile then, those projections, and the webbing runs from one spur to the next, around and around, but there are—patterns, odd patterns. It is not at all the simple webbing of a spider. I cannot quite see order in the patterns, in the traceries of the webs, but I feel sure the order is there; the meaning is waiting to be found.

"There are lights. Have I mentioned the lights? The lights are brightest around the center nexus, but they are nowhere very bright, a dim violet. Some visible radiation then, but not much. I would like to take an ultraviolet reading of this craft, but I do not have the instrumentation. The lights move. The veils seem to ripple, and lights can run constantly up and down the length of the spurs, at differing rates of speed, and sometimes other lights can be seen transversing the webbing, moving across the patterns. I do not know what the lights are. Some form of communication, perhaps. I cannot tell whether they emanate from inside the craft or outside. I—oh! There was another light just then. Between the spurs, a brief flash, a starburst. It is gone now, already. It was more intense than the others, indigo. I feel so helpless, so ignorant. But they are beautiful, my *volcryn* . . .

"The myths, they—this is really not much like the legends, not truly. The size, the lights. The *volcryn* have often been linked to lights, but those reports were so vague, they might have meant anything, described anything from a laser propulsion system to simple exterior lighting. I could not know it meant this. Ah, what mystery! The ship is still too far away to see the finer detail. It is so large, I do not think we shall get clear of it. It seems to have turned toward us, I think, yet I may be mistaken. It is only an impression. My instruments! If I only had my instruments. Perhaps the darker area in the center is a craft, a life capsule. The *volcryn* must be inside it. I wish my team were with me, and Thale, poor Thale. He was a class one. We might have made contact, might have communicated with them. The things we would learn! The things they have seen! To think how old this craft is, how ancient the race, how long they have been outbound . . . it fills me with awe. Communication would be such a gift, such an impossible gift, but they are so alien."

"*D'Branin,*" Agatha Marij-Black said in a low, urgent voice. "Can't you feel?"

Karoly d'Branin looked at her as if seeing her for the first time. "Can *you* feel them? You are a three—can you sense them now, strongly?"

"Long ago," the psipsych said, "long ago."

"Can you project? Talk to them, Agatha. Where are they? In the center area? The dark?"

"Yes," she replied, and she laughed. Her laugh was shrill and hysterical, and d'Branin had to recall she was a very sick woman. "Yes, in the center, d'Branin, that's where the pulses come from. Only you're wrong about them. It's not a *them* at all. Your legends are all lies, lies! I wouldn't be surprised if we were the first ever to see your *volcryn*, to come this close. The others, those aliens of yours, they merely *felt*, deep and distantly, sensed a bit of the nature of the *volcryn* in their dreams and visions, and fashioned the rest to suit themselves. Ships, and wars, and a race of eternal travelers, it is all—all—"

"Yes? What do you mean, Agatha, my friend? You do not make sense. I do not understand."

"No," Marij-Black said, "you do not, do you?" Her voice was suddenly gentle. "You cannot feel it, as I can. So clear now. This must be how a one feels, all the time. A one full of esperon."

"What do you feel? *What?*"

"It's not a *them*, Karoly. It's an *it*. Alive, Karoly, and quite mindless, I assure you."

"Mindless?" d'Branin said. "No, you must be wrong; you are not reading correctly. I will accept that it is a single creature if you say so, a single great marvelous star-traveler, but how can it be mindless? You sensed it—its mind, its telepathic emanations. You and the whole of the Crey sensitives and all the others. Perhaps its thoughts are too alien for you to read."

"Perhaps. But what I do read is not so terribly alien at all. Only animal. Its thoughts are slow and dark and strange, hardly thoughts at all, faint.

Stirrings cold and distant. The brain must be huge all right, I grant you that, but it can't be devoted to conscious thought."

"What do you mean?"

"The propulsion system, d'Branin. Don't you *feel?* The pulses? They are threatening to rip off the top of my skull. Can't you guess what is driving your damned *volcryn* across the galaxy? And why they avoid gravity wells? Can't you guess how it is moving?"

"No," d'Branin said, but even as he denied it, a dawn of comprehension broke across his face, and he looked away from his companion, back at the swelling immensity of the *volcryn*, its lights moving, its veils a-ripple, as it came on and on, across light-years, light-centuries, across eons.

When he looked at her, he mouthed only a single word. "Teke," he said.

She nodded.

Melantha Jhirl struggled to lift the injection gun and press it against an artery. It gave a single loud hiss, and the drug flooded her system. She lay back and gathered her strength and tried to think. Esperon, esperon—why was that important? It had killed Lasamer, made him a victim of his own latent abilities, multiplied his power and his vulnerability. Psi. It all came back to psi.

The inner door of the airlock opened. The headless corpse came through.

It moved with jerks, unnatural shufflings, never lifted its legs from the floor, It sagged as it moved, half-crushed by the weight upon it. Each shuffle was crude and sudden; some grim force was literally yanking one leg forward, then the next. It moved in slow motion, arms stiff by its sides.

But it moved.

Melantha summoned her own reserves and began to squirm away from it, never taking her eyes off its advance.

Her thoughts went round and round, searching for the piece out of place, the solution to the chess problem, finding nothing.

The corpse was moving faster than she was. Clearly, visibly, it was gaining.

Melantha tried to stand. She got to her knees with a grunt, her heart pounding. Then one knee. She tried to force herself up, to lift the impossible burden on her shoulders as if she were lifting weights. She was strong, she told herself. She was the improved model.

But when she put all her weight on one leg, her muscles would not hold her. She collapsed, awkwardly, and when she smashed against the floor, it was as if she had fallen from a building. She heard a sharp *snap,* and a stab of agony flashed up her arm, her good arm, the arm she had tried to use to break her fall. The pain in her shoulder was terrible and intense. She blinked back tears and choked on her own scream.

The corpse was halfway up the corridor. It must be walking on two broken legs, she realized. It didn't care. A force greater than tendons and bone and muscle was holding it up.

"Melantha . . . heard you . . . are . . . you . . . Melantha?"

"Quiet," she snarled at Royd. She had no breath to waste on talk.

Now she used all the disciplines she had ever learned to will away the pain. She kicked feebly, her boots scraping for purchase, and she pulled herself forward with her unbroken arm, ignoring the fire in her shoulder.

The corpse came on and on.

She dragged herself across the threshold of the lounge, worming her way under the crashed sled, hoping it would delay the cadaver. The thing that had been Thale Lasamer was a meter behind her.

In the darkness, in the lounge, where it had all begun, Melantha Jhirl ran out of strength.

Her body shuddered and she collapsed on the damp carpet, and she knew that she could go no further.

On the far side of the door, the corpse stood stiffly. The sled began to shake. Then, with the scrape of metal, it slid backward, moving in tiny sudden increments, jerking itself free and out of the way.

Psi. Melantha wanted to curse it, and cry. Vainly she wished for a psi power of her own, a weapon to blast apart the teke-driven corpse that stalked her. She was improved, she though despairingly, but not improved enough. Her parents had given her all the genetic gifts they could arrange, but psi was beyond them. The genes were astronomically rare, recessive, and—

—and suddenly it came to her.

"Royd," she said, putting all her remaining will into her words. She was weeping, wet, frightened. "The dial . . . *teke it,* Royd, teke it!"

His reply was faint, troubled. ". . . can't . . . I don't . . . mother . . . only . . . her . . . not me . . . no . . . mother . . ."

"Not mother," she said, desperate. "You always . . . say . . . *mother.* I forgot . . . forgot. Not your mother . . . listen . . . you're a *clone* . . . same genes . . . you have it too . . . power"

"Don't," he said. "Never . . . must be . . . sex-linked."

"No! It *isn't.* I know . . . Promethean, Royd . . . don't tell a Promethean . . . about genes . . . turn it!"

The sled jumped a third of a meter and listed to the side. A path was clear.

The corpse came forward.

". . . trying," Royd said. "Nothing . . . I *can't!*"

"She *cured* you," Melantha said bitterly. "Better than . . . she . . . was cured . . . prenatal . . . but it's only . . . suppressed . . . you *can!*"

"I . . . don't . . . know . . . how."

The corpse stood above her. Stopped. Its pale-fleshed hands trembled, spasmed, jerked upward. Long painted fingernails. Made claws. Began to rise.

Melantha swore. *"Royd!"*

". . . sorry . . ."

She wept and shook and made a futile fist.

And all at once the gravity was gone. Far, far away, she heard Royd cry out and then fall silent.

"The flashes come more frequently now," Karoly d'Branin dictated, "or perhaps it is simply that I am closer, that I can see them better. Bursts of indigo and deep violet, short and fast-fading. Between the webbing. A field, I think. The flashes are particles of hydrogen, the thin ethereal stuff of the reaches between the stars. They touch the field, between the webbing, the spurs, and shortly flare into the range of visible light. Matter to energy, yes, that is what I guess. My *volcryn* feeds.

"It fills half the universe, comes on and on. We shall not escape it, oh, so sad. Agatha is gone, silent, blood on her faceplate. I can almost see the dark area, almost, almost. I have a strange vision, in the center is a face, small, ratlike without mouth or nose or eyes, yet still a face somehow, and it stares at me. The veils move so sensuously. The webbing looms around us.

"Ah, the light, the light!"

The corpse bobbed awkwardly into the air, its hands hanging limply before it. Melantha, reeling in the weightlessness, was suddenly and violently sick. She ripped off the helmet, collapsed it, and pushed away from her own nausea, trying to ready herself for the *Nightflyer's* furious assault.

But the body of Thale Lasamer floated dead and still, and nothing else moved in the darkened lounge. Finally Melantha recovered, and she moved to the corpse, weakly, and pushed it, a small and tentative shove. It sailed across the room.

"Royd?" she said uncertainly.

There was no answer.

She pulled herself through the hole into the control chamber.

And found Royd Eris suspended in his armored suit. She shook him, but he did not stir. Trembling, Melantha Jhirl studied his suit and then began to dismantle it. She touched him.

"Royd," she said, "here, Feel. Royd, here, I'm here, feel it." His suit came apart easily, and she flung the pieces of it away. "Royd, *Royd.*"

Dead. Dead. His heart had given out. She punched it, pummeled it, tried to pound it into new life. It did not beat. Dead. Dead.

Melantha Jhirl moved back from him, blinded by her own tears, edged into the console, glanced down.

Dead. Dead.

But the dial on the gravity grid was set on zero.

"Melantha," said a mellow voice from the walls.

I have held the *Nightflyer's* crystalline soul within my hands.

It is deep red and multifaceted, large as my head, and icy to the touch. In its scarlet depths, two small sparks of smoky light burn fiercely and sometimes seem to whirl.

I have crawled through the consoles, wound my way carefully past safeguards and cybernets, taking care to damage nothing, and I have laid rough hands on that great crystal, knowing it is where *she* lives.

And I cannot bring myself to wipe it.

Royd's ghost has asked me not to.

Last night we talked about it once again, over brandy and chess in the lounge. Royd cannot drink, of course, but he sends his specter to smile at me, and he tells me where he wants his pieces moved.

For the thousandth time he offered to take me back to Avalon, or any world of my choice. If only I would go outside and complete the repairs we abandoned so many years ago, so the *Nightflyer* might safely slip into stardrive.

For the thousandth time I refused.

He is stronger now, no doubt. Their genes are the same, after all. Their power is the same. Dying, he too found the strength to impress himself upon the great crystal. The ship is alive with both of them, and frequently they fight. Sometimes she outwits him for a moment, and the *Nightflyer* does odd, erratic things. The gravity goes up or down or off completely. Blankets wrap themselves around my throat when I sleep. Objects come hurtling out of dark corners.

Those times have come less frequently of late, though. When they do come, Royd stops her, or I do. Together, the *Nightflyer* is ours.

Royd claims he is strong enough alone, that he does not really need me, that he can keep her under check. I wonder. Over the chessboard, I still beat him nine games out of ten.

And there are other considerations. Our work, for one. Karoly would be proud of us. The *volcryn* will soon enter the mists of the Tempter's Veil, and we follow close behind. Studying, recording, doing all that old d'Branin would have wanted us to do. It is all in the computer, and on tape and paper as well, should the system ever be wiped. It will be interesting to see how the *volcryn* thrives in the Veil. Matter is so thick there, compared to the thin diet of interstellar hydrogen on which the creature has fed so many endless eons.

We have tried to communicate with it, with no success. I do not believe it is sentient at all. And lately Royd has tried to imitate its ways, gathering all his energies in an attempt to move the *Nightflyer* by teke. Sometimes, oddly, his mother even joins with him in those efforts. So far they have always failed, but we will keep trying.

So goes our work. We know our results will reach humanity. Royd and I have discussed it, and we have a plan. Before I die, when my time is near, I will destroy the central crystal and clear the computers, and afterward I will set course manually for the close vicinity of an inhabited world. The *Nightflyer* will become a true ghost ship then. It will work. I have all the time I need, and I am an improved model.

I will not consider the other option, although it means much to me that Royd suggests it again and again. No doubt I could finish the repairs, and perhaps Royd could control the ship without me, and go on with the work. But that is not important.

I was wrong so many times. The esperon, the monitors, my control of the others; all of them my failures, payment for my *hubris.* Failure hurts. When I finally touched him, for the first and last and only time, his body was still warm. But *he* was gone already. He never felt my touch. I could not keep that promise.

But I can keep my other.

I will not leave him alone with her.

Ever.

Remembering Melody

Ted was shaving when the doorbell sounded. It startled him so badly that he cut himself. His condominium was on the thirty-second floor, and Jack the doorman generally gave him advance warning of any prospective visitors. This had to be someone from the building, then. Except that Ted didn't know anyone in the building, at least not beyond the trade-smiles-in-the-elevator level.

"Coming," he shouted. Scowling, he snatched up a towel and wiped the lather from his face, then dabbed at his cut with a tissue. "Shit," he said loudly to his face in the mirror. He had to be in court this afternoon. If this was another Jehovah's Witness like the one who'd gotten past Jack last month, they were going to be in for a very rough time indeed.

The buzzer buzzed again. "Coming, dammit," Ted yelled. He made a final dab at the blood on his neck, then threw the tissue into the wastebasket and strode across the sunken living room to the door. He peered through the eyehole carefully before he opened. "Oh, shit," he muttered. Before she could buzz again, Ted slid off the chain and threw open the door. "Hello, Melody," he said.

She smiled wanly. "Hi, Ted," she replied. She had an old suitcase in her hand, a battered cloth bag with a hideous red-and-black plaid pattern, its broken handle replaced by a length of rope. The last time Ted had seen her, three years before, she'd looked terrible. Now she looked worse. Her clothes — shorts and a tie-dyed T-shirt— were wrinkled and dirty, and emphasized how gaunt she'd become. Her ribs showed through plainly; her legs were pipestems. Her long stringy blond hair hadn't been washed recently, and her face was red and puffy, as if she'd been crying. That was no surprise. Melody was always crying about one thing or another. "Aren't you going to ask me in, Ted?"

Ted grimaced. He certainly didn't *want* to ask her in. He knew from past experience how difficult it was to get her out again. But he couldn't just leave her standing in the hall with her suitcase in hand. After all, he thought sourly, she was an old and dear friend. "Oh, sure," he said. He gestured. "Come on in."

He took her bag from her and set it by the door, then led her into the kitchen and put on some water to boil. "You look as though you could use a cup of coffee," he said, trying to keep his voice friendly.

Melody smiled again. "Don't you remember, Ted? I don't drink coffee. It's no good for you, Ted. I used to tell you that. Don't you remember?" She got up from the kitchen table, and began rummaging through his cupboards. "Do you have any hot chocolate?" she asked. "I like hot chocolate."

"I don't drink hot chocolate," he said. "Just a lot of coffee."

"You shouldn't," she said. "It's no good for you."

"Yeah," he said. "Do you want juice? I've got juice."

Melody nodded. "Fine."

He poured her a glass of orange juice, and led her back to the table, then spooned some Maxim into a mug while he waited for his kettle to whistle. "So," he asked, "what brings you to Chicago?"

Melody began to cry. Ted leaned back against the stove and watched her. She was a very noisy cryer, and she produced an amazing amount of tears for someone who cried so often. She didn't look up until the water began to boil. Ted poured some into his cup and stirred in a teaspoon of sugar. Her face was redder and more puffy than ever. Her eyes fixed on him accusingly. "Things have been real bad," she said. "I need help, Ted. I don't have any place to live. I thought maybe I could stay with you a while. Things have been real bad."

"I'm sorry to hear that, Melody," Ted replied, sipping at his coffee thoughtfully. "You can stay here for a few days, if you want. But no longer. I'm not in the market for a roommate." She always made him feel like such a bastard, but it was better to be firm with her right from the start, he thought.

Melody began to cry again when he mentioned roommates. "You used to say I was a *good* roommate," she whined. "We used to have fun, don't you remember? You were my friend."

Ted set down his coffee mug and looked at the kitchen clock. "I don't have time to talk about old times right now," he said. "I was shaving when you rang. I've got to get to the office." He frowned. "Drink your juice and make yourself at home. I've got to get dressed." He turned abruptly, and left her weeping at the kitchen table.

Back in the bathroom, Ted finished shaving and tended to his cut more properly, his mind full of Melody. Already he could tell that this was going to be difficult. He felt sorry for her — she was messed-up and miserably unhappy, with no one to turn to — but he wasn't going to let her inflict all her troubles on him. Not this time. She'd done it too many times before.

In his bedroom, Ted stared pensively into the closet for a long time before selecting the grey suit. He knotted his tie carefully in the mirror, scowling at his cut. Then he checked his briefcase to make sure all the papers on the Syndio case were in order, nodded, and walked back into the kitchen.

Melody was at the stove, making pancakes. She turned and smiled at him happily when he entered. "You remember my pancakes, Ted?" she asked. "You used to love it when I made pancakes, especially blueberry pancakes, you remember? You didn't have any blueberries, though, so I'm just making plain. Is that alright?"

"Jesus," Ted muttered. "Dammit, Melody, who said you should make *anything?* I told you I had to get to the office. I don't have time to eat with you. I'm late already. Anyway, I don't eat breakfast. I'm trying to lose weight."

Tears began to trickle from her eyes again. "But — but these are my special pancakes, Ted. What am I going to do with them? What am I going to *do?*"

"Eat them," Ted said. "You could use a few extra pounds. Jesus, you look terrible. You look like you haven't eaten for a month."

Melody's face screwed up and became ugly. "You bastard," she said. "You're supposed to be my *friend.*"

Ted sighed. "Take it easy," he said. He glanced at his watch. "Look, I'm fifteen minutes late already. I've got to go. You eat your pancakes and get some sleep. I'll be back around six. We can have dinner together and talk, all right? Is that what you want?"

"That would be nice," she said, suddenly contrite. "That would be real nice."

"Tell Jill I want to see her in my office, right away," Ted snapped to the secretary when he arrived. "And get us some coffee, willya? I really need some coffee."

"Sure."

Jill arrived a few minutes after the coffee. She and Ted were associates in the same law firm. He motioned her to a seat, and pushed a cup at her. "Sit down," he said. "Look, the date's off tonight. I've got problems."

"You look it," she said. "What's wrong?"

"An old friend showed up on my doorstep this morning," he said.

Jill arched one elegant eyebrow. "So?" she said. "Reunions can be fun."

"Not with Melody they can't."

"Melody?" she said. "A pretty name. An old flame, Ted? What is it, unrequited love?"

"No," he said, "no, it wasn't like that."

"Tell me what it was like, then. You know I love the gory details."

"Melody and I were roommates, back in college. Not just us — don't get the wrong idea. There were four of us. Me and a guy named Michael Englehart, Melody and another girl, Anne Kaye. The four of us shared a big old run-down house for two years. We were — friends."

"Friends?" Jill looked skeptical.

Ted scowled at her. "Friends," he repeated. "Oh, hell, I slept with Melody a few times. With Anne too. And both of them fucked Michael a time or two. But when it happened, it was just kind of — kind of *friendly,* you know? Our love life was mostly with outsiders. we used to tell each other our troubles, swap advice, cry on one another's shoulders. Hell, I know it sounds weird. It was 1970, though. I had hair down to my ass. Everything was weird." He sloshed the dregs of his coffee around in the cup, and looked pensive. "They were good times, too. Special times. Sometimes I'm sorry they had to end. The four of us were close, really close. I loved those people."

Watch out," Jill said, "I'll get jealous. My roommate and I cordially despised each other." She smiled. "So what happened?"

Ted shrugged. "The usual story," he said. "We graduated, drifted apart. I remember the last night in the old house. We smoked a ton of dope, and got very silly. Swore eternal friendship. We weren't ever going to be strangers, no matter what happened, and if any of us ever needed help, well, the other three would always be there. We sealed the bargain with — well, kind of an orgy."

Jill smiled. "Touching," she said. "I never dreamed you had it in you."

"It didn't last, of course," Ted continued. "We tried, I'll give us that much. But things changed too much. I went on to law school, wound up here in Chicago. Michael got a job with a publishing house in New York City. He's an editor at Random House now, been married and divorced, two kids. We used to write. Now we trade Christmas cards. Anne's a teacher. She was down in Phoenix the last I heard, but that was four, five years ago. Her husband didn't like the rest of us much, the one time we had a reunion. I think Anne must have told him about the orgy."

"And your house guest?"

"Melody," he sighed. "She became a problem. In college, she was wonderful; gutsy, pretty, a real free spirit. But afterwards she couldn't cut it. She tried to make it as a painter for a couple of years, but she wasn't good enough. Got nowhere. She went through a couple of relationships that turned sour, then married some guy about a week after she'd met him in a singles bar. That was terrible. He used to get drunk and beat her. She took about six months of it, and finally got a divorce. He still came 'round to beat her up for a year, until he finally got frightened off. After that Melody got into drugs, bad. She spent some time in an asylum. When she got out, it was more of the same. She can't hold a job, or stay away from drugs. Her relationships don't last more than a few weeks. She's let her body go to hell." He shook his head.

Jill pursed her lips. "Sounds like a lady who needs help," she said.

Ted flushed, and grew angry. "You think I don't know that? You think we haven't tried to help her? *Jesus.* When she was trying to be an artist, Michael got her a couple of cover assignments from the paperback house he was with. Not only did she blow the deadlines, but she got into a screaming match with the art director. Almost cost Michael his job. I flew to Cleveland and handled her divorce for her, gratis. Flew back a couple of months later, and spend quite a while there trying to get the cops to give her protection against her ex-hubby. Anne took her in when she had no place to live, got her into a drug rehabilitation program. In return, Melody tried to seduce her boyfriend — said she wanted to *share* him, like they'd done in the old days. All of us have lent her money. She's never paid back any of it. And we've listened to her troubles, God but we've listened to her troubles. There was a period a few years ago when she'd phone every week, usually collect, with some new sad story. She cried over the phone a lot. If *Queen for a Day* was still on TV, Melody would be a natural!"

"I'm beginning to see why you're not thrilled by her visit," Jill said dryly. "What are you going to do?"

"I don't know," Ted replied. "I shouldn't have let her in. The last few times she's called, I just hung up on her, and that seemed to work pretty well. Felt guilty about it at first, but that passed. This morning, though, she looked so pathetic that I didn't know how to send her away. I suppose eventually I'll have to get brutal, and go through a scene. Nothing else works. She'll make a lot of accusations, remind me of what good friends we were and the promises we made, threaten to kill herself. Fun times ahead."

"Can I help?" Jill asked.

"Pick up my pieces afterwards," Ted said. "It's always nice to have someone around afterwards, to tell you that you're not a son-of-a-bitch even though you just kicked an old dear friend out into the gutter."

He was terrible in court that afternoon. His thoughts were full of Melody, and the strategies that most occupied him concerned how to get rid of her most painlessly, instead of the case at hand. Melody had danced flamenco on his psyche too many times before; Ted wasn't going to let her leech off him this time, nor leave him an emotional wreck.

When he got back to his condo with a bag of Chinese food under his arm — he'd decided he didn't want to take her out to a restaurant — Melody was sitting nude in the middle of his conversation pit, giggling and sniffing some white powder. She looked up at Ted happily when he entered. "Here," she said. "I scored some coke."

"*Jesus,*" he swore. He dropped the Chinese food and his briefcase, and strode furiously across the carpet. "I don't *believe* you," he roared. "I'm a *lawyer,* for Chissakes. Do you want to get me disbarred?"

Melody had the coke in a little paper square, and was sniffing it from a rolled-up dollar bill. Ted snatched it all away from her, and she began to cry. He went to the bathroom and flushed it down the toilet, dollar bill and all. Except it wasn't a dollar bill, he saw, as it was sucked out of sight. It was a twenty. That made him even angrier. When he returned to the living room, Melody was still crying.

"Stop that," he said. "I don't want to hear it. And put some clothes on." Another suspicion came to him. "Where did you get the money for that stuff?" he demanded. "Huh, *where?*"

Melody whimpered. "I sold some stuff," she said in a timid voice. "I didn't think you'd mind. It was good coke." She shield away from him and threw an arm across her face, as if Ted was going to hit her.

Ted didn't need to ask whose stuff she'd sold. He knew; she'd pulled the same trick on Michael years before, or so he'd heard. He sighed. "Get dressed," he repeated wearily. "I brought Chinese food." Later he could check what was missing, and phone the insurance company.

"Chinese food is no good for you," Melody said. "It's full of monosodium glutamate. Gives you headaches, Ted." But she got to her feet obediently, if a bit unsteadily, went off towards the bathroom, and came back a few minutes later wearing a halter-top and a pair of ratty cutoffs. Nothing else, Ted guessed. A couple of years ago she must have decided that underwear was no good for you.

Ignoring her comment about monosodium glutamate, Ted found some plates and served up the Chinese food in his dining nook. Melody ate it meekly enough, drowning everything in soy sauce. Every few minutes she giggled at some private joke, then grew very serious again and resumed eating. When she broke open her fortune cookie, a wide smile lit her face. "Look, Ted," she said happily, passing the little slip of paper across to him.

He read it. OLD FRIENDS ARE THE BEST FRIENDS, it said. "Oh, shit," he muttered. He didn't even open his own. Melody wanted to know why. "You ought to read it, Ted," she told him. "It's bad luck if you don't read your fortune cookie."

"I don't want to read it," he said. "I'm going to change out of this suit." He rose. "Don't do anything."

But when he came back, she'd put an album on the stereo. At least she hadn't sold that, he thought gratefully.

"Do you want me to dance for you?" she asked. "Remember how I used to dance for you and Michael? Real sexy... you used to tell me how good I dance. I could of been a dancer if I'd wanted." She did a few steps in the middle of his living room, stumbled, and almost fell. It was grotesque.

"Sit down, Melody," Ted said, as sternly as he could manage. "We have to talk."

She sat down.

"Don't cry," he said before he started. "You understand that? I don't want you to cry. We can't talk if you're going to cry every time I say anything. You start crying and this conversation is over."

Melody nodded. "I won't cry, Ted," she said. "I feel much better now than this morning. I'm with you now. You make me feel better."

"You're *not* with me, Melody. Stop that."

Her eyes filled up with tears. "You're my friend, Ted. You and Michael and Anne, you're the special ones."

He sighed. "What's wrong, Melody? Why are you here?"

"I lost my job, Ted," she said.

"The waitress job?" he asked. The last time he'd seen her, three years ago, she'd been waiting tables in a bar in Kansas City.

Melody blinked him, confused. "Waitress?" she said. "No, Ted. That was before. That was in Kansas City. Don't you remember?"

"I remember very well," he said. "What job was it you lost?"

"It was a shitty job," Melody said. "A factory job. It was in Iowa. In Des Moines. Des Moines is a shitty place. I didn't come to work, so they fired me. I was strung out, you know? I needed a couple days off. I would have come back to work. But they fired me." She looked close to tears again. "I haven't had a good job in a long time, Ted. I was an art major. You remember? You and Michael and Anne used to have my drawings hung up in your rooms. You still have my drawings, Ted?"

"Yes," he lied. "Sure. Somewhere." He'd gotten rid of them years ago. They reminded him too much of Melody, and that was too painful.

"Anyway, when I lost my job, Johnny said I wasn't bringing in any money. Johnny was the guy I lived with. He said he wasn't gonna support me, that I had to get some job, but I couldn't. I *tried*, Ted, but I couldn't. So Johnny talked to some man, and he got me this job in a massage parlor, you know. And he took me down there, but it was crummy. I didn't want to work in no massage parlor, Ted. I used to be an art major."

"I remember, Melody," Ted said. She seemed to expect him to say something.

Melody nodded. "So I didn't take it, and Johnny threw me out. I had no place to go, you know. And I thought of you, and Anne, and Michael. Remember the last night? We all said that if anyone ever needed help..."

"I remember, Melody," Ted said. "Not as often as you do, but I remember. You don't ever let any of us forget it, do you? But let it pass. What do you want this time?" His tone was flat and cold.

"You're a lawyer, Ted," she said.

"Yes."

"So, I thought — " Her long, thin fingers plucked nervously at her face. "I thought maybe you could get me a job. I could be a secretary, maybe. In your office. We could be together again, every day, like it used to be. Or maybe," — she brightened visibly — "maybe I could be one of those people who draw pictures in the courtroom. You know. Like of Patty Hearst and people like that. On TV. I'd be good at that."

"Those artists work for the TV stations," Ted said patiently. "And there are no openings in my office. I'm sorry, Melody. I can't get you a job."

Melody took that surprisingly well. "All right, Ted," she said. "I can find a job, I guess. I'll get one all by myself. Only — only let me live here, okay? We can be roommates again."

"Oh, Jesus," Ted said. He sat back and crossed his arms. "No," he said flatly.

Melody took her hand away from her face, and stared at him imporingly. "Please, Ted," she whispered. "Please."

"No," he said. The word hung there, chill and final.

"You're my *friend,* Ted," she said. "You *promised.*"

"You can stay here a week," he said. "No longer. I have my own life, Melody. I have my own problems. I'm tired of dealing with yours. We all are. You're nothing but problems. In college, you were fun. You're not fun any longer. I've helped you and helped you and helped you. How fucking much do you want out of me?" He was getting angrier as he talked. "Things change, Melody," he said brutally. "People change. You can't hold me forever to some dumb promise I made when I was stoned out of my mind back in college. I'm not responsible for your life. Tough up, dammit. Pull yourself together. I can't do it for you, and I'm sick of all your shit. I don't even like to see you anymore, Melody, you know that?"

She whimpered. "Don't say that, Ted. We're friends. You're special. As long as I have you and Michael and Anne, I'll never be alone, don't you see?"

"You *are* alone," he said. Melody infuriated him.

"No I'm not," she insisted. "I have my friends, my special friends. They'll help me. You're my *friend,* Ted."

"I used to be your friend," he replied.

She stared at him, her lip trembling, hurt beyond words. For a moment he thought that the dam was going to burst, that Melody was finally about to break down and begin one of her marathon crying jags. Instead, a change came over her face. She paled perceptibly, and her lips drew back slowly, and her expression settled into a terrible mask of anger. She was hideous when she was angry. "You bastard," she said.

Ted had been this route too. He got up from the couch and walked to his bar. "Don't start," he said, pouring himself a glass of Chivas Regal on the rocks. "The first thing you throw, you're out on your ass. Got that, Melody?"

"You scum," she repeated. "You were never my friend. None of you were. You lied to me, made me trust you, used me. Now you're all so high and mighty and I'm nothing, and you don't want to know me. You don't want to help me. You never wanted to help me."

"I did help you," Ted pointed out. "Several times. You owe me something close to two thousand dollars, I believe."

"Money," she said. "That's all you care about, you bastard."

Ted sipped at his scotch and frowned at her. "Go to hell," he said.

"I could, for all you care." Her face had gone white. "I cabled you, two years ago. I cabled all three of you. I needed you, you promised that you'd come if I needed you, that you'd be there, you promised that and you made love to me and you were my friend, but I cabled you and you didn't come, you bastard, you didn't come, none of you came, none of you came." She was screaming.

Ted had forgotten about the telegram. But it came back to him in a rush. He'd read it over several times, and finally he'd picked up the phone and called Michael. Michael hadn't been in. So he'd reread the telegram one last time, then crumbled it up and flushed it down the toilet. One of the others could go to her this time, he remembered thinking. He had a big case, the Argrath Corporation patent suit, and he couldn't risk leaving it. But it had been a desperate telegram, and he'd been guilty about it for weeks, until he finally managed to put the whole thing out of his mind. "I was busy," he said, his tone half-angry and half-defensive. "I had more important things to do than come hold your hand through another crisis."

"It was *horrible*," Melody screamed. "I needed you and you left me all *alone*. I almost *killed* myself."

"But you didn't, did you?"

"I could have," she said, "I could have killed myself, and you wouldn't even have cared."

Threatening suicide was one of Melody's favorite tricks. Ted had been through it a hundred times before. This time he decided not to take it. "You could have killed yourself," he said calmly, "and we probably wouldn't have cared. I think you're right about that. You would have rotted for weeks before anyone found you, and we probably wouldn't even have heard about it for half a year. And when I did hear, finally, I guess it would have made me sad for an hour or two, remembering how things had been, but then I would have gotten drunk or phoned up my girlfriend or something, and pretty soon I'd have been out of it. And then I could have forgotten all about you."

"You would have been sorry," Melody said.

"No," Ted replied. He strolled back to the bar and freshened his drink. "No, you know, I don't think I would have been sorry. Not in the least. Not guilty, either. So you might as well stop threatening to kill yourself, Melody, because it isn't going to work."

The anger drained out of her face, and she gave a little whimper. "Please, Ted," she said. "Don't say such things. Tell me you'd care. Tell me you'd remember me."

He scowled at her. "No," he said. It was harder when she was pitiful, when she shrunk up all small and vulnerable and whimpered instead of accusing him. But he had to end it once and for all, get rid of this curse on his life.

"I'll go away tomorrow," she said meekly. "I won't bother you. But tell me you care, Ted. That you're my friend. That you'll come to me. If I need you."

"I won't come to you, Melody," he said. "That's over. And I don't want you coming here any more, or phoning, or sending telegrams, no matter what kind of trouble you're in. You understand? Do you? I want you out of my life, and when you're gone I'm going to forget you as quick as I can, 'cause lady, you are one hell of a bad memory." Melody cried out as if he had struck her. "NO!" she said. "No, don't say that, remember me, you have to. I'll leave you alone, I promise I will, I'll never see you again. But say you'll remember me." She stood up abruptly. "I'll go right now," she said. "If you want me to, I'll go. But make love to me first, Ted. Please. I want to give you something to remember me by." She smiled a lascivious little smile, and began to struggle out of her halter top, and Ted felt sick.

He set down his glass with a bang. "You're crazy," he said. "You ought to get professional help, Melody. But I can't give it to you, and I'm not going to put up with this anymore. I'm going out for a walk. I'll be gone a couple of hours. You be gone when I get back."

Ted started for the door. Melody stood looking at him, her halter in her hand. Her breasts looked small and shrunken, and the left one had a tattoo on it that he'd never noticed before. There was nothing even vaguely desirable about her. She whimpered. "I just wanted to give you something to remember me by," she said.

Ted slammed the door.

It was midnight when he returned, drunk and surly, resolved that if Melody was still there, he would call the police and that would be the end of that. Jack was behind the desk, having just gone on duty. Ted stopped and gave him hell for having admitted Melody that morning, but the doorman denied it vehemently. "Wasn't nobody got in, Mister Cirelli. I don't let in anyone without buzzing up, you ought to know that. I been here six years, and I never let in nobody without buzzing up." Ted reminded him forcefully about the Jehovah's Witness, and they ended up in a shouting match.

Finally Ted stormed away and took the elevator up to the thirty-second floor.

There was a drawing taped to his door.

He blinked at it furiously for a moment, then snatched it down. It was a cartoon, a caricature of Melody. Not the Melody he'd seen today, but the Melody he'd known in college; sharp, funny, pretty. When they'd been roommates, Melody had always illustrated her notes with little cartoons of herself. He was surprised that she could still draw this well. Beneath the face, she'd printed a message.

I LEFT YOU SOMETHING TO REMEMBER ME BY.

Ted scowled down at the cartoon, wondering whether he should keep it or not. His own hesitation made him angry. He crumbled the paper in his hand, and fumbled for his keys. At least she's gone, he thought, and maybe for good. If she left the note, it meant that she'd gone. He was rid of her for another couple of years at least.

He went inside, tossed the crumbled ball of paper across the room towards a wastebasket, and smiled when it went in. "Two points," he said loudly to himself, drunk and self-satisfied. He went to the bar and began to mix himself a drink.

But something was wrong.

Ted stopped stirring his drink, and listened. The water was running, he realized. She'd left the water running in the bathroom.

"Christ," he said, and then an awful thought hit him: maybe she hadn't gone after all. Maybe she was still in the bathroom, taking a shower or something, freaked out of her mind, crying, whatever. "Melody!" he shouted.

No answer. The water was running, all right. It couldn't be anything else. But she didn't answer.

"Melody, are you still here?" he yelled. "Answer, dammit!"

Silence.

He put down his drink and walked to the bathroom. The door was closed. Ted stood outside. The water was definitely running. "Melody," he said loudly, "are you in there? Melody?"

Nothing. Ted was beginning to be afraid.

He reached out and grasped the doorknob. It turned easily in his hand. The door hadn't been locked.

Inside the bathroom was filled with steam. He could hardly see, but he made out that the shower curtain was drawn. The shower was running full blast, and judging from the amount of steam, it must be scalding. Ted stepped back and waited for the steam to dissipate. "Melody?" he said softly. There was no reply.

"Shit," he said. He tried not to be afraid. She only talked about it, he told himself; she'd never really do it. The ones who talk about it never do it, he'd read that somewhere. She was just doing this to frighten him.

He took two quick strides across the room and yanked back the shower curtain.

She was there, wreathed in steam, water streaming down her naked body. She wasn't stretched out in the tub at all; she was sitting up, crammed in sideways near the faucets, looking very small and pathetic. Her position seemed half-foetal. The needle spray had been directed down at her, at her hands. She'd opened her wrists with his razor blades, and tried to hold them under the water, but it hadn't been enough, she'd slit the veins crosswise, and everybody knew the only way to do it was lengthwise. So she'd used the razor elsewhere, and now she had two mouths, and both of them were smiling at him, smiling. The shower had washed away most of the blood; there were no stains anywhere, but the second mouth below her chin was still red and dripping. Trickles oozed down her chest, over the flower tattooed on her breast, and the spray of the shower caught them and washed them away. Her hair hung down over her cheeks, limp and wet. She was smiling. She looked so happy. The steam was all around her. She'd been in there for hours, he thought. She was very clean.

Ted closed his eyes. It didn't make any difference. He still saw her. He would always see her.

He opened them again; Melody was still smiling. He reached across her and turned off the shower, getting the sleeve of his shirt soaked in the process.

Numb, he fled back into the living room. God, he thought, God. I have to call someone, I have to report this, I can't deal with this. He decided to call the police. He lifted the phone, and hesitated with his finger poised over the buttons. The police won't help, he thought. He punched for Jill.

When he had finished telling her, it grew very silent on the other end of the phone. "My god," she said at last, "how awful. Can I do anything?"

"Come over," he said. "Right away." He found the drink he'd set down, took a hurried sip from it.

Jill hesitated. "Er — look, Ted, I'm not very good at dealing with corpses," she said. "Why don't you come over here? I don't want to — well, you know. I don't think I'll ever shower at your place again."

"Jill," he said, stricken. "I need someone right now." He laughed a frightened, uncertain laugh.

"Come over here," she urged.

"I can't just *leave* it there," he said.

"Well, don't," she said. "Call the police. They'll take it away. Come over afterwards."

Ted called the police.

"If this is your idea of a joke, it isn't funny," the patrolman said. His partner was scowling.

"Joke?" Ted said.

"There's nothing in your shower," the patrolman said. "I ought to take you down to the station house."

"Nothing in the shower?" Ted repeated, incredulous.

"Leave him alone, Sam," the partner said, "He's stinko, can't you tell?"

Ted rushed past them both into the bathroom.

The tub was empty. Empty. He knelt and felt the bottom of it. Dry. Perfectly dry. But his shirt sleeve was still damp. "No," he said, "no." He rushed back out to the living room. The two cops watched him with amusement. Her suitcase was gone from its place by the door. The dishes had all been run through the dishwasher, no way to tell if anyone had made pancakes or not. Ted turned the wastebasket upside down, spilling out the contents all over his couch. He began to scrabble through the papers.

"Go to bed and sleep it off, mister," the older cop said. "You'll feel better in the morning."

"C'mon," his partner said. They departed, leaving Ted still pawing through the papers. No cartoon. No cartoon. No cartoon.

Ted flung the empty wastebasket across the room, and it caromed off the wall with a ringing metallic clang.

He took a cab to Jill's.

It was near dawn when he sat up in bed suddenly, his heart thumping, his mouth dry with fear.

Jill murmurred sleepily. "Jill," he said, shaking her.

She blinked up at him. "What?" she said. "What time is it, Ted? What's wrong?" She sat up, pulling up the blanket to cover herself.

"Don't you hear it?"

"Hear what?" she asked.

He giggled. "Your shower is running."

That morning he shaved in the kitchen, even though there was no mirror. He cut himself twice. His bladder ached, but he would not go past the bathroom door, despite Jill's repeated assurances that the shower was not running. Dammit, he could *hear* it. He waited until he got to the office. There was no shower in the washroom there.

But Jill looked at him strangely.

At the office, Ted cleared off his desk, and tried to think. He was a lawyer. He had a good, analytical mind. He tried to reason it out. He drank only coffee, lots of coffee.

No suitcase, he thought. Jack hadn't seen her. No corpse. No cartoon. No one had seen her. The shower was dry. No dishes. He'd been drinking. But not all day, only later, after dinner. Couldn't be the drinking. Couldn't be. No cartoon. He was the only one who'd seen her. No cartoon. I LEFT YOU SOMETHING TO REMEMBER ME BY. He'd crumpled up her cable, and flushed her away. Two years ago. Nothing in the shower.

He picked up his phone. "Billie," he said, "get me a newspaper in Des Moines, Iowa. Any newspaper, I don't care."

When he finally got through, the woman who tended the morgue was reluctant to give him any information. But she softened when he told her he was a lawyer, and needed the information for an important case.

The obituary was very short. Melody was identified only as a "massage parlor employee." She'd killed herself in her shower.

"Thank you," Ted said. He set down the receiver. For a long time he sat staring out of his window. He had a very good view; he could see the lake, and the soaring tower of the Standard Oil building. He pondered what to do next. There was a thick knot of fear in his gut.

He could take the day off, and go home. But the shower would be running at home, and sooner or later he would have to go in there.

He could go back to Jill's. If Jill would have him. She'd seemed awfully cool after last night. She'd recommended a shrink to him as they shared a cab to the office. She didn't understand. No one would understand... unless... he picked up the phone again, searching through his circular file. There was no card, no number; they'd drifted that far apart. He buzzed for Billie again. "Get me through to Random House in New York City," he said. "To Mr. Michael Englehart. He's an editor there."

But when he finally connected, the voice on the other end of the line was strange and distant. "Mister Cirelli? Were you a friend of Michael's? Or one of his authors?"

Ted's mouth was dry. "A friend," he said. "Isn't Michael in? I need to talk to him. It's . . . urgent."

"I'm afraid Michael's no longer with us," the voice said. "He had a nervous breakdown, less than a week ago."

"Is he . . .?"

"He's alive. They took him to a hospital, I believe. You know. Maybe I can find you the number."

"No," Ted said, "no, that's quite all right." He hung up.

Phoenix directory assistance had no listing for an Anne Kaye. Of course not, he thought. She was married now. He tried to remember her married name. It took him a long time. Something Polish, he thought. Finally it came to him.

He hadn't expected to find her at home. It was a school day, after all. But someone picked up the phone on the third ring. "Hello," he said. "Anne, is that you? This is Ted, in Chicago. Anne, I've got to talk to you. It's about Melody. Anne, I need help." He was breathless.

There was a giggle. "Anne isn't here right now, Ted." Melody said. "She's off at school, and then she's got to visit her husband. They're separated, you know. But she promised to come back by eight."

"Melody," he said.

"Of course, I don't know if I can believe her. You three were never very good about promises. But maybe she'll come back. Ted. I hope so. I want to leave her something to remember me by."